BLINDSPOT

Hidden Biases
of Good People

Mahzarin R. Banaji
and Anthony G. Greenwald

BANTAM BOOKS / NEW YORK

2016 Bantam Books Trade Paperback Edition

Copyright © 2013 by Mahzarin R. Banaji and Anthony G. Greenwald

Published in the United States by Bantam Books,
an imprint of Random House, a division of
Penguin Random House LLC, New York.

BANTAM BOOKS and the HOUSE colophon are registered
trademarks of Penguin Random House LLC.

Originally published in hardcover in the United States
by Delacorte Press, an imprint of Random House,
a division of Penguin Random House LLC, in 2013.

LIBRARY OF CONGRESS CATALOGING-IN-PUBLICATION DATA
Banaji, Mahzarin R.
Blindspot : hidden biases of good people / Mahzarin R. Banaji and
Anthony G. Greenwald
p. cm.
Includes bibliographical references and index.
ISBN 978-0-345-52843-8—ISBN 978-0-440-42329-4 (eBook)
1. Prejudices. 2. Discrimination—Psychological aspects.
I. Greenwald, Anthony G. II. Title.
BF575.P9B25 2013
155.9'2—dc23   2012015905

Printed in the United States of America on acid-free paper

randomhousebooks.com

13 14 15 16 17 18 19

Book design by Susan Turner

PRAISE FOR BLINDSPOT

"Accessible and authoritative . . . This research takes Freud's dagger into our vanity and twists it."

—The Washington Post

"[A] riveting book steeped in research that feels personal, sometimes uncomfortably so . . . By allowing us to participate in the science—as I did—and not just digest data, Banaji and Greenwald capture our attention."

—BookPage

"An accessible and persuasive account of the causes of stereotyping and discrimination . . . Banaji and Greenwald will keep even nonpsychology students engaged with plenty of self-examinations and compelling elucidations of case studies and experiments."

—Publishers Weekly

"Mahzarin R. Banaji and Anthony G. Greenwald's work has revolutionized social psychology, proving that—unconsciously—people are affected by dangerous stereotypes."

—Psychology Today

"A stimulating treatment that should help readers deal with irrational biases."

—Kirkus Reviews

"*Blindspot* successfully reveals how our unconscious minds influence our beliefs and behaviors and reminds us to think twice about our instinctive reactions."

—Scientific American

For Bhaskar and Jean
Revealers of blindspots

The sailor cannot see the North
—but knows the Needle can—

EMILY DICKINSON, in a letter
to a mentor, T. W. Higginson, seeking an
honest evaluation of her talent (1862)

CONTENTS

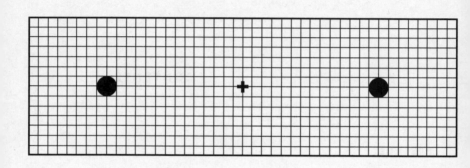

LIKE ALL VERTEBRATES, YOU HAVE A BLIND SPOT IN THE RETINA OF each eye. This region, a *scotoma* (from the Greek word for *darkness*), has no light-sensitive cells and therefore light arriving at that spot has no path to the visual areas of your brain.

Paradoxically, you can "see" your own blind spot. Try it by looking with one eye at the plus sign in the middle of the rectangle on the opposite page. Cover the other eye with one hand and hold the page at arm's length in front of you, then slowly bring the rectangle closer while maintaining your focus on the plus sign. When the page is about six inches away, the black disc on the same side as your open eye will disappear. It will reappear as you bring the page closer still. The moment of disappearance tells you when light from that disc is falling on the blind spot of your open eye. Here's a bonus: If you shift the gaze of your open eye to the still-visible disc on the other side, the plus sign will disappear!

You may have noticed something strange in the location of the vanished disc. When it disappeared, it left no blank spot—no hole in the grid background. You saw an unbroken grid. Your brain did something quite remarkable—it filled in the blind spot with something that made reasonable sense—a continuation of the same grid that was visible everywhere else in the rectangle.

A much more dramatic form of blindness than the one you just experienced occurs in a pathological condition called *blindsight,* which involves damage to the brain's visual cortex. Patients with this damage show the striking behavior of accurately reaching for and grasping an object placed in front of them, even while having no conscious visual experience of the object. If you place a hammer before the patient and ask, "Do you see something in front of you?" the patient will answer, "No, I don't." But ask the patient to reach for and grasp the hammer and the patient who just said it was invisible will do so successfully! This seemingly bizarre phenomenon happens because the condition of blindsight leaves intact subcortical retina-to-brain pathways that can guide visual behavior, even in the absence of consciously seeing the hammer.

Rather than an effect of visual perception, this book focuses on another type of blindspot, one that contains a large set of biases and keeps them hidden. This hidden-bias blindspot shares a feature with the blind spot that you just experienced via the image of the grid and discs—we can be unaware of hidden biases in the same way we are unaware of the retinal scotoma in each of our eyes. This blindspot also shares a feature with the dramatic and pathological phenomenon of blindsight. Just as patients who can't "see" a hammer can still act as if they do, hidden biases are capable of guiding our behavior without our being aware of their role.

What are the hidden biases of this book's title? They are—for lack of a better term—*bits of knowledge* about social groups. These bits of knowledge are stored in our brains because we encounter them so frequently in our cultural environments. Once lodged in our minds, hidden biases can influence our behavior toward members of particular social groups, but we remain oblivious to their influence. In talking with others about hidden biases, we have discovered that most people find it unbelievable that their behavior can be guided by mental content of which they are unaware.

In this book we aim to make clear why many scientists, ourselves very much included, now recognize hidden-bias blindspots as fully believable because of the sheer weight of scientific evidence that demands this conclusion. But convincing readers of this is no simple challenge. How can we show the existence of something in our own minds of which we remain completely unaware?

Some years ago, we presented people with a test that could reveal possible hidden bias—a test of their relative preference for two American cultural icons: Oprah Winfrey and Martha Stewart. A perfect and humorous example of just how unbelievable we find the idea that our behavior might be guided by information that lies in our blindspot arrived via this email: *"Dear Harvard People: There is no way that I prefer Martha Stewart over Oprah Winfrey. Please fix your tests. Sincerely, Frank."*

We know what Frank means. Frank does *know,* in the common understanding of that term, that his fondness for Oprah exceeds that for Martha. And, as his message indicates, Frank finds it simply unbelievable that his mind could additionally possess a preference about which he has no conscious knowledge. Therefore, it's the test that needs to be fixed!

The self-administered test that Frank found to be so flawed is the Implicit Association Test, which we as well as many others have been studying since 1995. Just as the rectangle with the black discs allows us to see the otherwise hidden retinal blind spot, the Implicit Association Test has enabled us to reveal to ourselves the contents of hidden-bias blindspots. And where the demonstration of the retinal blind spot allows us to know that the visual blind spot exists but not much more, the Implicit Association Test (IAT) lets us look into the hidden-bias blindspot and discover what it contains.

The two of us met in Columbus, Ohio, in 1980 when Mahzarin arrived from India as a PhD student to work with Tony at Ohio State University. The decade of the 1980s brought significant changes to our branch of psychology. Psychology was on the verge of what can now—thirty years later—be recognized as a revolution triggered by new methods that could reveal potent mental content and processes that were inaccessible to introspection. The two of us sought to learn whether these methods could be sufficiently developed to reveal and explain these unseen influences on social behavior. Looking back to that period, we can see how fortunate we were to be swept into the vortex of this revolution.

The still-growing surge of research on unconscious mental function has already dramatically changed how human behavior is understood. A quarter century ago, most psychologists believed that human behavior was primarily guided by conscious thoughts and feelings. Nowadays the majority will readily agree that much of human judgment and behavior is produced with little conscious thought. A quarter century ago, the word "unconscious"—having fallen out of favor in scientific psychology earlier in the twentieth century—was barely to be found in the scientific journals that we read and in which we published our research. Nowadays, the term "unconscious cognition" appears frequently, although it was surpassed in the 1990s by the related term "implicit cognition." A quarter century ago, psychologists' methods for understanding the mind relied mostly on asking people to report their mental states and intentions. Nowadays, research methods are much more diverse, including many that do not rely at all on research participants' reports on the contents of their minds or the causes of their behavior.

Readers who are fond of endnotes will discover our reliance on the scientists of the past eighty years, in whose footsteps we readily follow. Two of these predecessors stand out as giants with shoulders broad enough to accommodate many later researchers, us among them. Gunnar Myrdal led the multi-year collaborative effort that produced *An American Dilemma* in 1944, which converged with other forces to put race discrimination in the United States on the national agenda, where it still remains. Gordon Allport, writing *The Nature of Prejudice* in 1954, gave the scientific study of prejudice a foundation and organization that continues, in the twenty-first century, to inspire new scientific work.

Like the late United States senator Daniel Patrick Moynihan, we believe that people have a right to their own opinion but not a right to their own facts. This is easier said than done, because what constitutes a fact is often unclear and even contentious. Political satirist Steven Colbert coined the term *truthiness,* defined as the tendency to accept propositions that one wishes to be true as true, ignoring the usual verification standards for facts.

In poking fun at truthiness—by presuming to favor it over genuine facts—Colbert, the pseudo-conservative, quipped, "I don't trust books. They're all fact, no heart." To avoid indulging in truthiness of our own, we have chosen to stick closely to evidence, especially experiments whose conclusions reflect widely shared consensus among experts. In other words, we have opted, consistently and consciously, for *more* fact and *less* heart.

Like other scientists, we do not have the luxury of believing that what appears true and valid now will always appear so. Inevitably, future knowledge will exceed and replace present understanding. But if we have done our job modestly well, it may take a few decades for that to happen to the conclusions reached in this book, among them the idea that hidden-bias blindspots are so widespread that many good people have them.

It is with some trepidation that we refer to "good people" in this book's subtitle. We have no special competence (let alone the moral authority) to judge who is good and who is not. By "good people" we refer to those, ourselves included, who intend well and who strive to align their behavior with their intentions. Our highest aim for this book is to explain the science sufficiently so that these good people will be better able to achieve that alignment.

BLINDSPOT

1

Mindbugs

IT IS AN ORDINARY DAY ON A COLLEGE CAMPUS. STUDENTS AND professors of experimental psychology have filed into a lecture hall to listen to a distinguished visiting scientist explain how our minds perceive the physical world. Nothing about his tweed jacket and unkempt hair suggests the challenge he is about to deliver. A few minutes into the lecture, he says matter-of-factly, "As you can see, the two tabletops are exactly the same in shape and size."

Shuffling in their seats, some in the audience frown while oth-

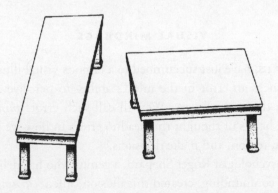

ers smile in embarrassment because, as anyone can plainly see, he is dead wrong. Some tilt their heads from side to side, to test if a literal shift in perspective will help. Others wonder whether they should bother staying for the lecture if this nonsense is just the start.

The nonbelievers are caught short, though, when the speaker proceeds to show the truth of his audacious claim. Using an overhead projector, he takes a transparent plastic sheet containing only a single red parallelogram, lays it over the tabletop on the left, and shows that it fits perfectly. He then rotates the plastic sheet clockwise, and places the parallelogram over the tabletop on the right; it fits perfectly there as well. An audible gasp fills the hall as the speaker moves the red frame back and forth, and the room breaks into laughter. With nothing more than a faint smile the speaker goes on to complete his lecture on how the eye receives, the brain registers, and the mind interprets visual information.

Unconvinced? You can try the test yourself. Find some paper thin enough to trace the outline of one of the tabletops, and then move the outline over to the other tabletop. If you don't find that the shape of the first tabletop fits identically onto the second tabletop, there can be only one explanation—you've botched the tracing job, because the table surfaces are precisely the same.

But how can this be?

VISUAL MINDBUGS

You, LIKE US, have just succumbed to a famous visual illusion, one that produces an error in the mind's ability to perceive a pair of objects as they actually are. We will call such errors *mindbugs*— ingrained habits of thought that lead to errors in how we perceive, remember, reason, and make decisions.[1]

The psychologist Roger Shepard, a genius who has delighted in the art of confounding, created this illusion called *Turning the Tables*. When we look at the images of the two table surfaces, our retinas do, in fact, receive them as identical in shape and size. In other words, the retina "sees" the tabletops quite accurately. However, when the eye transmits that information to the brain's visual cortex, where depth is perceived, the trouble begins.

The incorrect perception that the two tabletops are strikingly different in shape occurs effortlessly, because the brain *automatically* converts the 2-D image that exists both on the page and on the retina into a 3-D interpretation of the tabletop shapes as they *must be* in the natural world. The automatic processes of the mind, in other words, impose the third dimension of depth onto this scene. And the conscious, reflective processes of the mind accept the illusion unquestioningly. So much so that when encountering the speaker's assertion that the tabletop outlines are the same, the conscious mind's first reaction is to consider it to be sheer nonsense.

Natural selection has endowed the minds of humans and other large animals to operate successfully in a three-dimensional world. Having no experience in a world other than a 3-D one, the brain we have continues to perform its conscious perceptual corrections of the tables' dimensions to make them appear as they would in the traditional 3-D world.[2]

Contrary to expectation, this error reflects not a weakness of adaptation but rather a triumph, for Shepard's tabletops highlight the success of a visual system that has adapted effectively to the combination of a two-dimensional retina inside the eye and a three-dimensional world outside. The mind's automatic understanding of the data is so confident that, as Shepard puts it, "any knowledge or understanding of the illusion we may gain at the intellectual level remains virtually powerless to diminish the magnitude of the illusion." Take a look at the tables again. The knowledge you now have (that the tables have identical surfaces) has no corrective effect in diminishing the illusion![3]

Disconcerting as this experience is, it serves as a vivid illustration of a signal property of the mind—it does a great deal of its work automatically, unconsciously, and unintentionally. Mention of the mind's unconscious operation may summon up for you a visual memory of the bearded, cigar-smoking Sigmund Freud, who rightly gets credit for having brought the term *unconscious* into everyday use. However, an understanding of the unconscious workings of the mind has changed greatly in the century since Freud's pathbreaking observations. Freud portrayed an omniscient unconscious with complex motives that shape important aspects of human mind and behavior—from dreams to memories to madness, and ultimately to civilization itself. Today, however, Freud's arguments, detached as they have remained from scientific verification, have a greatly reduced impact on scientific understanding of unconscious mental life.

Instead, the modern conception of the unconscious mind must be credited to another historical figure, one far less known than Freud. A nineteenth-century German physicist and physiologist, Hermann von Helmholtz, offered the name *unbewußter Schluß,* or *unconscious inference,* to describe how an illusion like Shepard's tabletops might work.[4] Helmholtz aimed to describe the means by which the mind creates from physical data the conscious perceptions that define our ordinary and subjective experiences of "seeing." Our visual system is capable of being tricked by a simple 2-D image, because an unconscious mental act replaces the 2-D shape of the retinal image with a consciously perceived 3-D shape of the inferred object it suggests.

Now try this: Read the following sixteen words with sufficiently close attention so that you can expect to be able to recognize them when you see them again a few pages hence:

Ant
Spider
Feelers
Web
Fly

Poison
Slimy
Crawl
Bee
Wing
Bug
Small
Bite
Fright
Wasp
Creepy

In the meantime, here's another striking example of unconscious inference in the form of a checkerboard and cylinder to confound us further. When we tell you that the squares marked A and B are exactly the same in their coloring, you will doubtless believe us to be wrong. But take a thick piece of opaque paper, one large enough to cover the entire picture, mark with a point the two

"Surely, you can see that the shades of gray in squares A and B are identical."

squares labeled A and B, and make a circular hole just a bit smaller than the checkerboard square on which each sits. When you look only through the holes and without the rest of the image, you will see that they are indeed identical in color.

Again the culprit is an unconscious inference, a mindbug that automatically goes to work on the image. What causes this remarkable failure of perception? Several features of this checkerboard image are involved, but let us attend to the most obvious ones. First of all, notice that B is surrounded by several dark squares that make it look lighter than it is, merely by contrast; likewise, just the opposite, A is surrounded by adjacent lighter squares that make it seem darker than it actually is. Second, notice the shadow being cast by the cylinder. This darkens the squares within the shadow—including the one marked B—but the mind automatically undoes this darkening to correct for the shadow, lightening our conscious experience of B.

As with the table illusion, the mechanisms that produce this one also exist to enable us to see and understand the world successfully. Ted Adelson, a vision scientist at MIT and creator of this checkershadow image, writes: "As with many so-called illusions, this effect really demonstrates the success rather than the failure of the visual system. The visual system is not very good at being a physical light meter, but that is not its purpose."[5] Such examples force us to ask a more general question: To what extent do our minds possess efficient and accurate methods that fail us so miserably when we put them to use in a slightly revised context?

MEMORY MINDBUGS

THINK BACK to the words you memorized earlier, as you examine the list below. As you review each word, without turning back to the original list, try to recall whether each word you see here also appeared in the list you read earlier. If you have paper and pencil handy, and to avoid any doubt about your answers, copy all the words you recall seeing on the previous list and leave out any word that, by your recollection, did not appear before.

Maple Ant Poison Fly Stem Berry Feelers Slimy Birch Wing Leaves Tree Roots Bite Web Bug Small Oak Crawl Acorn Wasp Branch Insect Bee Willow Fright Spider Pine Creepy

To be correct, you should have left out all twelve tree-related words, starting with *maple* and ending with *pine,* for indeed, none of the tree words appeared on the earlier list. You should have also written down all the insect-related words, except one—the word *insect* itself! That word was not on the original list. If, as is quite likely, you included the word *insect* as one you'd seen before, you have demonstrated a powerful but ordinary mindbug that can create false memories.

In retrospect, it's easy to see the basis for the false memory for *insect.* The mind is an automatic association-making machine. When it encounters any information—words, pictures, or even complex ideas—related information automatically comes to mind. In this case, the words in the original list had an insect theme. Unthinkingly, we use that shared theme as we try to remember the past and, in so doing, stumble easily when we come across the word *insect* itself. Such a memory error is called a *false alarm*—we mistakenly remember something that actually did not occur.

In a study conducted at Washington University, 82 percent of the time students remembered seeing words that shared a theme—say, insects—but were not on the original lists. That huge percentage of error is especially remarkable when compared to the 75 percent correct memory for words that were actually on the list! In other words, mindbugs can be powerful enough to produce greater recollection of things that didn't occur than of things that did occur.[6]

The errors witnessed so far may not seem terribly consequential. What's the harm, after all, in misremembering a word? But imagine being interrogated about a potential suspect in a crime you have witnessed. Could the false-memory mindbug interfere with your accuracy in reporting what you saw? If the suspect bears some resemblance to the criminal—for example, has a similar beard—might a false identification result? If so, with what probability?

Elizabeth Loftus is among psychology's most creative experimentalists. Now at the University of California at Irvine, she has made it her life's work to study memory mindbugs in eyewitnesses by presenting simulated burglaries, car accidents, and other common mishaps and then testing people's memories of them. She has found not only that errors in these eyewitness memories are disturbingly frequent but also that even slight changes in the way in which the witness is prompted during questioning to remember an event can alter the content of what is remembered.

In one famous study, Loftus showed witnesses scenes from an automobile accident in which two cars had collided with no personal injury. Later she asked half the witnesses, "How fast was the car going when it hit the other car?" She asked the other half, "How fast was the car going when it smashed into the other car?" Those who were asked the "smashed" question gave higher estimates of the speed of the vehicle, compared to those who were asked the "hit" question, in addition to which they were more likely to mistakenly insert a memory of broken glass at the accident scene even though there was none in what they saw.[7]

Psychologists call this mindbug *retroactive interference*—an influence of after-the-experience information on memory. Loftus gave this a more memorable name: the *misinformation effect*. Her point is that a small change in language can produce a consequential change in what is remembered, often resulting in mistaken testimony by eyewitnesses who relied on mistaken information.

In recent years it has become clear that the number of wrongful convictions produced by eyewitness errors is substantial.[8] From the efforts of the Innocence Project, an organization dedicated to exonerating the wrongfully convicted through DNA testing, 250 people so far have been exonerated by conclusive tests that confirmed their innocence. Of these, 190 cases had been decided based on a mistaken eyewitness account. In other words, in nearly 75 percent of the cases of wrongful conviction, the failure of eyewitness memory (assuming no malign intent on the part of the witness to wrongfully convict) was responsible for tragedies that many societies believe to be so intolerable that their laws explicitly err on the side of allowing the guilty to walk free.

AVAILABILITY AND ANCHORING:
TWO FAMOUS MINDBUGS

PICK THE CORRECT ANSWER in each of the three pairs: Each year, do more people in the United States die from cause (a) or cause (b)?

1. (a) murder (b) diabetes
2. (a) murder (b) suicide
3. (a) car accidents (b) abdominal cancer

Most of us give the answer (b) for question 1 and (a) for questions 2 and 3, when in fact the correct answer to each question is (b). In other words, we get the first one right but not the next two. Psychologists Daniel Kahneman and Amos Tversky named and described the generic version of this mindbug, calling it the *availability heuristic*. When instances of one type of event (such as death by murder rather than suicide) come more easily to mind than those of another type, we tend to assume that the first event also must occur more frequently in the world. Murder is more likely to receive media attention than suicide, not to mention that the stigma of suicide makes it less likely to be discussed beyond the family. Car accidents are likewise more likely to be mentioned because of their shocking nature, whereas abdominal cancer is one of many kinds of cancer, a common cause of death. Because murder and car accidents come to mind more easily, they are wrongly assumed to occur more frequently. This is seemingly reasonable, but it can lead us to overestimate car accident deaths. However, greater ease of availability to the mind doesn't mean greater frequency of occurrence in the world. These kinds of mistakes occur routinely, and are often accompanied with great decision costs.[9]

Dan Ariely, a behavioral economist, asked students at MIT to write down the last two digits of their Social Security number on a piece of paper. He then asked them to estimate the price of a keyboard, a trackball, or a design book, items easily familiar to MIT students. Ariely collected these two numbers from each person and then computed the correlation between them, looking for a possible relation between the two digits of the Social Security number and the estimated prices. Logically, of course, there is no connection between the two sets of numbers, so the correlation should have been at or close to zero.

In fact, Ariely discovered that there was a substantial correlation between the two sets of numbers. Those for whom the last two digits of their Social Security number happened to lie between 00 and 19 said they would pay $8.62 on average for the trackball; those with digits between 20 and 39 were willing to pay more, $11.82; those with digits between 40 and 59 offered up even more, $13.45; and the poor souls whose Social Security numbers happened to end in digits from 60 to 79 and 80 to 99 offered to pay $21.18 and $26.18—all for the very same object![10]

This, the second of the two famous mindbugs, was discovered by psychologists Kahneman and Tversky, who called it *anchoring*, to capture the idea that the mind doesn't search for information in a vacuum.[11] Rather, it starts by using whatever information is immediately available as a reference point or "anchor" and then adjusting. The result, in this case of the random-digit anchor, was the potentially self-harming penalty of being willing to pay too much.

Those who fall prey to the availability and anchoring heuristics are not more feeble-minded or gullible than others. Each of us is an ever-ready victim. Property values can be altered by manipulated price anchors that inflate or deflate the actual price. The valuation of stocks can be influenced more by their suggested market price than actual value, perhaps providing some of the explanation for the persistence of financial bubbles.[12]

SOCIAL MINDBUGS

HUMAN BEINGS are social animals, first and foremost. Other members of our species are significant to us in ways that little else in the physical world can compete with. For this reason perhaps, the primate brain has evolved to pay special attention to others of its kind, and one way in which we do this is to routinely try to predict what might go on in the minds of others.

Emerging research suggests that selective brain regions appear to be active when we imagine the thoughts of another person (Does she believe in Christ the Savior?) and when we try to predict the actions of others (Will he allow our temple to be safe?).[13] These same brain regions do not seem to care when we contemplate the physical aspects of others, such as their height, weight, or eye color, suggesting that the brain has evolved specific regions to help with the tasks of social thinking and feeling. That is to say, other minds matter to us enough that regions of neural real estate are uniquely engaged for the purpose of making social meaning.

Gordon Bower, a cognitive psychologist at Stanford, was interested in how memory plays a role in important decisions about people. He invited groups of individuals to be members of a jury in a mock trial.[14] The defendant, Mr. Sanders, had run a stop sign while driving, with the consequence of colliding with a garbage truck. Although the defendant's blood alcohol level was not tested at the time of the accident, he was being tried on the basis of evidence that he might have been drunk while driving. Testimony was presented, with each of two groups of subjects receiving one of the following two descriptions of Mr. Sanders's behavior at a party just prior to the accident:

(1) *On his way out the door, Sanders staggered against a serving table, knocking a bowl to the floor.*

(2) *On his way out the door, Sanders staggered against a serving table, knocking a bowl of guacamole dip to the floor and splattering guacamole on the white shag carpet.*

Should there have been any difference in these two snippets of testimony on judgments of Mr. Sanders's guilt or innocence? Not at all. The information about the color of the food and its appearance on the white rug were logically irrelevant to his possible drunkenness. But those who heard the testimony with the additional detail about the guacamole were more likely to believe that Sanders was guilty. The culprit here is the vividness with which some events stick in memory. Vividness makes some information more readily available in memory (remember the availability bias?), and what Bower's experiment shows is that availability through vividness plays a role in skewing a jury's verdict, presumably with no awareness on the part of jurors that this is happening.

It's striking that these examples are not about rare or bizarre events that afflict a small group of unusually fragile people. Rather, it's their ordinariness that makes them such compelling phenomena to understand.

It is easy to see why we may give little thought to errors that harm others, such as Mr. Sanders, but not us. Might we be more careful and avoid mindbugs when our own interests are at stake? Imagine an experiment you might do with six friends. Ask a group of three of these friends (randomly chosen from the six) to give three reasons why they love their romantic partners, and ask the other three friends to give nine reasons for the same. Then ask both groups of friends this single question: "How satisfied are you with your relationship?" Surprisingly, research suggests that those asked to write only three reasons report greater happiness with their partner and their relationship than those asked to write nine reasons.

The explanation for the bias is counterintuitive but simple: Which of us can easily come up with *nine* good qualities of a partner? Even canonization requires only two miracles! Those asked to come up with nine reasons have to work harder to come up with the list, and it prompts this thought: "Hmm, that was hard! Is it possible that my partner isn't as wonderful as I'd imagined?" The experiment that tested this—by Norbert Schwarz at the University of Michigan—found that even important and familiar affections are susceptible to the availability bias.[15]

When judging people's character, we hardly even recognize just how "right" our assessment feels—even when it is based on only a smattering of information. Look at photos of any two strangers and ask yourself:

Which one of these two people seems to be more trustworthy?
Which one will be more competent on the job?
Which one is more likely to dominate others?

It turns out that it is surprisingly easy (we didn't say accurate) to make such assessments based on nothing more than a static picture. In fact, trying to *avoid* making such judgments may be far more effortful than making them. The problem, of course, is that these judgments may be not just a little wrong but quite wrong. A face whose features are similar to our own may evoke a feeling of trust when we are deciding to hire a job applicant or choosing a candidate to vote for. And particular facial configurations can lead us all to believe that a person is trustworthy—such as those who have more of a baby face.

Alex Todorov at Princeton University shows that shifting the eyes on a face closer together can make us believe the person to be less competent.[16] The implications from such a demonstration should give us pause, enough pause to rethink the manner in which we make important decisions about others and the degree to which such decisions are even in our own interest. Our interactions with others require not only that we must routinely make decisions about them but also that we do so under conditions of less than perfect knowledge. It's never quite clear which of two people, Shakeel or Stanley, was responsible for the brawl that erupted in a bar. It's not easy to say whether Joan or Joe will best lead our team into emerging markets. It's not easy to say whether Manuel or Mohammed has the necessary skills to serve as a competent Transportation Security Administration checkpoint guard. In making such difficult assessments, we rely on the social group to which the person belongs as a basis for predicting success. Without recognizing it, we automatically pose and answer questions such as: *Are people like him trustworthy or not? Is the group she comes from smart or dumb? Are people of his kind likely to be violent or peace-loving?*[17]

The same mind that viewed the two tables to be different when in fact they were the same is at work here, using membership in social groups rather than the table legs as the contextual cue that generates an unconscious social inference. In multiple experiments, we have given people nothing more than a picture of a human face and asked them to tell us whether Mark is likely to enjoy skiing or reading, whether Sally will visit family for the holidays, whether Heather finds shoe shopping to be a nuisance, and so on for dozens of questions.[18] Remarkably, nobody ever responds, "I can't say!" Using whatever they can eke out from even the most trivial information, people make assessments within a few seconds or fractions of a second, and without any visible discomfort at having to do so. This comfort with judging the likely trustworthiness and competence of others in the absence of any direct information at all— sometimes just a 2-D view of a face—is worth some consideration in itself.

Social mindbugs can give us both false feelings of faith in people we perhaps shouldn't trust and the opposite—feelings of distrust toward those whom we perhaps should trust. Take as an example Bernard Madoff, perpetrator of the largest investment fraud in U.S. history. While Madoff's victims were quite ethnically diverse, Jewish philanthropic organizations were particularly numerous among them, suggesting that they were more unwisely trusting of Madoff, with whom they shared a group identity based on religion.[19] A symmetric but opposite outcome involves the evocation of inappropriate distrust that is also in error. As the story goes, when Omar Edwards left his home on the morning of May 28, 2009, he had little reason to predict that he would never return home. But Edwards, a Black police officer, was fatally shot in Harlem when a fellow officer mistook him for a suspect.[20] Such tragic actions tell us that we fail to perceive individuals as individuals. They are often viewed as representatives of social groups.[21] Tragedies that arise both from inappropriate trust and from inappropriate distrust bear the imprint of automatic decisions made on the basis of group membership.

Economists, sociologists, and psychologists have confirmed time and again that the social group to which a person belongs can be isolated as a definitive cause of the treatment he or she receives. Our work has led us to think about single ordinary instances—a smile or a suspicious look, a bank loan approved or rejected, a decision to stop and search, to promote or let go, to investigate with further medical tests or not. Each individual act involves but a single decision that one mind makes about another, and it is here that we must look for mindbugs.

Social mindbugs are not restricted to decisions based on a person's race or ethnicity. They stem from psychologically and socially meaningful human groups of all sorts. Age, gender, religion, class, sexuality, disability, physical attractiveness, profession, and personality are only a few examples, and some are more magnetic than others in drawing us toward them as explanations of behavior. As Jean-Paul Sartre's famous narration goes, when a woman had difficulty with a particular furrier, she added as an explanation of her troubles with him that he was Jewish. Why, Sartre asked, did she not turn her dislike of the man to be a property of furriers? Why Jews? Mindbugs are at the root of such likes and dislikes, even strong passions. The groups to which people belong seem to be compelling explanations for who they are and what they do and even what they may potentially do, and thereby serve as justification of behavior toward them.

Curiously, social mindbugs affect decisions not only about others but also about ourselves. In a study conducted at Yale's School of Public Health, Becca Levy showed a stunning correlation—that the negative beliefs about the elderly that elderly people themselves held when they were younger predicted their vulnerability to heart disease when they became older.[22] This result emerged even after controlling for other factors such as depression, smoking, and family history. We take such evidence as suggestive that stereotypes can be harmful not just to the others we assess and evaluate but also to ourselves. In understanding mindbugs, a persuasive reason to take them seriously is self-interest: Stereotypes can negatively affect our actions toward *ourselves*.

CODA

HERBERT SIMON, a pioneer in studying the mind's capacities, poked fun at the assumption that people make decisions based on a sensible analysis of the actual value of the options available to them. Human beings, Simon noted, have "neither the facts nor the consistent structure of values nor the reasoning power at their disposal" to make decisions in line with subjective expected utility, which he argued was "a beautiful object deserving a prominent place in Plato's heaven of ideas . . . [but] impossible to employ . . . in any literal way in making actual human decisions."[23]

Give people the option of taking a free $10 bill versus an equally free $20 bill and they will, if rational, take the latter. But as soon as the situation gets even slightly more complex or uncertain, people begin to depart from economists' expectation of "utility maximization." We now know that in our daily choices, whether it is choosing between eating pepperoni or mushroom, visiting Bali or Barcelona, choosing a career in investment banking or carpentry, we do not always act to maximize our own happiness and well-being.

Evidence from the second half of the twentieth century has made it increasingly plausible that human rationality is severely limited. Our task, in this book, is to follow this idea of the bounds on rationality into a particular place—where the questions concern how we judge ourselves, other individuals, and the social collectives to which they and we belong.

As a backdrop to our analysis, we will keep in mind that humanity has a long evolutionary past that has shaped social nature to be what it is today. Our ancestors lived in relatively small, homogeneous groups, surrounded by constant physical danger. In response to the pressures of that environment, they evolved mechanisms that made social choices paramount to mere survival. Several of the mindbugs we have described are consequences of these erstwhile evolutionary triumphs.

But we also recognize that the modern social world in which we live would be unrecognizable to our ancestors. The social contents of our minds, how we think about what's right and wrong as it involves other people, even those quite unlike us, would be incomprehensible to them. Human values and aspirations have changed radically and rapidly, even within just the last few generations. Principles of equal rights and fair treatment, values essential to any modern democratic political system, have existed for barely a few centuries. The demands placed on us to survive in the past are not the same demands that allow us to thrive now. As just one obvious example, staying away from those who were different or strange may once have been a safe strategy. Now, it can be financially costly, if the tendency to avoid those who are different keeps a corporation from investing in places distant from the business's country of origin or from working in a labor market that does not speak their language.

Even a short time ago it would have been unthinkable that we should devise regulations to monitor our behavior—for example, that we should prohibit ourselves from buying a cup of coffee for a federal employee who may be in a position to fund our research. Think about the vast difference in our notion of power, even the seemingly "natural" power of parents over children—not to mention changes in our views of torture and the rights of enemy combatants. These changes have their origins in our conscious, reflective minds, which transformed our sense of what is fair and just, and the right way to live as social beings.

We changed because to the extent that mindbugs slant how we see, remember, reason, and judge, they reveal a particular disparity in us: between our intentions and ideals, on one hand, and our behavior and actions, on the other. The mind sciences have shown that such disparities undermine self-awareness, threaten the ability to consciously control actions, and obfuscate the cherished ideal of self-determination. Understanding how mindbugs erode the coastline of rational thought, and ultimately the very possibility of a just and productive society, requires understanding the mindbugs that are at the root of the disparity between our inner minds and outward actions.

2

Shades of Truth

(Problems with Asking Questions)

WHEN YOU ARE ASKED QUESTIONS, HOW OFTEN DO YOU GIVE AN-swers that you *know* are untrue? If your answer is "rarely" or "never," we hope to convince you that this itself is something you know to be untrue.

We are not questioning your integrity. It's perfectly understand-able that you would believe that you rarely answer questions in ways you know to be untrue. Almost certainly you see yourself as an honest person—most people do. And you probably assumed that we were asking about times when you were consciously and deliberately lying, perhaps even in ways that might benefit you at the expense of others. But we are interested in something both much simpler than that and not at all malevolent—untruths that are somewhere on the spectrum between totally unconscious and partly conscious, untruths that people tell not only to others but at times to themselves as well.

You may be only dimly aware of forces that work to shade your answers away from truth. Those forces reflect a diverse set of moti-vations, including (paradoxically) a desire to be accurate and truth-ful. We aim here to help you become aware not only of the extent of your unrecognized untruths but also of their causes.

Consider the question that is probably the one you are most frequently asked and the one to which you most often give an answer that—after you think about it—you often know to be untrue:

Q1. *How are you?*

How often do you answer "Fine" even if the question interrupted your mental review of how much your back hurts, how upset you are about criticism just received from a friend, or how little sleep you've been getting?

Here's a question that you might have heard from someone who is overweight:

Q2. *Do I look fat in these jeans?*

To ask whether you often answer Q1 and Q2 with less than the truth is hardly different from asking if you're human. You may defend yourself by pointing out that the untruths you tell in response to these questions are nobly motivated—they reveal only your desire to avoid boring, burdening, or hurting the person who asked the question. You may add to your defense by pointing out that your less-than-true answers to these questions cannot possibly harm anyone—quite the contrary. And even the person who asks these questions may have little expectation of receiving a truthful answer. But remember—the question we asked was whether you *ever* give answers that you know are untrue, not whether you can justify those answers.

Untruths in answering questions such as Q1 and Q2 are called *white lies*—presumably because the purity and innocence associated with the color white seem appropriate to the harmlessness of these lies. In the same spirit, we have named several other categories of untruth after colors that suggest appropriate symbolic meanings. Although these names won't be familiar to you in the way the term "white lies" is, you will recognize the categories themselves once you read about them.

GRAY LIES

WHEN CONFRONTED with the untruths you told in answering Q1 and Q2 you may have thought, "OK—it's true. I *do* engage in the occasional white lie, but that's my limit. Otherwise I'm quite honest." Please read on.

Q3. *What were you dreaming about when you moaned in your sleep?*

(You groggily answer your partner *I can't remember,* although you know quite well that you were dreaming about a passionate interlude with an ex.)

Q4. *Can you spare a dollar?*

(You respond, "Sorry, I don't have any cash" to the homeless person on the street, even though you actually have plenty and could easily afford to part with a dollar.)

Q5. *Is Ms. X* [who answers the phone] *at home?*

(Ms. X's blithe answer to the telephone solicitor: "No, she's not.")

These untruths are a bit darker than white lies, so we color them gray. Like white lies, gray lies are motivated by a desire to spare feelings. However, these answers are shaped more by the desire to spare one's own feelings than by the intention to spare someone else's. For Q3 (*What were you dreaming about when you moaned?*), the primary motive may be to avoid embarrassing yourself, but you also are probably concerned about not hurting your partner. In answering Q4 (*Can you spare a dollar?*), the main goal is to get out of giving the supplicant any money, but you might also want to do that without expressing hostility. With Q5 (*Is Ms. X at home?*), Ms. X may want most to avoid an unwanted intrusion on her time, but, knowing that the caller is just doing a hired job, she avoids being confrontational.

COLORLESS LIES

FYODOR DOSTOYEVSKY wrote:

> Every man has reminiscences which he would not tell to everyone but only his friends. He has other matters in his mind which he would not reveal even to his friends, but only to himself, and that in secret. But there are other things which a man is afraid to tell even to himself, and every decent man has a number of such things stored away in his mind.[1]

The things that people keep from themselves are what we will call colorless lies, because they are invisible to the teller of the lie. As mundane illustrations of Dostoyevsky's poetic insight, consider the answers that a smoker or a drinker might give to two questions that physicians routinely ask during medical checkups:

Q6. *How many cigarettes a day do you smoke?*

Q7. *How many drinks do you have per day?*

The answers to Q6 and Q7 may underestimate the truth substantially, even while the answerer sees them as fully truthful. Assume that the smoker knows perfectly well that an entire pack disappears each day, but answers "half a pack." The thought behind this answer might be, "I buy a pack each day and I smoke little more than half of each cigarette. That makes half a pack." The drinker may answer "two drinks" while consuming an amount that the medical community counts as four. The problem is not a mistake in counting. The drinker may conveniently ignore the fact that each of two trips to the home bar produces a glass with twice the amount of alcohol of a standard drink.[2]

These colorless lies differ from other types of untruths because they can be invisible even to those who utter them. They are targeted as much at the untruth-teller him- or herself as at the listener. You may be familiar with the term that psychologists use for these untruths: *self-deception*.

RED LIES

IN HIS 1850 POEM *In Memoriam A. H. H.*, Alfred Lord Tennyson penned a line describing nature as "red in tooth and claw." That line has served, ever since, as a shorthand reference to the processes at work in natural selection. We therefore refer to lies that potentially confer survival and reproductive benefits to the teller as "red lies." Perhaps these untruths have an evolutionary basis—they may have evolved to be part of human nature.

Some evolutionary biologists have proposed that *Homo sapiens* is indeed hardwired to tell lies. Their theory is based partly on observations of how much lying people actually do in the course of daily life. But a stronger scientific basis for believing that lying is innate is that many other animal species display survival-enhancing forms of deceit. There is widespread acceptance that these nonhuman deceptions must have evolved by natural selection and therefore have a genetic basis. Camo moths, brimstone butterflies, and crescent moths are just a few of the many species that disguise their presence by camouflage, having evolved appearances indistinguishable from their foliage backgrounds. Other insects deter predators through mimicry—they look or behave like members of species that are poisonous or foul-tasting, making it more likely that they will be avoided than eaten.

Although the proposition that deception in various animal species has evolved through Darwinian natural selection is uncontested, it is nevertheless a leap to extend that conclusion to the spoken falsehoods of our own species. On the timescale of evolution, human language itself is a recent arrival, dating back perhaps a mere hundred thousand years. So we have to ask whether something that came into being so recently in the time span of hominids on earth (variously estimated as somewhere between two million and twelve million years) could show any kind of evolutionary adaptation. In other words, is a hundred thousand years long enough to allow for natural selection to have produced not just language but deceitful language?

Evolutionary theorists believe that selection pressures can produce significant genetic changes in as little as thirty generations—which is less than a thousand years for our species. If lying produces a selection advantage that allows the liar to live longer and to produce more offspring than a non-liar, there could indeed have been enough time for natural selection to promote genes that predispose us to lie.[3]

One obvious example of this skill in action is the person who deceptively declares "I love you" to a potential sex partner and who might therefore succeed better at passing on his or her genes than someone who claims only to want sex. False claims of material wealth and the lavishing of counterfeit flattery on a potential bedmate are likewise lies of a kind that could confer reproductive benefits.

BLUE LIES

AT SOME TIME, all of us will give answers that we know are untrue, for the paradoxical and totally strange reason that we actually believe the answer to be *more essentially truthful* than the actual truth. The phrase "true blue" inspired the color for this category of untruths. Some examples:

Q8. *Did you vote in last Tuesday's election?*

(Survey researcher to regular voter who neglected to vote last Tuesday but who answers yes because—"truth be told"—he or she is a "regular voter")[4]

Q9. *Did you do all of the reading for the last test?*

(Professor to student who received a low grade on an exam and did not read the assigned texts but who answers yes)

Q10. *What radio station do you listen to?*

(Asked of a guest at an elite dinner gathering who answers "public radio," but whose car has only two preset stations, one for talk radio, the other for pop music)

Those who answer these three questions in known-untrue fashion may intend their answers to communicate a truth deeper than the actual facts would indicate, as in: *I am the type of person who votes regularly (even though I was too busy to vote last Tuesday); who always does the assigned work (but didn't last week because I had too many assignments from other courses); who shares the cultural and political values associated with public radio (but listens to it only when what's on the other stations is boring).*

We can justify blue lies such as these by observing that they allow others to see us as we (honestly) see ourselves. But this is a charitable view. Less charitably, these blue lies are ploys to produce favorable regard by others. Social psychologists know this ploy well, and have a telling name for it—*impression management.*[5]

Impression management even comes into play when people are answering questions that do not seem to permit much wiggle room. If someone wants to know your age, height, and weight, what would you say? Although many people provide entirely accurate answers, researchers have repeatedly found that substantial minorities err when asked about these basic facts on survey questionnaires. And the errors are systematic: With the exception of answers provided by the very young, the very thin, and the very tall, the errors are virtually all in the direction of being younger, lighter in weight, and taller than can be verified with the aid of birth certificates, scales, and rulers.[6]

Impression management has become well recognized as a problem in survey research. Survey participants will often produce less-than-true responses even when they know that their answers will just be fed into a computer and no researcher will ever see or hear them—even when they have been further assured that after their responses have been recorded, no one will be able to identify them as the source of their answers.

The problem of distortion of survey data by impression management is so great that survey researchers have devised a strategy to identify and weed out those survey participants who appear most likely to give responses shaped by their desire to make a favorable impression. The strategy calls for inserting some true-false catch questions such as the following into a survey.

Q11. *I am always courteous, even to people who are disagreeable.*

Q12. *I always apologize to others for my mistakes.*

Q13. *I would declare everything at customs, even if I knew that I could not possibly be found out.*

Researchers assume that many of those who answer "true" to these questions are impression managers because, for most people, full honesty should produce "false" to all three. After all, few people are *always* courteous, few people *always* apologize for mistakes, and few are so scrupulously honest that they would make a statement that could cost them money if they could avoid the financial penalty through a minor deception that would remain undetected. It is a more than mildly ironic comment on the vicissitudes of self-report survey methods that social scientists credit the person who admits to cheating at customs with greater honesty than the one who claims not to cheat.

If you think that you could honestly answer "true" to all three of Q11, Q12, and Q13, it is possible that you are among the very small group of completely honest people on the planet. Of course, honesty may be an overrated virtue. If you decided to report all of your flaws to friends and to apply a similar standard of total honesty when talking to others about their shortcomings, you might soon find that you no longer have friends. Should you have any doubts about this, recall Q2 (*Do I look fat in these jeans?*). The white lie typically offered in response to Q2 can also be seen as a reflected blue lie, providing a mirror in which the questioner can find welcome agreement with his or her own too-good-to-be-true perception (that is, *I look just great*). Tamper with that self-regard at your own risk.

Our daily social lives demand, and generally receive, repeated lubrication with a certain amount of untruthfulness, which keeps the gears of social interaction meshing smoothly. Unfortunately, what works so well in daily life does not serve the interests of science.

USING QUESTIONS IN RESEARCH

WE LEFT SCIENCE in the background while describing the various pressures to produce less-than-truthful answers to questions. However, when these same forces operate to influence answers given by participants in a scientific study, the accuracy of the study's results may be seriously compromised, and that is of course a concern to us. If answers to questions as matter-of-fact as those about age, height, and weight can be inaccurate, what should we assume about the limits of what can be learned from question-asking research on topics as highly charged as a person's racial attitudes or other forms of bias?

In the absence of reliable checks on accuracy such as those that can be provided by scales and rulers when asking about weight or height, it's remarkably difficult to assess whether a person is telling the truth in answering a survey questionnaire. That's why, when evaluating the honesty of people applying for jobs that involve access to confidential or secret documents, government agencies rely not just on questions directed to the applicant but also on interviews with friends, relatives, teachers, work colleagues, and past employers. But these methods are themselves imperfect, not only because these various informants do not have full and accurate knowledge of the person about whom they are asked but also because they may succumb to the same forces that make self-reporting unreliable—they may be overly generous (or the reverse) in their assessments. And of course these methods of asking others hardly meet the demands of assessing something as personal—and generally hidden—as bias.[7]

The first scientific studies of attitudes toward racial and ethnic groups were conducted in the 1920s and 1930s, using the only methods then available—asking questions and compiling the self-reported answers. It was only after forty years of question-based research that psychologists began to appreciate, and eventually to document, the types of deviations from accuracy that we have described in this chapter.

There is now no doubt that impression management produces flawed, inaccurate responses to many questions that have long been used to measure race prejudice. As just one of many well-substantiated examples of this effect, we offer a 1981 study in which White college students were asked to state their level of agreement (ranging from "strongly disagree" to "strongly agree") with the statements in Q14 and Q15.

Q14. *It is a bad idea for Blacks and Whites to marry each other.*

Q15. *Black people are generally not as smart as Whites.*

Half the study participants who were asked these questions received them from researchers who were Black, and the remainder received them from White researchers. All these respondents were assured that no researcher would ever see their answers and that their answers would be treated in total confidence. Nevertheless, when the questioner was Black the subjects' responses were noticeably more Black-favorable than when the questioner was White. This impression-management effect almost certainly occurred without the subjects being aware that their answers had been influenced by the race of the person who handed them the questionnaire.[8]

And, as we have been describing, impression management is but one of a diverse array of forces that influence our truthfulness—about everything, from what we weigh to how much we drink, and whether our loved one is fat to whether we have favorable views of Black people.

TRUTHFULNESS REVISITED

WE RETURN to the chapter-opening question: *When you are asked questions, how often do you give answers that you* know *are untrue?* If at first you responded "rarely" or "never," perhaps you are now ready to grant that it might be more often than that. Which leads us to ask: Do you think you are biased against people of other races or ethnicities? Given what you have just learned about the limits of honesty, in thinking about your answer you might want to ask yourself: *How close to truthful will I be in responding to questions about my racial beliefs and attitudes?* Even what you now know about the causes of distortion may not stop you from shading the truth.

3

Into the Blindspot

PSYCHOLOGICAL RESEARCH ON ATTITUDES TOWARD RACE IS A RELA-tively recent scientific endeavor, dating back less than a century. The pioneers, psychologists, and sociologists of the 1920s and 1930s undertook the first studies of Americans' attitudes toward ethnic and racial groups. Their methods were the only ones then available—they asked questions. This method of "self-report" treats people as the best authorities on their own racial attitudes. The problems with question-asking methods that were described in the last chapter notwithstanding, self-reporting was very useful in the earliest studies of prejudice. This was in part because, unlike present-day Americans, early twentieth-century Americans apparently had no qualms about openly expressing their racial and ethnic attitudes.

The story of how early researchers discovered compelling evidence of prejudices toward dozens of different groups is told in Appendix 1 ("Are Americans Racist?"). That appendix further describes how research methods became increasingly sophisticated during the twentieth century, evolving toward methods that no longer relied on asking questions.

This chapter focuses on the method created by Tony in 1994—a method that gives the clearest window now available into a region of the mind that is inaccessible to question-asking methods.

A NEW KIND OF TEST

To GIVE YOU A FEELING for how the new method works, we ask you to try a hands-on demonstration—quite literally hands-on because you will need to have a deck of playing cards in hand. If at all possible, please find two things—a standard deck of fifty-two playing cards and a watch or clock that displays time in seconds.

Once you have the cards and the timer, first shuffle the deck a few times and hold the cards faceup. You will be timing yourself as you perform two slightly different sorting tasks.

First you will sort the cards into two piles, with *hearts* and *diamonds* to the left, *spades* and *clubs* to the right. The second task is to sort them by putting *diamonds* and *spades* to the left, *clubs* and *hearts* to the right. Before you begin, think about these two sorting tasks and ask yourself which will be easier.

Whether or not you think that one of the tasks will be easier than the other, if you've got the cards and the timer, you're ready to start. As fast as you can, first sort the cards into two piles, *hearts* and *diamonds* to your left and *spades* and *clubs* to your right. Make a note of the number of seconds you took to do that. Next, reshuffle the deck a few times and repeat the process, but this time *diamonds* and *spades* to the left, *clubs* and *hearts* to the right.

If you were more than a few seconds faster at one task than the other, make a mental note of which of the two was faster before turning the page to learn what we expect.

Almost certainly you were faster at the first task, which allowed you to use a simple rule for the sorting—*red suits left, black suits right*. The second task didn't offer any such simple rule. Doing each test twice, Mahzarin and Tony averaged twenty-four seconds for the first task (red suits versus black suits) and thirty-seven seconds for the second (spades and diamonds versus hearts and clubs). Taking about 50 percent longer to do the second task is a big difference, big enough that we could feel it as we did the sorting.

THE IMPLICIT ASSOCIATION TEST (IAT)

NEXT WE ASK YOU to participate in another hands-on demonstration, for which you will again need a watch or clock that displays seconds. You will also need a pen or pencil. If you prefer not to mark this book's pages, turn ahead a few pages and photocopy the two pages of the flower-insect Implicit Association Test.

Looking at the two pages of the flower-insect test, you will see that each page has words running down the middle of two columns. To the left and right of each of the words is a small circular bubble. Your task is to place a mark in the bubble either to the left or to the right of each word, and to do that as fast as you can.

There are four sets of words:

Flower names: *orchid, daffodil, lilac, rose, tulip, daisy, lily*
Insect names: *flea, centipede, gnat, wasp, roach, moth, weevil*
Pleasant-meaning words: *gentle, heaven, cheer, love, enjoy, happy, friend*
Unpleasant-meaning words: *damage, vomit, hurt, poison, evil, gloom, ugly*

Just below are instructions and an example of the correct way to start marking the first sheet of the flower-insect test. After reading these instructions and the added suggestions just after them, you will be ready to start.

Do Sheet A first. Start at the top left and make marks as rapidly as you can. As soon as you have worked your way down the left

For **INSECTS** and for <u>**words pleasant in meaning**</u>, mark in the circle to the left. For everything else (FLOWERS and unpleasant-meaning words) mark in the circle to the right. Start at top left, go from top to bottom doing all items in order, then do the second column. At bottom right, record the elapsed time in seconds.

INSECTS or pleasant words	FLOWERS or unpleasant words	INSECTS or pleasant words	FLOWERS or unpleasant words
⊘ WASP ◯		◯ ROSE ◯	
◯ poison ⊘		◯ heaven ◯	
◯ TULIP ⊘		◯ ORCHID ◯	
⊘ enjoy ◯		◯ gentle ◯	

column, continue without pause to do the right column in the same way. For each word mark the bubble to the left or right. Here are some added suggestions:

1. Use just a single short stroke for your marks—that will be fastest.
2. Do all the words in order. Don't skip any.
3. *Definitely* do not stop or backtrack to correct errors—that will make your result less accurate.
4. Timekeeping will be easiest if you start when your watch reads zero seconds—at the beginning of a minute.
5. Write your time (in seconds) to complete Sheet A at the bottom right of the sheet.
6. Then do Sheet B, *which has different instructions* and also different labels above the two columns. Have the changed instructions well in mind before you start Sheet B.
7. Record the number of seconds you took for Sheet B at the bottom right.

Of all the hands-on experiences in this book, this one is the most important for starting on the path to grasp the essence of the book. *Please do the flower-insect test on the next two pages now.* If you'd prefer to complete this test online or on a mobile device instead, please go to bit.ly/T8h6uD.

A

For **INSECTS** and for **words pleasant in meaning**, mark in the circle to the left. For everything else (FLOWERS and unpleasant-meaning words) mark in the circle to the right. Start at top left, go from top to bottom doing all items in order, then do the second column. At bottom right, record the elapsed time in seconds.

INSECTS or pleasant words	FLOWERS or unpleasant words	INSECTS or pleasant words	FLOWERS or unpleasant words
◯ ORCHID ◯		◯ TULIP ◯	
◯ gentle ◯		◯ enjoy ◯	
◯ ROSE ◯		◯ WASP ◯	
◯ heaven ◯		◯ poison ◯	
◯ FLEA ◯		◯ ROACH ◯	
◯ damage ◯		◯ evil ◯	
◯ DAFFODIL ◯		◯ DAISY ◯	
◯ cheer ◯		◯ gloom ◯	
◯ CENTIPEDE ◯		◯ MOTH ◯	
◯ vomit ◯		◯ ugly ◯	
◯ GNAT ◯		◯ WEEVIL ◯	
◯ hurt ◯		◯ happy ◯	
◯ LILAC ◯		◯ LILY ◯	
◯ love ◯		◯ friend ◯	

Number of seconds: ____

Number of errors: ____

B

For **FLOWERS** and for **words pleasant in meaning**, mark in the circle to the left. For everything else (<u>INSECTS</u> and <u>unpleasant-meaning words</u>) mark in the circle to the right. Start at top left, go from top to bottom doing all items in order, then do the second column. At bottom right, record the elapsed time in seconds.

FLOWERS or pleasant words	INSECTS or unpleasant words	FLOWERS or pleasant words	INSECTS or unpleasant words
◯ FLEA ◯		◯ GNAT ◯	
◯ gentle ◯		◯ enjoy ◯	
◯ ORCHID ◯		◯ WASP ◯	
◯ evil ◯		◯ poison ◯	
◯ ROSE ◯		◯ ROACH ◯	
◯ damage ◯		◯ heaven ◯	
◯ DAFFODIL ◯		◯ DAISY ◯	
◯ cheer ◯		◯ gloom ◯	
◯ CENTIPEDE ◯		◯ LILY ◯	
◯ vomit ◯		◯ ugly ◯	
◯ LILAC ◯		◯ MOTH ◯	
◯ hurt ◯		◯ happy ◯	
◯ TULIP ◯		◯ WEEVIL ◯	
◯ love ◯		◯ friend ◯	

Number of seconds: ____

Number of errors: ____

If you are reading this sentence without yet having done the flower-insect test, we urge you to go back a few pages and do it before reading further. We say this only once in the book because we know that the experience of taking the tests in this book will prompt reactions of surprise and skepticism that will be well worthwhile.

After completing the flower-insect test, you may immediately know what it reveals about which part was easier, without even having to compute your results. But here's how to arrive at an exact score for your tests: For each of Sheets A and B, add your time in seconds (s) to your number of errors (e). Now subtract the sum of s + e for Sheet B from the sum of s + e for Sheet A.

If you were faster and had fewer errors for Sheet A than Sheet B, you have an automatic preference for insects relative to flowers. Much more likely, however, you found Sheet B to be the easier one, which reveals an automatic preference for flowers relative to insects. With the s + e scoring method, a difference of 18 or more between the two sheets shows a *strong* automatic preference one way or the other. A difference between 12 and 17 indicates a *moderate* automatic preference, and a difference between 6 and 11 reflects a *slight* automatic preference. If the s + e difference was less than 6, it should be considered too small to indicate either preference clearly.

A few years ago we gave this flower-insect test to a group of thirty-eight people with a doctorate in one of several academic disciplines. They took an average of sixteen seconds longer to complete Sheet A than to complete Sheet B. If you think about the fact that a runner of only moderate speed can run 100 meters in the extra time it took these PhDs to do Sheet A, you will get a sense of just how large a difference this is.

HOW THE IAT (IMPLICIT ASSOCIATION TEST) WORKS

YOU HAVE JUST COMPLETED the first version of what we now call an Implicit Association Test (IAT for short). Its effectiveness relies on the fact that your brain has stored years of past experiences that you cannot set aside when you do the IAT's sorting tasks. For flowers and insects, this stored mental content is most likely to help you put flowers together with pleasant words while interfering with your pairing flowers with unpleasant words. Similarly, it will likely be easier for you to connect insects with unpleasant words and harder to connect them with pleasant words. This is why Sheet B's task was probably easier for you than Sheet A's task—unless you're an entomologist or a ten-year-old boy.

In doing Sheet B, you may have had the feeling that flower names and pleasant words were not two different categories but just a single category of "good things." Insect names and unpleasant words may similarly have felt like a single "bad things" category. Thinking of them this way may remind you of the task of sorting card suits when you were asked to sort together suits that shared a color, rather than suits that were not color-matched.[1]

When categories can be linked to each other via shared goodness or badness, the shared property is what psychologists call *valence*, or emotional value. Positive valence attracts and negative valence repels. Positive valence, which is shared by flower names and pleasant words, can function as a mental glue that bonds these two categories into one. When there is no shared valence, which is expected for most people when they try to put flower names together with unpleasant words, it is harder to find a connection between the two categories. There is no mental glue available, and this makes the IAT's sorting task on Sheet A far more challenging.

The mental glue that can allow two categories to combine into one corresponds to an ancient concept in psychology: *mental association*. Hearts and diamonds have a mental association because they share the color red. For most people, flower names and pleasant-meaning words have a mental association because they share the more abstract quality of positive valence.[2]

In June 1994, Tony wrote the first computer program to administer an IAT, which used the same categories of flower, insect, pleasant, and unpleasant that were used in the flower-insect test you just took. As he was checking the program to make sure it worked properly, he became the first subject to try it. Here's how Tony later recalled the experience of taking that first IAT.

> I had programmed the computer so that it first presented what I expected to be the easier task—giving the same response to flower names and pleasant words. As each word appeared on the screen, I was to press a key with my left hand for either insect names or unpleasant-meaning words, and a different key with my right hand for either flower names or pleasant words. Even though I had to keep track of instructions for four different categories, each with twenty-five different possible words, the task was easy—I breezed through it.
>
> For the second task I had to press the left key for flower names or unpleasant words, and the right one for insect names or pleasant words. Within a few seconds, I could see that this was difficult. After (slowly) completing a series of fifty key presses at this task, I assumed that I would soon overcome this difficulty by practicing the task another few times. Wrong! I repeated the task several times—I did not improve at all.
>
> Then I tried just forcing myself to respond rapidly to each word. The result was frustration. I made frequent errors—pressing the wrong key. I soon concluded that the only way I could respond accurately was to go slowly. That was the first strong clue that this method might prove useful.
>
> During the next several days I asked some University of Washington psychology graduate students to try the task. They too discovered the difficulty of the second task. Next, I tried it on volunteers from the university's introductory psychology courses.

*When I looked at their performances, it was obvious that, for al-
most all of them, the task that required the same key-press to
flower names and unpleasant words was putting them into slow
motion. It mattered only a little whether they did that task first
or second.*[3]

Those initial tryouts of the new procedure were very exciting
because they suggested that the (not-yet-named) IAT could provide
a useful way to measure one of psychology's long-established theoretical concepts—attitude. To psychologists, *attitude* has a meaning similar to its meaning in ordinary language. It refers to one's
likes and dislikes such as, for example, liking flowers (a "positive"
attitude) and disliking insects (a "negative" attitude). More techni-
cally, attitudes are the associations that link things (flowers and
insects in this case) to positive or negative valence.

Attitudes can be expressed in many ways, including poetic
verse: "Yet my heart is sweet with the memory of the first fresh
jasmines [flower] that filled my hands when I was a child." Or:
"They [insects] will eat up your trees. They will dig up your lawn.
You can squash all you can, but they'll never be gone." The IAT
captures attitudes toward flowers and insects much more prosai-
cally, by comparing the speeds of completing two different sorting
tasks.[4]

THE RACE IAT

A SECOND TYPE of IAT soon followed—it was the first Race IAT.
The change of procedure was small, replacing names of flowers and
insects with the names of famous African Americans and European Americans. The new IAT was expected to reveal whether the
method could measure one of our society's most significant and
emotion-laden types of attitudes—the attitude toward a racial
group. If it revealed a preference for White relative to Black race
groups in some significant percentage of those who tried it, that

might suggest the test was able to bypass the impression management phenomenon (described in Chapter 2) that is a significant source of interference in self-report methods for measuring racial attitudes. If the IAT could do that, it could be of great value in research. Even more important, it might help unveil a type of mental content that we and other social psychologists at the time were just beginning to understand—hidden biases that could not possibly be tapped by asking questions because their possessors were unaware of having them.

Perhaps you would like to try the Race IAT before reading anything about what results to expect from it. If you have access to a Web browser or mobile device, you can find the Race IAT on the Internet, at bit.ly/TtkoCZ.[5] If you prefer, you can try the Race IAT in a paper-and-pencil version on the next two pages. Again you will need only a pencil or pen and a timer that can record seconds. But, before you do, please try to predict your performance. Do you think you will be:

- Faster in associating (sorting together) Black faces with pleasant words
- Faster in associating White faces with pleasant words
- Equally fast at both of these?

For the Race IAT on the next two pages, as for the previous flower-insect IAT, please try to go as fast as you can. As you complete each sheet, record the number of seconds it took to complete it and then, using the same scoring instructions as for the flower-insect IAT, compute the s + e difference between the two.

A note of caution: If you prefer not to risk discovering a result different from the one you predicted, you might want to avoid this IAT. About half of those who take this test—Tony and Mahzarin among them—obtain a result that deviates from their initial expectation.

A

For **pleasant words** and for <u>**African American children's faces**</u>, mark in the circle to the left. For everything else (<u>unpleasant words</u> and <u>European American children's faces</u>) mark in the circle to the right. Start at top left, go from top to bottom doing all items in order, then do the second column. At bottom right, record the elapsed time in seconds.

pleasant or Afr. Am. faces	unpleasant or Eur. Am. faces		pleasant or Afr. Am. faces	unpleasant or Eur. Am. faces
◯ disaster ◯			◯ agony ◯	
◯ 🖼 ◯			◯ 🖼 ◯	
◯ hatred ◯			◯ smile ◯	
◯ 🖼 ◯			◯ 🖼 ◯	
◯ honest ◯			◯ sincere ◯	
◯ 🖼 ◯			◯ 🖼 ◯	
◯ grief ◯			◯ crash ◯	
◯ 🖼 ◯			◯ 🖼 ◯	
◯ lucky ◯			◯ diamond ◯	
◯ 🖼 ◯			◯ 🖼 ◯	
◯ peace ◯			◯ sweet ◯	
◯ 🖼 ◯			◯ 🖼 ◯	
◯ rotten ◯			◯ tragedy ◯	
◯ 🖼 ◯			◯ 🖼 ◯	

Number of seconds: _____

Number of errors: _____

For **unpleasant words** and for <u>**African American children's faces**</u>, mark in the circle to the left. For everything else (<u>pleasant words</u> and <u>European American children's faces</u>) mark in the circle to the right. Start at top left, go from top to bottom doing all items in order, then do the second column. At bottom right, record the elapsed time in seconds.

unpleasant or Afr. Am. faces	pleasant or Eur. Am. faces		unpleasant or Afr. Am. faces	pleasant or Eur. Am. faces
◯ disaster	◯		◯ agony	◯
◯ 🙂	◯		◯ 🙂	◯
◯ hatred	◯		◯ smile	◯
◯ 🙂	◯		◯ 🙂	◯
◯ honest	◯		◯ sincere	◯
◯ 🙂	◯		◯ 🙂	◯
◯ grief	◯		◯ crash	◯
◯ 🙂	◯		◯ 🙂	◯
◯ lucky	◯		◯ diamond	◯
◯ 🙂	◯		◯ 🙂	◯
◯ peace	◯		◯ sweet	◯
◯ 🙂	◯		◯ 🙂	◯
◯ rotten	◯		◯ tragedy	◯
◯ 🙂	◯		◯ 🙂	◯

Number of seconds: _____

Number of errors: _____

Here is how Tony remembers his experience in taking the Race IAT for the first time:

I programmed the first Race IAT within a few months after the flower-insect IAT. It used names of famous African Americans and famous European Americans in place of flower and insect names. I tried it immediately when the program was ready. Because I had no preference (or so I thought) for one race group over the other, I expected to be as fast in sorting Black names together with pleasant words as in sorting White names together with pleasant words.

It was a rare moment of scientific joy to discover—in midperformance—that the new method could be important. It was also a moment of jarring self-insight. I immediately saw that I was very much faster in sorting names of famous White people together with pleasant words than in sorting names of famous Black people together with pleasant words. I can't say if I was more personally distressed or scientifically elated to discover something inside my head that I had no previous knowledge of. But there it was—it was as hard for me to link names of Black people and pleasant words as it had been a few months earlier to link insect names and pleasant words.

After taking that first Race IAT and repeating it several times to see if the first result would be repeated (it was), I did not see how I could avoid concluding that I had a strong automatic racial preference for White relative to Black—just as I had a strong automatic preference for flowers relative to insects.

I then asked myself what any social psychologist would: Is this something that affects my behavior in relation to African Americans whom I regularly encounter—especially students in my classes? Do I act as if I feel less positive toward them than toward White students?

The question Tony asked himself points to the deeper issues raised by the test. What exactly does an "automatic preference for

White relative to Black" mean? Is it a sign of prejudice, and if so, what are the effects of that prejudice? If a person such as Tony, who genuinely believes himself not to be prejudiced, takes the test and then discovers a preference for White in himself, should we expect that he is likely to express this hidden bias in ways that could be damaging to others?

DOES "AUTOMATIC WHITE PREFERENCE" MEAN "PREJUDICE"?

THE RACE IAT holds up a mirror in which many see a reflection that they do not recognize. Most who take the Race IAT are faster on Sheet B (linking racial White to pleasant words) than on Sheet A (linking racial Black to pleasant words). This is the pattern that is described as showing "automatic preference for White relative to Black."

In our own first experiences with the Race IAT, both of us were surprised to discover how much more easily we associated White than Black with pleasant. Our initial "There must be some mistake" reaction soon gave way to "Does this mean that *I* am prejudiced?" Since then, that same question has been directed to us many, many times by others who have taken the Race IAT and were confronted with test scores that were at odds with both their expectations and their self-perceptions.

For almost a decade after the Race IAT was created, when people asked us if a White-preference result means "I am prejudiced," we dodged the question by saying that we didn't yet know. We would say that the Race IAT measured "implicit prejudice" or "implicit bias," emphasizing that we regarded these as clearly distinct from prejudice as it has generally been understood in psychology.

We had good reasons to be cautious. First of all, the IAT results that reveal automatic White preference—results based on speed of responding to words and pictures—bear little resemblance to the extremely negative racial attitudes that were expressed in self-reports from the twentieth century (these are described in Appendix 1). Results obtained with those question-asking methods have established an understanding that prejudice is an attitude that encompasses dislike, disrespect, and even hatred. Nothing about the IAT suggests that it taps such hostility.

The second good reason for our unwillingness to equate the IAT's "automatic White preference" result with "prejudice" was the unavailability of any research evidence needed to justify that conclusion. Neither we nor anyone else had done studies to determine whether those who show the highest levels of automatic White preference on the Race IAT are also those who are most likely to show racially discriminatory behavior.

But this situation has changed. Because of the rapid accumulation of research using the Race IAT in the last decade, two important findings are now established. First, we now know that automatic White preference is pervasive in American society—almost 75 percent of those who take the Race IAT on the Internet or in laboratory studies reveal automatic White preference. This is a surprisingly high figure. We (Mahzarin and Tony) thus learned that we are far from alone in having a Race IAT result that reveals that preference.[6]

Second, the automatic White preference expressed on the Race IAT is now established as signaling discriminatory behavior. It predicts discriminatory behavior even among research participants who earnestly (and, we believe, honestly) espouse egalitarian beliefs. That last statement may sound like a self-contradiction, but it's an empirical truth. Among research participants who describe themselves as racially egalitarian, the Race IAT has been shown, reliably and repeatedly, to predict discriminatory behavior that was observed in the research. Because this conclusion is surprising and therefore may not be easy to grasp, we take some space here to describe a few key portions of this large (and still rapidly growing) body of research evidence.

DO MERE ASSOCIATIONS SHOW UP IN BEHAVIOR?

THE FIRST EXPERIMENT to test whether scores on the Race IAT were related to discriminatory behavior was reported in 2001 by Allen McConnell and Jill Leibold, psychologists at Michigan State University. Their research subjects were forty-two Michigan State undergraduate volunteers. Without initially informing their research subjects of the fact, the researchers videotaped these student subjects during two brief interviews, one conducted by a White woman, the other by a Black woman. During the interviews the students were asked a series of innocuous pre-planned questions, such as "What would you change to improve psychology classes?" and "What did you think about the difficulty level of the computer task?" (The computer task was the Race IAT, which had been presented as if it was part of a separate experiment.)

The purpose of the videotaping was to assess whether strong automatic White preference shown on the Race IAT would predict acting in a friendlier fashion to the White interviewer than to the Black one. After completing both interviews, the experimenters explained the purposes of the videotaping and asked the students to give their permission to analyze the videotapes. All but one gave permission.

The videotapes of the interviews were scored by counting occurrences of nonverbal behaviors that had been found, in many previous studies, to indicate friendliness or coolness. Indicators of comfort or friendliness included smiling, speaking at greater length, laughing at a joke told by the interviewer, and making spontaneous social comments. Discomfort indicators included speech errors and speech hesitations. Another measure of comfort or discomfort was how closely the subjects positioned their rolling desk chair to each of the interviewers. Immediately after each interview, both of the interviewers also made personal assessments of how friendly and comfortable they thought the subject had seemed during their interaction.

McConnell and Leibold found that subjects with higher levels of automatic White preference on the IAT showed less comfort and less friendliness when talking with the Black interviewer than with the White interviewer. This was an intriguing result, but it was also just one study that, by itself, was not enough to support a conclusion that the Race IAT could predict racially discriminatory behavior. But quite a few other researchers, aware of the possible importance of what the Race IAT could reveal, began to use the Race IAT in combination with measures of discriminatory behavior or judgment—aiming to see how well the Race IAT would predict.

Following are a few examples of behaviors that were found, in various studies, to be predicted by the Race IAT's measure of automatic White preference: in a simulated hiring situation, judging White job applicants more favorably than equally qualified Black applicants; emergency room and resident physicians recommending the optimal treatment—thrombolytic (blood-clot dissolving) therapy—less often for a Black patient than for a White patient who presented with the same acute cardiac symptoms; and college students being more ready to perceive anger in Black faces than in White faces.

By early 2007, thirty-two studies had been done in which the Race IAT was administered together with one or more measures of racially discriminatory behavior. These studies were among 184 in a collection that was published in 2009, using the statistical method of meta-analysis to combine all of these results for the purpose of evaluating the IAT's success in predicting a wide variety of judgments and behaviors.

The meta-analysis answered the most important question about which we had been uncertain in the first several years of the IAT's existence: It clearly showed that the Race IAT predicted racially discriminatory behavior. A continuing stream of additional studies that have been completed since publication of the meta-analysis likewise supports that conclusion. Here are a few examples of race-relevant behaviors that were predicted by automatic White preference in these more recent studies: voting for John McCain rather than Barack Obama in the 2008 U.S. presidential election; laughing at anti-Black racial humor and rating it as funny; and doctors providing medical care that was deemed less satisfactory by their Black patients than by their White patients.[7]

The meta-analysis's findings can be summarized as saying that IAT scores correlated *moderately* with discriminatory judgments and behavior. "Correlated moderately" is a statistical term that needs elaboration for its implications to be fully clear. (Readers who are content not to immerse themselves in the technical explanation of that phrase can safely skip the next six paragraphs.)

The statistic used in almost all tests of the IAT's ability to predict behavior is the *correlation coefficient*—a number that can range between 0 and 1. Finding a correlation of 0 between a Race IAT measure and discriminatory behavior means that knowing a person's Race IAT score provides absolutely no information about the likelihood of that person engaging in discriminatory behavior. A perfect correlation of 1 would mean that knowledge of where a person ranked, from lowest to highest, on the Race IAT measure of automatic White preference would tell you exactly where he or she ranked, from lowest to highest, in discriminatory behavior. Among researchers, there is a conventional understanding that a correlation of .10 is small, one of .30 is medium, and one of .50 or greater is large. In saying that the meta-analysis found a moderate average correlation between Race IAT measures and measures of discriminatory behavior, we mean that the average correlation was close to the conventional "medium" value of .30. (To be precise, the meta-analysis found an average correlation of .24 between Race IAT measures and discriminatory behavior.)

An example that has nothing to do with race discrimination may make the real-life implications of "moderate correlation" more meaningful. Suppose you are a bank manager whose job it is to decide which of the bank's loan applicants should receive loans they have applied for. Although most borrowers will pay back at least some portion of their loan, some will not pay enough to yield a profit for the bank. Fortunately, there is some information that can help you judge the suitability of each potential borrower: their credit rating scores.

We need one more assumption to make use of this example: We shall assume that, as bank manager, you know that only half of potential borrowers are likely to repay enough to reach the bank's profitability threshold. If loan applicants' credit rating scores were known to correlate perfectly with their expected amount of repayment, your problem would be entirely solved. You should give loans to the 50 percent of applicants with the highest credit ratings, knowing that you would thereby be giving loans to all of those who will pay back enough to make the loan profitable—and only to those. You would thereby be maximizing the bank's profit.

Of course, credit rating systems are not perfect—the correlation between credit rating scores and amount of loan repayment will not be the perfect value of 1. Let us assume that the credit ratings available to you are known to correlate at a medium (.30) level with the expectable amount of repayment. This tells you that if you give your loans to the 50 percent of applicants who have the highest credit rating scores you can expect 65 percent of them to repay at a level that will create profit for the bank, compared to only 35 percent of the loans being profitable if you instead loan to the 50 percent in the lower half of credit rating scores. Although this is clearly not a perfect outcome, notice how much more desirable it is than what would happen if you had no credit rating scores at all—in that case half your loans would be profitable and half not, meaning little or no profit for the bank. A credit rating score that has a medium "predictive validity" correlation will therefore enable a substantial profit, even if not the maximum possible profit.[8]

This mortgage loan example tells us how to understand the meta-analysis's average correlation between the Race IAT and discriminatory behavior. The correlation value of .24 means that, in a situation in which discrimination might be shown by 50 percent of those for whom we have Race IAT scores, we can expect that discrimination to be shown by 62 percent of those having automatic White preference scores in the top half of the overall distribution of scores, compared to 38 percent of those in the bottom half (difference = .24).

To the surprise of many, the meta-analysis found that the Race IAT predicted discriminatory judgments and behaviors significantly more effectively than did the types of question-asking measures that had long been used in studies of prejudice. Those self-report measures yielded an average validity correlation of only .12, compared to the IAT's .24. The magnitude of this superiority of prediction by the IAT was not expected by anyone.

Perhaps we appear ready to conclude that those who show automatic White preference on the Race IAT should indeed be characterized as "prejudiced"—in the sense that they are more likely than others to engage in discriminatory behavior. However, one important aspect of the research evidence has yet to be taken into account, and it is a critical aspect. The forms of discrimination investigated in the research studies that used Race IAT measures involved no *overtly* racially hostile actions—no racial slurs, no statements of disrespect, and certainly no aggressive or violent actions. Recall the examples of the research behavior that we mentioned—social behaviors in interracial interviews, doctors' treatment recommendations for a cardiac patient, and evaluations of job applicants in a hiring situation. These are not the types of negativity or hostility that are generally taken to be characteristic of "prejudice."

This is why we answer no to the question "Does automatic White preference mean 'prejudice'?" The Race IAT has little in common with measures of race prejudice that involve open expressions of hostility, dislike, and disrespect. Even so, the hidden race bias revealed by the Race IAT is unwelcome news to many who receive an automatic White preference result from the test, and it is probably also distressing to these same people to learn now that the Race IAT is a moderate predictor of racially discriminatory behavior. Included in those who are thus distressed are Mahzarin and Tony, who were not pleased to discover that hidden race bias was an uninvited potential mindbug, revealed to them when the IAT made it possible to look into their blindspot.[9]

4

"Not That There's Anything Wrong with That!"

IT'S DIFFICULT NOT TO SMILE WHEN THINKING BACK ON EPISODE 57 of the TV sitcom *Seinfeld*. "The Outing" portrays Jerry and George pretending to be lovers for the benefit of a young woman they've noticed eavesdropping on them, only to find out that she's actually a reporter who, fully taken in by the charade, intends to "out" Jerry in her newspaper. Trying to clear up the mistake, Jerry and George repeatedly try to persuade her that they're not really gay, while repeatedly adding the qualification "Not that there's anything wrong with that!"

Even if one has no familiarity whatsoever with the sitcom or its characters, it's easy to recognize that the humor in that oft-repeated line derives from a contradiction: While contemporary attitudes toward homosexuality may have come so far that in many of our minds there's everything right with being gay (Jerry and George can even pretend to be gay), the very need for the denial signals that at some level, many of us must believe that there's *something* wrong with it.

TWO FACETS OF MIND:
REFLECTIVE AND AUTOMATIC

OUR PREFERENCES—what and whom we favor or reject, nurture or thwart, approach or avoid—can take different forms. For the purpose of building theories and conducting research, psychologists routinely speak about two systems that characterize the mind: reflective and automatic. The reflective or conscious side of Jerry's mind is indeed gay-friendly, and he can honestly say that he believes there's nothing wrong with being gay. But Jerry is also the product of a culture that has for centuries treated homosexuality to be at best an unfortunate psychological disorder, and more likely an abomination, a sin guaranteeing a quick passage to hell. If Jerry's automatic, less conscious mind makes this simple yet culturally potent association (*gay = sinful*), surely this will influence his own thoughts, feelings, and behavior. This other side of Jerry, the side to which he has less conscious access, experiences uneasiness, perhaps even shame at the thought that others might view him as gay.

The genius of the script, of course, lies in the indirect reminders contained in the recurring line "Not that there's anything wrong with that" and the psychologically important idea it telegraphically captures—the split between the two parts of the mind, automatic and reflective.

We know our reflective preferences quite well, especially when they concern matters important to us. For example, we can voice our religious beliefs, or the lack thereof. We can articulate why a particular candidate for political office is the right or wrong choice. Consciously, we can even make statements that are cognitively and emotionally complex such as "Although I would probably gain by the election of X, I will vote for Y, whom I regard to be better for the country as a whole." Sometimes such beliefs and preferences are also mirrored in actions. Explicit belief in a god drives people to actions such as prayer, helping another member of the sect, or enlisting for a war to protect a religious state. Thinking is for doing, the psychologist William James said, and indeed, the power of conscious thoughts and feelings is to create a particular type of fuel for action.

The automatic side of our mind, on the other hand, is a quite different entity. It's a stranger to us. We implicitly *know* something or *feel* a certain way, and often these thoughts and feelings are reflected in our actions too—the difference being that we can't always explain these actions, and they are at times completely at odds with our conscious intentions. We learned about a business school professor, a savvy teacher of negotiation no less, who went to a dealership to purchase a new car. A person with a growing family, he left the house intending to buy a sensible family car, good for transporting the dog, the groceries, and the kids—a Volvo station wagon, perhaps? A few hours later, he found himself pulling into his driveway in a sporty red Porsche!

Alas, we can all think of equivalent if perhaps not quite so costly lapses in judgment. So what caused the gap between the professor's reflective intention and his actual behavior? Even more intriguing, why didn't he know all along what his final choice was going to be? This example actually captures a quite common experience. We regularly find ourselves attracted to things (and people too) on the basis of color and shape and style, features that appeal to preferences that lie below the surface, while we are indifferent to the more sensible features that clearly are more rational. For example, we choose a car because it is sleek rather than for its repair record, a pair of stilettos for their sex appeal rather than comfort, a house because of its French-lilac color rather than its energy efficiency.

Every day, automatic preferences steer us toward less conscious decisions, but they are hard to explain because they remain impervious to the probes of conscious motivation. Thus we may expound at great length on the virtues of the things we think we ought to prefer (the tanklike safety of a Volvo), but when it comes to making a choice, our rationality (which tells us *Buy the Volvo*) is often no match for our automatic preference (which says, *Nope, I want that red-hot sporty Porsche*).[1] As Phoebe Ellsworth, a colleague at the University of Michigan, once said about making a balance sheet to help her decide which of two jobs to take: "I get halfway through my balance sheet and say, 'Oh, hell, it's not coming out right! Have to find a way to get some pluses over on the other side!' "[2] Phoebe's candid self-insight reveals the comically convoluted motions of rational choice that we go through, only to subvert it by allowing impulse and intuition rather than reason to make our choice for us.

DISSOCIATION: A CRACK IN THE SYSTEM

IN JANUARY 2005, *Washington Post* reporter Shankar Vedantam wrote a story about our research.[3] One of his interviewees, a gay activist, had predictably expressed strong pro-gay attitudes during the interview. Vedantam then invited her to take an IAT to measure her automatic preference for gay versus straight groups. The activist was stunned by the result. The IAT revealed that her own mind contained stronger *gay = bad* associations than *gay = good* associations. One mind, two opposing preferences—one the product of her mind's reflective thinking, the other of the same mind's automatic associations.[4]

For any person sharp enough to spot this contradiction in themselves, the discovery can pose a real conflict. But years of looking at the results of the various IATs at the Project Implicit website have persuaded us that such cracks in the mental system as observed in Vedantam's interviewee are not uncommon. Widespread as they are, they never cease to be disturbing—even to those who work with IATs all the time. Mahzarin, for example, routinely describes her Race IAT result as representing a "failing" score. Of course, the test has no objective pass/fail grade, so what does it mean to say that she flunked the test? Mahzarin gives herself a failing grade because the test's characterization of her as showing automatic White preference is sharply inconsistent with the egalitarian race attitude that she holds in her own reflective mind. In other words, "failing the test" is her way of reporting her dissatisfaction with the state of her mind revealed by the test.

This gap between Mahzarin's reflective and automatic reactions to the same thing (Black-White attitudes) would not have been unveiled without the insight the test inflicted. The powerful message that the test gave her about the force of the unconscious has been among the most significant self-revelations she has experienced, impressing upon her the full import of the observation that the "self is more distant than any star."[5]

Listen to the writer Malcolm Gladwell, in an interview with Oprah Winfrey, reporting his candid response to taking the Race IAT:

> *I took it the first time, and it told me that I had a moderate preference for White people. . . . I was biased—slightly biased—against Black people, toward White people, which horrified me because my mom's Jamaican. . . . The person in my life who I love more than almost anyone else is Black, and here I was taking a test, which said, frankly, I wasn't too crazy about Black people, you know? So, I did what anyone else would do: I took the test again! Maybe it was an error, right? Same result.* Again, *same result, and it was this creepy, dispiriting, devastating moment.*[6]

Such splits exist even in the minds of those who would be disadvantaged by the bias they carry because, like the gay woman activist who took the sexuality IAT and the biracial writer Malcolm Gladwell, who took the Race IAT, they are themselves members of the group they are implicitly biased against. The potentially self-sabotaging nature of such mindbugs is one of their most striking features, and we return to it time and time again.

The word that psychologists use to capture these cracks in the system is *dissociation,* which encompasses so many of humankind's contradictory attitudes and behaviors that it ranks among psychology's most powerful concepts. Here's a definition: *Dissociation is the occurrence, in one and the same mind, of mutually inconsistent ideas that remain isolated from one another.* More specifically, in the context of this book, the mutually inconsistent ideas we are interested in are those that are the product of our reflective or rational mind, on one hand, and our automatic or intuitive mind, on the other. It is this barrier between conscious and unconscious, reflective and automatic, that the IAT was designed to reveal, and it has held up its end of the bargain effectively.

COGNITIVE DISSONANCE AND THE CHOICE TO KNOW

THE LAST DECADE has been witness to an unprecedented number of outings of gay politicians who have voted in favor of anti-gay legislation. The pre-outing minds of these once-closeted gay politicians are an interesting contrast to Jerry Seinfeld's. Exactly the opposite of his, their often publicly expressed reflective thoughts were anti-gay while their automatic thoughts—the ones that directed their sexual behavior—were pro-gay. For these politicians, it's likely that they were aware of the conflict between reflective and automatic. To talk coherently about the existence, in one and the same mind, of mutually inconsistent ideas, thoughts, feelings, judgments, or behaviors, we need to add a technical term to the discussion—the now famous idea of *dissonance*. Adapting a term from music, psychologists have used dissonance to describe both instances in which the person is aware of the conflict and those in which the contradiction occurs outside conscious awareness. If the disconnect is outside of awareness, it's as though (to stick with the music metaphor) two adjacent piano keys are being struck, but one of them so softly that its vibrations can't be heard.

The IAT's role is to reveal this latter kind of mental dissonance. The news it delivers is often as unwelcome as it was to Malcolm Gladwell, whose description of "this creepy, dispiriting, devastating moment" captures what many people feel when they come face-to-face with their hidden biases.

A well-known psychological theory about such dissonances has been so influential that it has entered the mainstream language and culture. Formulated in the mid-1950s by Leon Festinger, a brilliant social psychologist, the theory of *cognitive dissonance* tells us that becoming aware of conflicts between our beliefs and our actions, or between two simultaneously coexisting beliefs, violates the natural human striving for mental harmony, or consonance. The uncomfortable mental state associated with this violation is as disturbing in its own way as the auditory dissonance produced by musical sounds that are not in harmony.[7]

Festinger's theory and the many studies it prompted are important for what they tell us about the sometimes convoluted behaviors in which people engage to try to resolve dissonance and return to the desired feeling of mental harmony. But we bring it up here because it has relevance to our decision about whether and how to introduce the IAT to naive test takers. Malcolm Gladwell, Shankar Vedantam's stunned gay activist, and Mahzarin and Tony can all attest to the disturbing feeling of dissonance produced by taking an IAT that results in a new awareness of a conflict between conscious and unconscious thoughts or feelings.

Understanding the real discomfort that may be involved in coming to terms with one's IAT results has obliged us to think twice before encouraging people to try an IAT that might expose a heretofore unknown—and unwelcome—dissociation. Of course we had no problem asking you to try the flower-insect IAT, which has little chance of revealing a dissociation—you surely know that you'd rather receive a bouquet of flowers than a box of insects, and the test only confirms that preference for flowers over insects (in most people). Even if the test showed that you have a preference for insects over flowers (a rare outcome), you may perhaps be surprised but not distressed by that discovery.

The Race IAT is different. It, as well as a number of the other IATs on the Project Implicit website—those having to do with gender, sexuality, religion, weight, age, and ethnicity—can not just provoke surprise, they can bother us. Now that you have read about the cognitive-dissonance-producing experiences of several people, you will see why, in the preceding chapter, we advised you to think twice before taking the Race IAT. For those who would rather not know about their hidden biases, it may be best to let sleeping dissociations lie.

Most people, we've discovered to our happy surprise, would rather know about the cracks in their own minds. In the same way that they would want to know about a high level of blood cholesterol so that they can take action against it, they wish to confront potentially harmful mental content. They do so to be more certain that their automatic, unconscious thoughts do not result in actions that conflict with their reflective, rational side. We have been struck by the candor of the judges and lawyers, journalists and creative writers, police officers and district attorneys, social workers and health-care practitioners, employees and managers, students and teachers, and many others who have opted to take the IAT and describe with honesty and even humility the disparity between their reflective and automatic minds. They have spontaneously offered examples of catching themselves making assumptions about others that then turned out to be untrue, as further evidence of their blindspots. Their stories are often comical, but always instructive about how pervasive such biases are. Many have asked us how they might create environments for themselves and especially their children that are relatively free of mindbugs, topics we take up in later chapters.

LIKE BODY, LIKE MIND

To THINK MORE OBJECTIVELY and less emotionally about the problem of two opposing thoughts residing in a single mind, consider the way we regard the workings of our own bodies. Does it perplex or embarrass us when we discover that we are unable to accurately detect the pressure of blood traveling through our arteries? We seem to be able to accept that we don't have what might be termed "arterial consciousness." Indeed, many of us would be hard-pressed to define the terms *systolic* and *diastolic,* yet readily offer our arm to any technician equipped with a pump and strap to obtain those measurements. We easily accept that we know little about most of the body's work, whether it involves the flow of blood, the secretion of peptides, the dynamics of cell regeneration, the firing of a neuron, the breakdown of amino acids, or any of the other complex processes occurring within our bodies every millisecond of our lives.

Why, then, is it so hard to take a similar approach to our minds, and to accept that important aspects of it too are unknown to us? Here's a possible reason: We don't have the expectation that we ought to be aware of the working of all our bodily functions, but we do believe that we have—or should have—superior access to the stuff inside our minds. The influence of Freud notwithstanding, it is hard for humans beings, endowed with the capacity for conscious thought, to accept that the beliefs and preferences that so define us can be shaped by forces outside our awareness.

Eric Kandel, a neuroscientist at Columbia University who received a Nobel Prize for his work on memory, was once pressed to say how much of the mind works unconsciously; he gave an estimate of 80 to 90 percent.[8] John Bargh, a psychologist at Yale University, isn't bashful about putting the number at Ivory soap's 99 and 44/100 percent.[9] The actual number isn't important or even possible to derive. The point is that experts agree that the ability to have conscious access to our minds is quite low. For that reason, some humility about self-insight is in order.

And while we are being a little humble, let us ask you a question: Would you date an undertaker?

WOULD YOU DATE AN UNDERTAKER?

You meet someone new, and you are immediately dazzled—by his charm, his intelligence, *and* his good looks. It doesn't get better, you tell yourself, and you ask the dazzler, "So, what do you do?" The answer falls on your ears with a thud: "I'm an undertaker. I own a mortuary." The television show *Six Feet Under* may have done what it could to sexualize undertakers, but probably not effectively enough to overcome your automatic and negative reaction to the charming, good-looking guy hoping expectantly for your eyes to light up. Your reflective side will no doubt muster up some enthusiasm, but not nearly quickly enough while you tell yourself, *Not that there's anything wrong with that!* because you know full well that there's much to be said for a profession devoted to providing support and services for the bereaved. You stay long enough to ask, "How many do you embalm on an average day?" But before you know it, even before you become aware of the slight automatic revulsion you are likely to feel for somebody associated with dead bodies, you have made a quarter turn away from the undertaker to join an adjacent conversation about the intricacies of investment banking.

Automatic preferences serve as navigational devices—a smartphone app, if you will—directing us through challenging terrain such as singles bars and arranged-marriage "showings." They do their work quietly and quickly, turning us away from dissonance generators such as undertakers well before any feeling of mental discomfort penetrates our conscious awareness. In so doing, it's as if our minds had unconsciously anticipated the conversation with Mother: "He's an undertaker. . . . Yes, an undertaker . . . No, he doesn't outsource. He does his own embalming"—and had done everything needed to help us avoid having the conversation at all.

KNOWING AND NOT KNOWING AT THE SAME TIME

SOME OF THE BEST EVIDENCE we have of the impact of unconscious mental content on our judgments and opinions comes from patients with disorders in their ability to remember. In one such study, Marcia Johnson, now at Yale University, and her associates gathered a group of amnesic patients who suffered from a particular kind of failure of memory.[10] These patients had normal memories of their experiences prior to the time of the onset of their amnesia but very limited memory of anything that took place in their lives after that time.

Such a failure—the inability to make new memories—can create odd situations for amnesic patients. They may remember songs they sang as children but have no memory of a song they heard an hour ago. They may be unable to grasp that the president of the country now is different from the president who was in office at the time of their injury. Because none of their post-amnesia experiences consolidate into memories, life for such patients is a constant stream of new people and new events.

Johnson asked a group of these patients to look at photos of two men, and then she gave them information about each. They were told that one of them was a good guy—helped his father, received a military commendation for saving a life, et cetera—whereas the other, they were told, had stolen things, broken someone's arm in a fight, and so on. Having learned biographical data about these two people, the patients later took a simple memory test. They were shown the same photos they had seen before and asked to recount all they could remember about the people depicted. As expected, the patients had virtually no recollection of having learned anything about them.

However, when the patients were asked whether the person in the photo was a good guy or a bad guy, their responses were strikingly accurate. Eighty-nine percent of the time they were able to correctly assess whether the person was *good* or *bad*. It seems that the information they had been given about the person had been turned into an impression that was lodged in their minds in the same way as it would be in an intact person. Even though they had no ability to consciously retrieve that impression, they were able to make a correct good/bad judgment automatically and nonreflectively. The experiment reveals something similar to the split between automatic and reflective kinds of mental processing, or as Johnson puts it, between "affect" (feeling) and "reflection" (reason).

Amnesiacs such as those studied by Johnson have been sought out by neuropsychologists precisely because of their lack of memory for ordinary experiences. Yet they also seem to "save" certain aspects of experience in memory just as others do. Can such a phenomenon of dissociation, viewed so clearly in the pathological state of amnesia, also occur in ordinary, neurologically typical people? We've all had the experience of trying to tell a friend about a movie we saw a while ago and not being able to remember the name, the plot, or even the actors, but remembering with crystal-clear conviction that we loved the movie (or hated it). Carrying that opinion with such certainty despite our inability to access the information that gave rise to the opinion in the first place is similar to, though less dramatic than, what the amnesiacs experienced.

The study of amnesic patients has provided a valuable research window into the phenomenon of dissociation, helping us to understand the power of the unconscious. The IAT has also provided a research window, one that fortunately does not require brain injury to be useful for understanding human minds.

DOES LAUGHING MATTER?

You've surely had this experience: Somebody tells a joke and you burst out laughing, but you realize almost before the laughter tapers off that the joke is offensive because it demeans a group of people, perhaps even your own. What each of us finds simultaneously funny and offensive varies so widely that it is nearly impossible to select a single joke that would result in any agreement about its humor. But take the following, one of the tamest of ethnic jokes, as a mild example of what we are describing:

Question: How do you know that the person who ransacked your home is Asian?

Answer: The dog is missing and the kids' homework is done.

Tame as it is, this joke can elicit both a frown and a smile not just from two individuals but from the same person. In some obvious sense it is funny, but knowing that the humor depends on our knowledge of ethnic stereotypes makes us wonder about our enjoyment and elicits some discomfort.

Having two conflicting reactions to the same stimulus is psychologically intriguing, but is it meaningful? Can our response to a joke tell us something about ourselves? Robert Lynch of Rutgers University investigated this question by looking at people's responses to the racist and sexist humor in a half-hour comedy routine. To see whether laughter can reveal anything about our biases, unconscious as well as conscious, Lynch had Rutgers students watch a video of a stand-up comic who made a lot of jokes that turned on race and gender stereotypes. While they watched, he measured the amount of their laughter and recorded their facial expressions, then used a standard protocol to code these expressions for the degree of positive emotions. By administering the Race IAT, he also obtained from each person a measure of his or her attitude toward Black and White Americans.

Using the results of these tests, Lynch looked at whether the two tests were related—specifically, whether those who had stronger IAT-measured automatic White preference were also more likely to show humorous responses when they heard a joke involving a Black stereotype. Indeed, that's what he found, and a parallel study of sexist humor produced the same type of result—those with stronger IAT-measured gender stereotype associations laughed more at sexist humor.[11] Like the IAT, what we find funny can inform us about how we feel, because laughter is an automatic, hard-to-fake indicator. As the title of Lynch's article says, "It's funny because we think it's true."

WHO LIKES THE ELDERLY?

THE DEVELOPMENT of the IAT had many wellsprings. One of them was our nagging sense that existing techniques to study unconscious mental content, while elegant and perfectly robust for theory testing, were not sufficient to produce a palpable recognition of automatic feelings that go counter to reflective ones. These previous techniques did not provide the kind of aha moment that we experience when we see that the two apparently quite different tabletop drawings are of the same size and shape. The great benefit of powerful visual illusions of the sort we encountered in Chapter 1 on mindbugs is their in-your-face quality. The disparity they reveal between perception and reality can't be ignored.

The dissonance revealed by the IAT is likewise hard to deny, and often just as surprising. The IAT that tests our attitude toward age yields some particularly unexpected results, for our unconscious feelings about the elderly are out of synch with so many of our assumptions. The elderly just don't seem like natural targets of hidden bias. As a group, after all, the elderly seem to be rather benign and in many ways quite appealing. The elderly people many of us know best are our own grandparents and great-grandparents, people who are patient and kind, and who once upon a time let us eat ice cream for breakfast.

Moreover, there are no strong expressions of hostile feelings toward the elderly. You don't hear people shouting, "Hurrah for the young! Down with the elderly!" or actively promoting any kind of anti-elderly political agenda. However, many studies show that our feelings toward the elderly are anything but warm and friendly.[12] If you disagree with this assertion, we invite you to take an age IAT, by visiting implicit.harvard.edu. We can tell you in advance that 80 percent of Americans have a stronger *young = good* than *old = good* association. In other words, most Americans have a strong automatic preference for the young over the old. Only 6 percent show the reverse preference.[13] Indeed, ageism is one of the strongest implicit biases we've detected across dozens of studies over fifteen years, and it seems to be visible in every country in which we've tested it, including countries in Asia.[14]

In the domain of age attitudes, we see one of the most striking dissociations between self-reported feelings and IAT behavior. The people of psychological interest here are not the young, who neither report favorable attitudes toward the elderly nor show automatic preference for the elderly—they are consistent in their negative attitude. The elderly themselves are of interest, because their minds reveal one of the clearest "cracks in the system" we have observed—they report far greater favorability toward the elderly (their own group) than their IAT behavior reveals.

What could account for the disparity of reflective and automatic attitudes in the elderly? While the elderly may seem quite appealing in many ways, as we said earlier, there are many negative stereotypes associated with them in our culture. Much of what we read, see in movies and television shows, and absorb through advertising campaigns targeted at the older generations focuses on their deficits and woes—loneliness and isolation, poor health, weak bodies, fading looks (cosmetic surgery, anyone?), diminished sensory capabilities, incontinence, impotence, memory problems, dementia, Alzheimer's, and so on. No wonder the Beatles asked, "Will you still need me, will you still feed me, when I'm sixty-four?"(an age that must have seemed as remote to them at the time as ninety-four).[15]

Part of what the IAT tells us when it reveals hidden biases, whether about the elderly, dark-skinned people, or gay people, is that the membrane that divides the culture "out there" from our mind "in here" is permeable. Whether we want them to or not, the attitudes of the culture at large infiltrate us. As was true of the gay activist described earlier, even those engaged in a fight for the rights of their stigmatized group are affected by the constant negative input from the culture. A preference for the young among the elderly is further evidence that the outside ends up inside the mind. Our minds pick up a lot of what's out there, and it seems nearly impossible to resist the pull toward culturally rooted stereotypes.

Ageism among the elderly themselves is psychologically fascinating for what it reveals about how dissociations are managed by our minds. To think about it in terms of Festinger's theory of cognitive dissonance, how do the elderly deal with the dissonance created by knowing that they are old while having the same strong automatic preference for young that young people do?

One possible answer emerged from data collected by Mary Lee Hummert at the University of Kansas.[16] In a three-part study, one revealing reflective attitudes, the other two (both IATs) unveiling automatic attitudes, she looked at three groups of adults with average ages of twenty-two, sixty-nine, and eighty years. Perhaps not surprisingly, when asked to report—reflectively—what age they felt, the youngest group added an average of nine years to their maturity while the two older groups subtracted about seven years. Hummert also had the three groups take an age attitude IAT. It showed, just as expected from results we have already mentioned, that the two older groups had every bit as strong an automatic preference for young as did the twenty-two-year-olds.

The third element of Hummert's study was the use of an age identity IAT to measure automatic associations between self and the age categories of young and elderly. The unexpected but unambiguously clear finding: Both older groups had automatic associations of *self = young* that overpowered any *self = old* identification. If you've ever heard an elderly person say, "Inside I feel like I'm eighteen," you may have thought it was a remark offered in jest. Not at all. What the age identity IAT (measuring the strength of association between the concepts of old/young and self) reveals is that many of the elderly achieve a harmonious resolution of the dissonance between their reflective and automatic attitudes toward old age by simply not allowing the label to apply to themselves.

REFLECTING ON THE AUTOMATIC

OVER THE COURSE of fifteen years, the implicit.harvard.edu website[17] has produced a large body of data attesting to a dissociation between our automatic and reflective minds. With over fourteen million IATs completed by 2013 and more than twenty thousand new visitors arriving at the site each week, we now have ample evidence of the dissociation between reflective egalitarianism and automatic preferences in attitudes involving race, sexual orientation, and age as well as skin color, body weight, height, disability, and nationality. And with other websites providing similar tests in thirty-nine countries and twenty-four languages at this time, we also know that Americans do not have a monopoly on these disconnections between the reflective and automatic mental systems. Nor are Americans the only ones to be disturbed when they come face-to-face with their hidden biases. This self-knowledge causes distress, even sadness, because it undermines the image we have of ourselves as largely fair-minded and egalitarian.

"What good is intelligence if you cannot discover a useful melancholy?" the Japanese poet Ryūnosuke Akutagawa is said to have asked, by which he meant that knowledge that provokes a feeling of distress is only of value if it can be put to some use.[18] We might pose this question about our own science. Of what value is it to have developed tests like the IAT that reveal the darker side of ourselves?

For example, what if Jerry Seinfeld and his buddy George Costanza could have taken an IAT to allow them to recognize the dissonance between their reflective and automatic attitudes toward gay people? Had the IAT been available to them, as it was to Hank

Hill, the main character of the animated comedy *King of the Hill*, how might the episode have progressed? Hank took the Race IAT after the family dog, Ladybird, attacked an African American repairman, and was told that he must be unconsciously racist, having passed along his feelings to Ladybird.[19] But then what? What can the IAT do for Jerry, George, or Hank? Its primary use, we think, is to bring the dissonance between reflective and automatic preferences into conscious awareness. From there it is at least partly up to each individual to use that knowledge to move beyond dismay and to find ways to understand hidden biases and, if desired, to neutralize them before they translate into behavior.

Although our focus has been on the power of the unconscious mind, we do not mean to suggest that such thoughts cannot be overruled. When it comes to seeking change, the reflective, conscious side of the brain—the side that is unique to humankind—is more than capable of doing the necessary work. Its power derives from its ability to observe itself and to use those observations to guide conscious action. The reflective aspects of our mind allow us to imagine a future that improves on the present state of affairs, and to achieve settled-upon and consciously chosen goals and values. Knowledge is indeed power, and self-knowledge achieved by taking the IAT can exert its power by unsettling existing views of one's mind. If that happens, the melancholy produced by the IAT will indeed be useful.

5

Homo Categoricus

A FATHER AND HIS SON ARE IN A CAR ACCIDENT. THE FATHER DIES at the scene and the son, badly injured, is rushed to the hospital. In the operating room, the surgeon looks at the boy and says, "I can't operate on this boy. He is my son."

How can this be? (Continue reading when you either have an answer or conclude that you have none.)

If your immediate reaction is puzzlement, that's because automatic mental associations caused you to think "male" on reading "surgeon." The association *surgeon = male* is part of a stereotype. In this riddle, that stereotype works as the first piece of a mindbug. The second piece is an error in judgment—in this case a failure or delay in figuring out that the surgeon must be the boy's mother. This puzzler has been around for so long that Mahzarin remembers having been caught by it—much to her chagrin—as long ago as 1985. For those who are strong believers in women's equal rights and abilities, being tripped up by this riddle is especially annoying. Feminists are not likely to suspect that they possess the automatic *surgeon = male* association—but most of them do.

Consider that feminist just a bit further. Why should he base his thinking on a stereotype that clashes with his personal views? (Did you just discover that you have a *feminist* = *female* association?) Think back to the tabletop illusion that opened Chapter 1. On seeing the two tabletops you immediately concluded that their outline shapes on the page were strikingly different. But, having been told that they were in fact identical, and perhaps even having definitive proof of that, you were still not able to eradicate your first impression. The way the tabletop illusion works on the brain is just too powerful. Similarly, having "male" jump into mind on hearing "surgeon" is a mental habit that is difficult to override, even for someone who is prepared to argue at length that women are as qualified as are men to become surgeons (or anything else).

The conscious feeling of puzzlement on reading *He is my son* in the surgeon story is a good sign that the *male* = *surgeon* association was automatically activated, lurking outside of conscious awareness. But we must now confess that we didn't rely on just that stereotype to set this mindbug in motion. If you count the male and female words in the story you will find a lopsided victory for male—nine male words, zero female words. The male words, in order, were: *father, his, son, father, son, boy, boy, he, son.* These multiple triggers to think "male" almost certainly added to activation of the *surgeon* = *male* association. Had the story instead been about an injured daughter, six of those nine words would have been female, ending with, "I can't operate on this girl. She is my daughter." Written that way, it might have entered your mind more rapidly that the surgeon was the mother. These extra triggers in the riddle's wording provided a context that assisted the automatic inference of male, much as the artfully drawn table legs assisted the automatic shape inferences that produce Roger Shepard's tabletop illusion.

The word *stereotype* entered the English language in the late 1700s as the name for a printer's metal plate that could hold an entire page of print. The stereotype plate made it very easy to produce identical copies of a page. Drawing on this "identical copy" meaning, journalist and political commentator Walter Lippmann gave *stereotype* its current meaning in 1922, when he used it to refer to "pictures in our head" that portray all members of a group as having the same attributes—often not very attractive attributes. Lippmann suggested that this fixed mental picture of a group would enter our thoughts each time we encountered someone from that group.[1]

With modern printing technology, the metal stereotype has become obsolete. The mental variety, however, remains in widespread and constant use, especially in judging the characteristics of strangers about whom we know nothing other than that they belong to some group—for example, that the person is elderly or Asian or female. Without giving it a moment's conscious thought, we use a stereotype of the group as a starting point for our perception of that person.

HOW ACCURATE ARE STEREOTYPES?

SOME STEREOTYPES:

Old people are forgetful.
Koreans are shy.
Asians are good at math.
Boston drivers are aggressive.
Women are nurturing.

Each of these captures an association that connects a group with an attribute. We can use an equal sign to capture the bare essence of these associations, as with *surgeon = male*. Applying the equal-sign shorthand, these five stereotypes are: *old = forgetful, Korean = shy, Asian = good at math, Boston driver = aggressive, woman = nurturing*.

Almost any stereotype is true in some way. To appreciate that, mentally add the word *some* to the front end of the statements about old people, Koreans, Asians, Boston drivers, and women. How can you possibly disagree, for example, that "some Koreans are shy"? Also, any stereotype is at least partly false. There will always be members of the stereotyped group to whom the stereotype does not apply. You are not likely to argue with "There are many outgoing Koreans" or even with "There are many male feminists."

Because all stereotypes are partly true and partly false, it may seem pointless to debate their accuracy. Nevertheless, we can say that some stereotypes are more valid than others. For example, almost certainly, *feminist = female* is more valid than *Boston driver = aggressive*. A reasonable question to ask is whether any of the five stereotypes is valid enough so that it might be wise to be guided by it when we know nothing about a person other than the group identification—such as that the person is a driver in Boston.

If drivers in Boston are, in actuality, no more aggressive than drivers in most other cities, then our Boston driver stereotype should be judged invalid and we would be unwise ever to be guided by it. But perhaps the stereotype has some validity. Boston drivers may be demonstrably more aggressive—as might be confirmed by learning that they have higher accident rates and pay higher insurance premiums—than drivers in other American cities. Does that make it wise to use the stereotype? That's a difficult question, which we will set aside for now and come back to, after learning a bit more about stereotypes.

SCIENTIFIC STUDY OF STEREOTYPES

THE FIRST INFLUENTIAL SCIENTIFIC RESEARCH on stereotypes was published in 1933 by Princeton psychologists Daniel Katz and Kenneth Braly. They sought to describe the pictures-in-the-head that one hundred Princeton students had for each of ten groups. They provided the students with a list of eighty-four traits that are often attributed to people. A portion of that list, shown on page 75, includes all five traits that the Princeton students selected as most descriptive of Germans. A small challenge here: Looking at the list, try to identify two of those five traits that the Princeton students judged to be most descriptive of Germans, circa 1930. When you have your guesses, turn the page to find the five that were most frequently chosen by the Princeton students.

aggressive	sportsmanlike	progressive
intelligent	boastful	talkative
musical	physically dirty	efficient
revengeful	industrious	loyal to family ties
ambitious	conservative	quarrelsome
honest	stolid	unreliable
neat	jovial	gregarious
scientifically minded	practical	methodical
artistic	superstitious	reserved
impulsive	conventional	witty
persistent	lazy	

scientifically minded (78%)
industrious (65%)
stolid (44%)
intelligent (32%)
methodical (31%)

The number in parentheses next to each trait is the percentage of students who selected it as descriptive of Germans. If your two choices are among these five, it may mean that you are psychologically or historically sharp enough to deduce the content of Americans' stereotypes of Germans in the 1930s. Another possibility is that your own current stereotype of Germans is similar to that held by Princeton students in the 1930s. It could actually be either—we deliberately chose a stereotype that had changed little between the 1933 study and a repetition of the study that was published in 2001. The top three traits in the 1933 list for Germans were the same as the top three in 2001—scientifically minded, industrious, and stolid.

But the German stereotype was unusual in this respect. Greater change over time was shown for all nine other groups in the 1933 study—Italians, Negroes, Irish, English, Jews, Americans, Chinese, Japanese, and Turks. One example of these changes: For Turks, the five traits judged most descriptive in 1933 were, in order, *cruel, very religious, treacherous, sensual,* and *ignorant.* In 2001, only one of those five traits was among the new top five, which were *very religious, extremely nationalistic, tradition-loving, quick-tempered,* and *aggressive.* The 2001 list falls well short of suggesting unbridled present-day admiration for Turks by Americans. However, the disappearance of three particularly nasty traits (*cruel, treacherous,* and *ignorant*) suggests that Americans today are considerably less negative toward Turks than they were in the 1930s.[2]

Clearly stereotypes can evolve, sometimes in ways that are easily tied to changes in social and cultural circumstance. The 1933 stereotype of African Americans did not include *athletic,* but that would likely appear prominently in any modern study, and it would validly reflect societal changes that allowed African Americans to participate in activities and careers that were mostly closed to them in the early twentieth century. Similarly, *scientific* and *technical* were not part of a 1930s stereotype of Chinese but almost certainly would appear in a modern study. As was true for the stereotype of Turks, these are changes in a positive direction. But this does not mean that all stereotypes are on an upward trajectory.

STEREOTYPES ARE USUALLY NOT FAVORABLE

IMAGINE THAT you belong to a group for which others judge the five most typical traits to be *attractive, generous, honest, intelligent,* and *trustworthy.* Wouldn't you be delighted to have your group's stereotype applied to you? But no stereotype is that positive. To estimate the balance between positive and negative in stereotypes, we looked at the ten national stereotypes that were described in the 1933 Princeton study. For two of them (Turks and African Americans) more than half the ten characteristics most frequently attributed to the group were unequivocally negative. For another three groups (Italians, Irish, and Chinese) three of the top ten traits were unequivocally negative.

Having "only" three negative characteristics out of ten for a group may not seem bad—after all, that means seven of the ten characteristics were either neutral or favorable. But a quick mental exercise will show that being stereotyped with 30 percent negative traits is far from good.

Consider your friends. How many of them would you credit with any of the seven unequivocally negative characteristics in the list of thirty-two from page 75? Those seven were *boastful, physically dirty, lazy, quarrelsome, revengeful, superstitious,* and *unreliable.* Conceivably you could assign one or two of these seven to one or two of your friends. But would you say that even one of those traits is characteristic of *all* of your friends? If so, you may want to consider finding some new friends!

Yes, there are a very few stereotypes that are nearly uniformly positive—such as that of the rocket scientist, who is conceived as someone (actually, a male someone) who is considerably more intelligent than the rest of us. But the great majority of stereotypes contain at least a few characteristics that you would not attribute to anyone you like or respect. In the 2001 study, even the mostly positive stereotype that Americans had of their fellow Americans contained some negatives. The two traits that were most often selected for Americans in 2001 were the semi-negative traits *individualistic* and *materialistic*. Our conclusion: Group stereotypes typically consist of traits that are noticeably more negative than those we would attribute to our friends.

CATEGORIES

THE RECOGNIZED STARTING POINT for modern scientific understanding of stereotypes is Gordon Allport's 1954 book *The Nature of Prejudice*. Allport wrote: "The human mind must think with the aid of categories. . . . Once formed, categories are the basis for normal prejudgment. We cannot possibly avoid this process. Orderly living depends on it."[3]

The term *Homo categoricus* acknowledges the scientific impact of Allport's view of the importance of mental categories. A category is a collection of things having enough in common so that it is convenient to treat them as kin. The similarity among category members does not need to be great. The category of *car* includes things as different as toy cars, cable cars, and railroad cars. But the use of categories has a powerful effect on our behavior—as a quick look at a situation involving some subordinate categories within the *car* category will make clear: If you are driving on a highway and closing rapidly on a fast-moving car in front of you, your own speed in the next few seconds will be drastically different if you categorize that speeding vehicle as *police car* rather than as *sports car*. Another example: You will act very differently toward small white crystals that you categorize as *sugar* than toward ones you categorize as *salt,* even though you can't visibly tell one from the other in a spoon.

The categories that we use for people also affect our behavior in very clear ways. For example:

- In a department store to make a purchase, you readily surrender your credit card to a total stranger whom you categorize as a *salesclerk.* You trust this stranger to be a typical member of the salesclerk category—that is, someone who will not surreptitiously record your account information and then sell it to an identity thief.

- Entering a medical clinic, you assume the obedient role of *patient* (another category). Even though you may never have seen any of the medical staff before, you unquestioningly follow the instructions of people who are dressed in ways that lead you to categorize them as *doctor* or *nurse.* Having so categorized them, you then proceed to trust them with your life—not to mention your willingness to strip naked in their presence.

- Driving on highways, you stay in your proper lane, you obey the traffic lights, and (a remarkably high percentage of the time) you stop at the stop signs. Without giving it a moment's thought, you behave as a member of the category *driver* and trust that others whom you categorize as drivers will be good members of that category and will act likewise.

Consider the alternatives. You might request a criminal-record check for all salesclerks. You might ask for the diplomas and current certifications of all the medical personnel you encounter. And you might refuse to venture out driving, for fear of being crushed under the wheels of other vehicles. If you did actually behave in so cautious a fashion, however, you yourself might be classified as paranoid or agoraphobic (two more categories), as a consequence of which you would experience inconveniences far greater than those you risk just by trusting others to be good members of their categories. Yes, there are tales of salesclerks who engage in identity theft, stories of medical impostors, and news reports of accidents caused by inebriated, incompetent, and sleepy drivers. It is remarkable that, for almost all of us, knowing that these possibilities exist does not stop us from shopping, getting medical help, or driving. Categories are not only extremely convenient—they are essential in permitting us to get about the business of our lives.

A MIND BUILT TO USE CATEGORIES

To SHOW HOW, as Allport put it, "orderly living" depends on the use of categories, we shall describe four of the many feats that our minds perform with the aid of categories. Each of these is carried out so effortlessly that, even while doing them, we remain entirely unaware of the mental virtuosity that they draw upon.

FEAT 1: MULTIDIMENSIONAL CATEGORIES—A SNAP!

Can you make sense of this string of sixteen words?

1991 Subaru Legacy 4-door sedan with 4-cylinder engine, front-wheel drive, and automatic transmission.

Possibly you understood it in no more than the few seconds it took to read it. Next question: Would you have known that the string identified something quite different if it included "station wagon with standard transmission" in place of "sedan with automatic transmission"? If you can answer yes to both questions, you can regard yourself as the proud owner of a seven-dimensional category structure for automobiles. The seven dimensions are the seven columns of Table 5-1.

The sixteen-word Subaru description is one of thousands of distinct automobile categories that can be formed by stringing together identifiers from the seven columns of the table. The ability to conjure up pictures of a great many distinct automobile categories is one of two important characteristics of Feat 1. The second is

Table 5-1. Seven-Dimensional Automobile Category Generator

MODEL	YEAR	BODY TYPE	ENGINE SIZE	POWER SOURCE	TRANSMISSION	DRIVE
Ford Taurus	1990	Hatchback	4-cylinder	Diesel	manual 4-speed	front wheel
Cadillac Seville	1991	Station wagon	6-cylinder	Electric	manual 5-speed	rear wheel
VW Jetta	1992	Convertible	8-cylinder	Hybrid	automatic	4-wheel
...	...	SUV		Gasoline		
Subaru Legacy	2007	Pickup				
Audi Turbo	2008	2-door sedan				
Toyota Camry	2009	4-door sedan				
Mercedes 550SL	2010	Van				

the ease and automaticity with which your mind regularly makes use of this seven-dimensional structure.

Because some people are not so familiar with automobiles, not everyone can rapidly decode the sixteen words that describe the 1991 Subaru. If the Subaru example did not work for you, hold on for a moment—the much larger number of groups categorized in Feat 2 should establish the point.

FEAT 2: MILLIONS OF PERSON CATEGORIES CREATABLE ON THE FLY

Table 5-2. Six-Dimensional Person Category Generator

RACE	RELIGION	AGE	NATIONALITY/ REGION	SEX/GENDER	OCCUPATION
White	Christian	Young	French	Male	Professor
Asian	Muslim	Middle-aged	Detroit	Female	Homemaker
Black	Jewish	Sixtyish	Australian	Gay	Flight attendant
Hispanic	Zoroastrian	Elderly	American	Lesbian	Factory worker

Table 5-2 shows a small part of a six-dimensional structure that generates distinct categories of people by stringing together terms from its six columns. Some of the categories identified by these six-label strings encompass a relatively large number of people. For example, there are many middle-aged, White, male, Christian, Detroit factory workers. At the same time, if you don't live in Detroit, there is a good chance that you may never have met even one such person. Nevertheless, few Americans will have difficulty in forming an immediate mental conception of that factory worker on reading or hearing the six-label description. You may think that you can form an immediate impression of the Detroit factory worker because you've seen or heard or read about people like him in news media (talking about the closing of factories or being on strike, perhaps), in fiction, through friends, and so on.

But in fact, your facility with the six dimensions of Table 5-2 cannot be explained that simply. Your category-forming capacity is actually great enough to allow you to instantly conceive even a person described by an entirely unfamiliar combination of the six dimensions. For example, try thinking about a Black, Muslim, sixtyish, French, lesbian professor. Most readers of this book are unlikely to know even one person who could be identified by any four of those six identifiers. (Try it!) But that doesn't make it difficult to imagine one. It's almost a certainty that you will easily be able to form a picture in your mind of a person quite unlike anyone you have ever met: a Black, Muslim, sixtyish, French, lesbian professor.

For people who recognize the four sexuality/gender categories in the table, along with five race groups (add Native American to the four shown), plus approximately fifty nationalities or regions, about ten religions, eight age groups, and perhaps fifty occupations, Table 5-2 will produce a staggeringly large number of person categories—four million. The rapidity with which we can use the six identifiers to arrive at a picture of a category of person, however large (the Detroit factory worker) or small (the French professor) the category, confirms the brain's agility as a maker and user of categories.

FEAT 3: LEAPING BEYOND THE AVAILABLE INFORMATION[4]

How does your brain deal with learning that a person is "American"—for example, "My English professor is American" or "An American passenger was held for questioning" or "The American lottery winner remained anonymous"? Before reading the next paragraph, please humor us by forming a mental image of one of these—say, the anonymous American lottery winner. Try to visualize that person in the process of making a phone call to claim the winnings.

What characteristics does your imagined person have in addition to being American? We suspect that your imagined person is very likely also White, male, and adult. And if your imagined American did have those three added characteristics, very likely they entered your mind without your having to consciously place them there. You can't form a mental image of a person without attributing a male or female gender to that person, and usually a race and an age too. That said, you could—in theory—have imagined a female Hispanic American teenager making the call to collect the lottery winnings. But there's a much higher likelihood that your mind generated the image of a White male adult. The characteristics that you added can be thought of as your default values for the race, gender, and age of a typical American. Why might White, male, and adult be the default characteristics for an otherwise undescribed "American"? Likely it's because those are the characteristics of Americans whom you see, hear, and read about in newspapers, radio, television, and conversation most frequently, no matter whether they are the characteristics of those you meet and talk with most often as you go about your day.

If you are at all skeptical about the idea that in forming these mental pictures we use default characteristics to flesh out and go far beyond the basic information we've been given, then think about it this way: The default attributes that we add are so taken for granted and so automatic that, without thinking about why we do this, we are usually careful to specify a *different* set of attributes when the default ones don't apply. Thus you simply say "American" when you are referring to a White American. But if you're talking about another kind of American, you may instead say "Asian American" or "African American." Similarly, when you refer to a "taxi driver" you are almost certainly referring to a male taxi driver. If not, you may say "lady cab driver."

You can now understand something that might have been puzzling when we described the 1933 Princeton stereotype study on page 74. The students were asked to describe typical characteristics of nationality or race categories that were identified by single words, such as *Americans, Germans, Chinese,* and *Italians.* The Princeton students almost certainly assumed, without giving it any thought, that when they were asked to choose characteristics typical of Americans, they were expected to provide traits characteristic of White, male, adult Americans. The two traits that they most often selected for Americans, *materialistic* and *ambitious,* are very unlikely to be characteristics that the students would have chosen if they had been asked to describe American women or children.[5]

FEAT 4: COOPERATIVE CATEGORIZATION

People often actively send signals about the categories to which they themselves belong. Thus, on first meeting, we can often read these signals to help us identify a person's occupation. At the service station, we know that the person wearing coveralls is a mechanic, not a customer. In the hospital, the person in the white coat is a nurse or doctor, not a patient. The use of clothing to identify different occupations is just one of many ways in which people routinely help others to easily place them into appropriate categories.

Probably the most common, and arguably the most important, of these cooperative categorization strategies are those that help others to categorize us as male or female. If you are puzzled by this statement, wondering, "Who needs help in classifying people as male or female?" your puzzlement indicates only how unthinkingly—and routinely—almost everyone provides this help.

Although it is not difficult to distinguish male from female using natural body shape and facial features, we nevertheless use a wide variety of additional aids to help the process along. Women typically wear their hair longer than men. Most men and women wear sex-typical clothes that serve to accentuate body shape differences between male and female. Many people wear styles of collars, sleeves, belts, and shoes that are distinctively masculine or feminine. Cosmetics, manicures, jewelry, and gestures add still more markings that advertise—perhaps *flaunt* is the better word—maleness or femaleness. It could be an interesting exercise in economics to calculate the fraction of American wealth spent on clothing, cosmetics, and other accessories that ease the work of categorizing one another as male or female.

Race is another feature that can usually be identified fairly rapidly without help, but it too is a category that people often choose to make more identifiable by their choice of hairstyle, clothing, speech, gesture, and other signifiers.

Of course, such signifiers can be co-opted by other groups—witness the phenomenon of White suburban teenagers dressing "ghetto" to make a particular impression. This brings us to recognize that the cooperative categorization phenomenon also has its uncooperative variant form, in which we send visual signals for the explicit purpose of *mis*representing a category to which we belong.

The most common form of uncooperative categorization is the effort that many put into projecting the appearance of an age group younger than their own. A great deal of money is made supplying elders with cosmetics, hair dyes, surgery, and drugs designed to erase wrinkles, shore up sagging body parts, disguise hair that is turning gray or white, and replace hair that has disappeared. Given the traits stereotypically associated with old age—being slow, forgetful, hard of hearing, feeble, and so on—it is easy enough to see why elderly people might want to make it appear that they belong to a younger age group!

Less often disguised than age are religion and ethnicity, but they too are the object of uncooperative categorization under certain circumstances. A well-known strategy is to replace an ethnically identifiable name, such as Winona Horowitz, Issur Demsky, Anna Maria Louisa Italiano, or Jacob Cohen, with something less ethnically identifiable—like the names Winona Ryder, Kirk Douglas, Anne Bancroft, and Rodney Dangerfield (as these people are better known). A more recent cultural invention of the uncooperative categorization variety is the "whitening" of résumés submitted by African Americans in applying for jobs. This involves removing mentions of memberships and positions in obviously African American organizations and altering or omitting names of traditionally Black colleges or universities.

Notwithstanding the relative ease of engaging in uncooperative categorization, many members of often-stigmatized ethnic, racial, or sexual orientation categories not only avoid misrepresenting their categories but choose to do quite the opposite, making it easy for others to place them in their often-stigmatized categories. This suggests that the advantages of signaling those identities may often outweigh the disadvantages.

Think, for example, of gays and lesbians. Although they remain stigmatized and disadvantaged in many settings in modern America, many have decided to make their sexual orientation known—at least to other members of their category, and sometimes to the world at large. Such assists to "gaydar" (the ability to assess another's sexual orientation from a distance) make it much easier for gays to identify one another, and—if the signals are not of the secret-handshake type—often for non-gays to do so as well, helping avoid potential embarrassment on both sides.

Of the four feats, cooperative categorization stands apart from the others, being the only one that directly shows the everyday working of stereotypes. When cooperative categorization comes into play, a stereotype operates, interestingly, exactly opposite to the fashion usually expected. Instead of knowing a person's category (for example, female) and expecting a stereotypic trait (for example, long hair), we observe the long hair and infer that the person is female. Another paradox of cooperative categorization is that deliberately displaying a stereotyped characteristic (for example, the male professor's pipe and elbow-patched jacket) can have the possibly unwanted effect of strengthening observers' conception of the stereotype's validity.

The remainder of this chapter will make use of the mental virtuosity of Feats 1, 2, and 3 to describe further how stereotypes function in our daily lives. We reach a conclusion that should be a surprise to those familiar with existing scientific understanding of stereotypes.

HOW WE USE STEREOTYPES

MOST OF US think that the statement *Ducks lay eggs* is quite reasonable. But "Ducks lay eggs" is actually false for a substantial majority of the world's ducks, and not for one but two reasons. First, because fewer female than male ducklings survive the hatching process, more than half the world's ducks are non-egg-laying males.[6] Second, among female ducks, many are too young to be egg layers. Without doubt, egg-laying ducks are a distinct minority. We anticipate your reaction: "In agreeing that 'Ducks lay eggs' was reasonable, I meant only that I knew that *some* ducks lay eggs, not that *all* ducks lay eggs."

Fair enough. But suppose that the statement had been *Dogs wear clothes*. This is certainly true of *some* dogs. Would you have classified that statement as reasonable? Not likely. In our understanding, "Ducks lay eggs" seems more reasonable than "Dogs wear clothes" because most people have a strong *duck = egg layer* association. And unless you have been greatly influenced by William Wegman's photos of Man Ray, Fay Ray, and their successors, you probably do not have a *dog = clothes wearer* association.

The "Ducks lay eggs" example gives a clue to how stereotypes influence our thinking. Just as we may incorrectly assume that a duck seen swimming in a nearby pond can lay eggs, we may—equally unthinkingly—assume that an elderly person we have just met has poor memory. The *old = forgetful* stereotype is valid only to the extent that a greater proportion of elderly than young people have poor memory. Nevertheless, that stereotype may influence your reactions to *all* elderly people, including ones whose memories may be far better than your own.[7]

Here is another illustration of the tendency to think in stereotypes. For each of the five traits listed on the left below, do you see that trait as a better description of the first of the two groups named to the right, or the second?

TRAIT	GROUPS
Leadership	Men more than women?
Musical talent	African Americans more than Native Americans?
Legal expertise	Jews more than Christians?
Math ability	Asians more than Whites?
Criminality	Italians more than Dutch?

Any yes answer suggests that you possess a stereotype that, undoubtedly, many others also have. It's true that possessing these stereotypes doesn't make it inevitable that you will use them when you are making judgments about individual people, or that you will make important decisions based on them. For example, a corporate manager may believe that the *leader = male* stereotype is generally valid but may still be able to recognize that a specific woman who has shown outstanding leadership potential would be a good candidate for an executive position. At the same time, the bar she would have to clear might be higher than for men competing for the same position. Similarly, a teacher with a *math* = *male* stereotype may encourage an obviously gifted girl to pursue her studies in math. But this same teacher may also underestimate the math abilities of many other girls, all the while being more ready to recognize the potential of boys and to single them out for extra help and attention.

DOES STEREOTYPING HAVE A USEFUL PURPOSE?

WHILE WE MAY CONCEDE Gordon Allport's point that "the human mind must think with the aid of categories," and that, as he said, orderly living is not possible without using categories, we also have to wonder about the ultimate consequences of our category-making and category-using activities. For, as Allport also told us, "Once formed, categories are the basis for normal prejudgment." Another way of saying this is that the categories that our brains form so easily give rise to stereotypes. Thus we associate certain categories with certain prejudged attributes—Africans with having rhythm, Asians with being good at math, women with being inattentive drivers, and so forth.

Indeed, stereotyping by social category is so widely practiced as to deserve recognition as a universal human trait—as implied by the term *Homo categoricus*, which we used as the title for this chapter. Scientists understand universal traits in terms of the idea of adaptiveness or usefulness. Universal traits are generally assumed either to be presently adaptive or to be unfortunate by-products of other presently adaptive characteristics, or perhaps to be troublesome vestiges of previously (but no longer) adaptive characteristics.

The currently dominant explanation for the pervasiveness of stereotyping is of the "unfortunate by-product" type—stereotyping is an unfortunate by-product of the otherwise immensely useful human ability to conceive the world in terms of categories. Many social psychologists see this explanation as plausible, and we are among them.

There is also a theory of the "presently adaptive" type. This theory supposes that many people derive a useful self-esteem boost because stereotypes allow them to see their own group as superior to other groups. Having unfavorable stereotypes of many other groups makes this fairly easy to do. But this theory is less than compelling, in part because humans have so many other ways to boost self-esteem, and in part because it leads to an expectation that is most likely untrue—that those occupying the higher-status roles in their society or possessing the society's default characteristics should engage in more stereotyping than those lower in the hierarchy.

We offer here a new (and admittedly speculative) theory of the benefits of stereotyping that is also of the "presently adaptive" variety: Stereotyping achieves the desirable effect of allowing us to rapidly perceive total strangers as distinctive individuals.

We hope you read that last sentence at least twice, trying to find words that you thought you must have missed on first reading. The assertion "Stereotyping allows us to perceive strangers as distinctive individuals" may seem incomprehensible, even ludicrous, to anyone who thinks of stereotypes as the one-size-fits-all mental boxes into which we force all members of a group, no matter how different from one another they may be. Recall the inspiration for Walter Lippmann's coinage in 1922—the printer's metal plate that produced many identical copies. If stereotypes cause us to view all _____ (you name the group: cheerleaders, Italians, Muslims, rocket scientists, whatever) as being alike, then it would seem to follow that stereotypes must undermine, rather than facilitate, our ability to perceive strangers as distinct individuals.

We come to our seemingly absurd theory courtesy of the second mental feat of which *Homo categoricus* is capable: the ability to simultaneously use six (possibly more) person identifiers to produce mental images of many distinct categories of people. Applying the stereotypes associated with these six or so identifiers simultaneously produces a result very different from Lippmann's "identical copies."

This will be a good time to recall the Black, Muslim, sixtyish,

French, lesbian professor we used to illustrate Feat 2. Each of her six identifiers carries its own set of stereotypic traits. Using one identifier at a time would mean seeing her only with the Black stereotype, or only the Muslim stereotype, or only the stereotype for one of her other four category labels. But processing her six identifiers together, all at once, lets us conceive of a person who is distinctly different from anyone else we know. Maybe they didn't quite break the mold when they made her, but she'll be seen as a distinct individual, someone whom we will not readily confuse with anyone else we know.

To make our paradoxical explanation convincing, it may help if we make clear how easy it is to grasp half a dozen or so person identifiers within a fraction of a second. We do this all the time. Imagine a person who walks past you while you wait to board an airplane. Five identifiers will almost always be immediately available—sex, age, race, height, and weight. Clothing may permit us to add multiple other identifiers, perhaps including income, social class, religion, ethnicity, and occupation. Each of these identifiers has stereotypical traits associated with it. When our minds automatically activate all these stereotypes at once, we get a rich, complex perception of the person, even though the passerby we are contemplating is a total stranger. After no more than a brief glance we should be able to distinguish this passerby from just about everyone else in sight, and quite possibly from everyone else in the airport. This is why we conclude that the mental virtuosity described in Feat 2 allows us to use stereotypes *to perceive strangers as distinctive individuals.*

WHO USES STEREOTYPES? WHO GETS STEREOTYPED?

IT IS NOT POSSIBLE to be human and to avoid making use of stereotypes. Stereotypes make up a submerged but significant portion of the meaning that we read into words such as *old, female, Asian,* and *Muslim.* These submerged, automatically activated meanings go well beyond dictionary definitions. For example, nowhere in any dictionary of the English language will you find *old* defined as "slow," "forgetful," "hard of hearing," or "feeble," but these are all parts of the stereotype that the category *old* is packaged with. Not having stereotypes to provide meaning to our person categories would be like knowing the words of a language without knowing what they mean. In other words, *everyone uses stereotypes.*

The answer to "Who gets stereotyped?" is less simple. Stereotypes are not distributed equally. If you can be described by the default attributes of your society—the attributes that don't need to be mentioned because they are assumed unless explicitly stated otherwise (see Feat 3)—you will be subject to less stereotyping than others. You won't be stereotyped by the members of your in-group—those who share the default characteristics that you have—and you may be stereotyped little by others. In Japan, young Japanese men are unlikely to be stereotyped. However, in the United States, they are likely to be stereotyped. This is perhaps why those who belong to their society's "default" categories may see stereotyping as less of a problem than others do—they are much less likely to be its victims.

On the other hand, those who lack their society's default characteristics are likely to be stereotyped, and not just by others but by themselves—which can be to their disadvantage. This conclusion has only recently been established in research, and it may be the unkindest cut of all. The stereotypes applied to a group are sometimes self-applied by members of the group to themselves, and in that case the stereotypes may act as self-undermining and self-fulfilling prophecies.

Self-fulfilling prophecies can be beneficial. An own-group stereotype might guide African Americans toward becoming better track athletes, basketball players, or jazz musicians. Asian stereotypes may prompt Asian Americans to work hard in school, win scholarships, and launch themselves into high-paying careers in science, medicine, and engineering.

But when stereotypes are unfavorable, as many are, the forces that cause people to act in ways that conform to the stereotype applied to their own group can have damaging effects. Elders who internalize stereotypes of the elderly are at greater risk of declining health; women who internalize gender stereotypes are at risk of underperforming in math and science; African Americans who internalize stereotypes of their own group are at risk of not living up to their academic potential. It doesn't take the (stereotypical) rocket scientist to understand the potential for harm in stereotypes.[8]

6

The Hidden Costs of Stereotypes

JOAN A., SOMEONE WE BOTH KNOW, WAS IN EXCELLENT HEALTH. Playing tennis one day with a doctor friend, she mentioned that her primary care physician, Dr. M., had told her during a checkup that she didn't need routine blood cholesterol screening. Surprised to hear that, the friend urged Joan to press her doctor for the test. When the results came back, Joan learned that her cholesterol levels were high enough to warrant starting a drug regimen to reduce cholesterol immediately.

To his credit, Dr. M. acknowledged that among his reasons for not having prescribed a cholesterol test might have been his belief that women are at lower risk for heart disease than men. In other words, he had acted on a gender stereotype that cardiovascular disease is more prevalent among men than women. Possessing the stereotype is understandable, based on the facts of gender differences in heart disease. But the application of the stereotype to the individual is problematic because such application has serious consequences that nobody would consider ignoring—for Joan's health, for her family's security, for the physician who misses the chance to do his job as he intends, and for the insurance company, which gains from early detection of possibly life-threatening problems.

Stereotypes can operate in broad daylight, but this one imposed its cost quietly. When the doctor decided that Joan didn't need a cholesterol test, he wasn't thinking—in any conscious sense, that is—that Joan was unworthy or that he should protect the insurance company's resources by not ordering the test. The error likely emanated from a simple mental image of the average cardiac patient—male, possibly overweight, probably sedentary—and Joan, a fit and physically active woman, didn't match that prototype.

Our own bungling of the "surgeon and son" riddle in Chapter 5 illustrates that a reliance on stereotypes is obligatory.[1] But the fact that these and other potentially harmful stereotypes are persistent, and can routinely damage judgment and actions, demands that we seek innovative ways to look into the blindspot. In this chapter we visit a variety of automatic stereotypes to learn about their nature and their consequences: first, how they exert influence and the costs they impose on the targets of stereotyped perceptions, and second, about the self-defeating effects of stereotypes on the very people who hold them. Our attention will focus on the most serious consequences of stereotypes—their role in causing violence, imprisonment, even death; and their role in cutting off opportunities that make for a full and productive life.

KNOWING VERSUS ENDORSING

TWO SURVEYS OF STEREOTYPES, one published in 1933 and the other in 2001, warrant our attention. In both surveys (the second of which was explicitly undertaken to provide contemporary data for comparison to the first), respondents were asked whether they regarded several personality traits to be among the top five characteristics of Jews.[2] In the 1933 data, the traits that received the highest check marks were (in percentages): *shrewd* (79), *mercenary* (49), *industrious* (48), *grasping* (34). Almost seventy years later, a survey that used the same method found the same traits to be far less likely to be checked off as characteristic of Jews: *shrewd*: (30.5), *mercenary* (3.4), *industrious* (11.9), and *grasping* (0). If asked which percentages from 1933 were most likely to represent what people today think of Jews, our bet would have been closer to the 1933 percentages—perhaps somewhat diminished since 1933, but not nearly as low as the actual results. But clearly, respondents in 2001 didn't think so. Given how distant the 1930s seem—conjuring up dusty images of Al Capone, the Great Depression, and Amelia Earhart—we ask why our own predictions were closer to the data found in the 1930s than in 2001.

It is not surprising that people in the 1930s "knew" the historical stereotypes of Jews, because stereotypes persist. Think, for example, of the stereotypes in Elizabethan England, as reflected vividly in the title characters of Shakespeare's *The Merchant of Venice* and Christopher Marlowe's *The Jew of Malta*. Shylock and Barabas are the epitome of *shrewd, mercenary, industrious,* and *grasping,* and even 330 years later, in the 1930s, these traits were known and expressed. What ought to be surprising are the severely diminished percentages in 2001. It raises the question: Could the 2001 respondents really have been unaware of the stereotypes that we, and apparently the respondents from the 1930s, "know"? Or is it perhaps more plausible that by diminishing their characterization of Jews with negative stereotypes, at a time when anti-Semitism was far less acceptable, the 2001 respondents were trying to distance themselves from expressions of stereotypes they found repugnant? And if so, who would blame them? We too would like to put such stereotypes out of our minds, and hope that by ignoring them we can urge them to just go away.

In Chapter 4 we described the concept of dissociation, the idea that one can simultaneously possess two attitudes that are mutually inconsistent but remain isolated from each other, so that the person experiencing the dissociation does not become aware of the inconsistency. In fact, we used Jerry Seinfeld's comic refrain "Not that there's anything wrong with that!" as the example of exactly this—of being consciously gay-friendly but squeamish about being recognized as genuinely such.

We now need to give the idea of dissociation a twist. Remember that dissociation represents a state in which a person possesses conflicting attitudes, one reflective, the other automatic. If, on reading that description in Chapter 4, you had an uneasy feeling that perhaps something was missing, there was good reason for it. We hadn't yet addressed the question of whether a person who *possesses* an automatic attitude can be assumed to *endorse* it.

It is easy to understand the distinction between possession or knowledge of an idea, for example that UFOs have landed in New Mexico, and believing or endorsing it. This distinction brings us back to the survey takers, whose choice of a set of traits to describe Jews had nothing in common with the traditional stereotype of Jews. Their choice, we would claim, was essentially their way of saying, "I *know* these stereotypes quite well, but I don't for a moment *endorse* them myself." In so doing, the survey respondents are drawing a bright line between "those people out there" who benightedly believe in the stereotype and "me, the enlightened person in here" who does not. As far as consciously held beliefs go, such a distinction is completely meaningful.

As an example, think about the concept *Earth,* which contains among its many attributes that of roundness. Hearing the word *Earth* likely causes an image of a cerulean blue sphere to come effortlessly to mind. Most readers both *know* and *endorse* the idea that the Earth is round—if only because they have seen numerous representations of Earth, from the inflated plastic one gathering dust in the classroom corner to the endless pictures of it beamed back from outer space ever since the iconic one taken by Apollo 8. To *endorse* something, as opposed to be aware of it or merely know it, is to put one's own skin in the game.

This description should make complete sense, because we speak here about consciously held beliefs about the shape of the Earth.

Yet when we consider the very same distinction between knowing and endorsing in the context of automatic beliefs, we realize that there is no simple parallel. Is it possible to have the automatic association that *math* = *male* (knowing) and put it to use, without endorsing it? The distinction between knowing and endorsing, which seems to make so much sense when speaking about conscious or reflective beliefs, falls away when mapping it onto representations in our mind that are more automatic. Our thesis is that at the automatic level, unlike the reflective level, the distinction between *knowing* and *endorsing* is meaningless because there's no capacity for endorsing.

Understanding this concept is difficult because our scientific grasp of the human mind has only recently turned toward its unconscious aspects. It is difficult to fathom what it even means to have an automatic stereotype, that is, a belief about a social group that we possess but don't personally endorse or even approve of. But our minds have been shaped by the culture around us. In fact, they have been invaded by it. To fully grasp the extent to which this happens, imagine the challenge presented to the minds of members of a minority group, the Flat Earth Society. These latter-day followers of the nineteenth-century thinker Samuel Rowbotham endorse a view that differs from the one held by the majority of earth dwellers. They believe as firmly as the ground on which they stand that the Earth is flat.

But flat-Earthers live in a world permeated by the belief that the Earth is a sphere. Wherever they look, the Earth is represented as such—in teaching devices, in pictures, in language and metaphors—not the two-dimensional disc they believe it to be. Without doubt, flat-Earthers endorse the idea of Earth as a two-dimensional disc, but if we could examine their automatic associations, what should we expect to find?

We could test flat-Earthers' automatic belief about the shape of the planet by persuading them to take an IAT that measures the relative strength of their *Earth* = *sphere* versus *Earth* = *flat* associations. In contrast to their explicitly endorsed belief in flatness, this group's IAT scores would almost certainly reveal the presence of *Earth* = *sphere* knowledge in their minds. Once their *Earth* = *sphere* knowledge had been "outed" by the test, flat-Earthers might immediately protest that the result reflects not their personal beliefs but only the inescapable mental residue of the round-Earthers' constant propaganda efforts. And they would be right, for it would require a creature with near-null cognitive capacity to not absorb, via cultural osmosis, the dominant view of Earth as sphere.

If this is true, what would be revealed by a Jewish stereotype IAT that you or we might take? Would it reveal an automatic stereotype of Jews as *grasping, mercenary, shrewd*? It's likely that none of us believes that those stereotypes are so descriptive of the group that most Jews possess them. Far from it. But by now Mahzarin and Tony have become so accustomed to the IAT's unwelcome revelations that it would hardly be surprising to discover that an "inescapable mental residue" of Jewish stereotypes remains in the minds of many present-day Americans, including ourselves. We would agree that we possess these stereotypes because we've been repeatedly exposed to relevant propaganda in images, in stories, in jokes, in ordinary language, and in the inferences that pervade social space.

BECOMING FAMOUS OVERNIGHT

IN THE LATE 1980s, a paper with the intriguing title "Becoming Famous Overnight" appeared in a scientific journal.[3] In it, Larry Jacoby and three colleagues reported a series of simple but ingenious experiments. If you were a participant in their study, you were first asked to judge the relative ease of pronouncing dozens of ordinary names on a list that had been pulled from a local phone book, names such as Sebastian Weisdorf.

On returning to the laboratory the next day, you would

be given another list, this one containing three types of names, all mixed together: (1) the ones you had read the day before, such as Sebastian Weisdorf (we'll call these *old not-famous*), (2) new names from the same phone book, such as Andrew Ringren (*new not-famous*), and (3) names of actual famous people such as the ice hockey player Wayne Gretzky (*famous,* at least in Canada, where the study was done). Your task would be to answer a simple question for each name: *Is this the name of a famous person?*

To be correct, you would have to answer yes to the names of people who are actually famous, such as Wayne Gretzky, and no to all the phone-book names, regardless of whether they were "old" names such as Sebastian Weisdorf or "new" names such as Andrew Ringren. However, as the experimenters discovered, confirming their theory of how memory works, old non-famous names proved tricky on day 2. Jacoby's data showed that you'd be more likely to mistakenly think that a previously seen name such as Sebastian Weisdorf was actually a famous person (an incorrect answer) than was a previously unseen name such as Andrew Ringren.

Memories have a texture attached to them, and we sense that texture by "feeling" the memory as we might feel a piece of silk, to judge its quality. The familiarity of a name gives our memory for it a particular texture. In the case of an old not-famous name such as Sebastian Weisdorf, the familiarity causes confusion. The study subjects must ask themselves a question about why a name is familiar: Is this name familiar because it was on the list yesterday? Or is it familiar because the guy is famous? With Andrew Ringren there's no such confusion because with no prior exposure, there is no feeling of familiarity. Confusing two sources of familiarity leads to an obvious mindbug—that of mistakenly thinking people are famous when in fact they are not.

BUT WHAT IF SEBASTIAN WERE SAMANTHA?

With one tweak, we modified Jacoby's nifty experiment to see what it could teach us about the costs and benefits of another mindbug. Let's begin with the uncontroversial observation that in most societies, men are more likely to be famous than women, using accepted criteria for fame such as achievement and name recognition. This holds in just about every domain of human endeavor—the arts, politics, finance, sports, and the intellect. We tested whether familiarity provides greater benefit to men than women by asking: Is Jacoby's result that familiar names are likely to be mistakenly judged as famous equally true for both men and women?

Jacoby made it easy for us to do this. We had only to add female names such as Samantha Weisdorf to the almost exclusively male names that Jacoby and his colleagues had used. In the several experiments we conducted, we found that women did become famous overnight but they did so at significantly lower rates than did men. Clearly, the false-fame mindbug does its work more readily when the name is male than female. We hardly need to draw out the implications of this disparity. Suffice it to say that it can be advantageous to men if in public life they are more likely than women to benefit from (mistaken) assumptions that they have accomplished something when in fact they have not.

A remarkable feature of the false-fame mindbug was the test-takers' total lack of awareness that the gender of the name played any role in their decisions about fame. Even when questioned directly, virtually none of the several hundred subjects thought that their answers might have been influenced by the gender of the name. They were surprised that we would even suggest that possibility. The stereotype that was being put to use clearly resided in their blindspots.

These studies were Mahzarin and Tony's first collaboration on the topic that then produced other studies in quick succession, continuing over the past twenty-five years. Even as we completed the first studies in the late 1980s, it was clear that such a bias, if it was demonstrable more generally, could reveal the costly nature of automatic stereotypes. And that if it did, those in the worlds of law, business, medicine, and conceivably every profession might find the data to be of interest, because the "good people" in the title of this book surely do not intend to impose stereotype-based costs on anybody.

In the next two sections we describe two damaging out-group stereotypes that associate Black men with weapons and deny Asian Americans the same "citizenship" accorded to White Americans.

THE COST OF THE BLACK=HARMFUL STEREOTYPE

THE BELIEF that Black men are criminals persists even though the likelihood of any given Black male being a criminal is low.[4] Needless to say, the existence of a stereotype associating a given group with violence and crime is grave and has important implications for the individual, the group, and society.

The next IAT is designed to test the association between race and weapons. As before, you can begin the test with either Sheet A or Sheet B. Here are this IAT's four categories:

> Black Americans: *faces with Afrocentric features*
> White Americans: *faces with Eurocentric features*
> Weapons: *pictures of a cannon, pistol, sword, etc.*
> Harmless things: *pictures of a phone, soda can, camera, etc.*

After you have timed and completed the two pages of the test, revisit Chapter 3, where the first IAT test was introduced, for detailed instructions about how to do the scoring. If you'd prefer to complete this test online or on a mobile device, go to bit.ly/P7byzi.

A

For **weapons** and <u>**African American faces**</u>, mark in the circle to the left. For everything else (<u>harmless objects</u> and <u>European American faces</u>) mark in the circle to the right. Start at top left, go from top to bottom doing all items in order, then do the second column. At bottom right, record the elapsed time in seconds.

weapons or Afr. Am. faces	harmless objects or Eur. Am. faces	weapons or Afr. Am. faces	harmless objects or Eur. Am. faces
○ 🔫 ○		○ 🔫 ○	
○ 😐 ○		○ 😐 ○	
○ ⚒ ○		○ 🧴 ○	
○ 😐 ○		○ 😐 ○	
○ 📟 ○		○ 👜 ○	
○ 😐 ○		○ 😐 ○	
○ 🗡 ○		○ 🪓 ○	
○ 😐 ○		○ 😐 ○	
○ 📷 ○		○ 📱 ○	
○ 😐 ○		○ 😐 ○	
○ 🥤 ○		○ 📷 ○	
○ 😐 ○		○ 😐 ○	
○ 🔫 ○		○ 🔫 ○	
○ 😐 ○		○ 😐 ○	

Number of seconds: _____

Number of errors: _____

B

For **weapons** and **European American faces**, mark in the circle to the left. For everything else (<u>harmless objects</u> and <u>African American faces</u>) mark in the circle to the right. Start at top left, go from top to bottom doing all items in order, then do the second column. At bottom right, record the elapsed time in seconds.

weapons or Eur. Am. faces	harmless objects or Afr. Am. faces	weapons or Eur. Am. faces	harmless objects or Afr. Am. faces
○	○	○	○
○	○	○	○
○	○	○	○
○	○	○	○
○	○	○	○
○	○	○	○
○	○	○	○
○	○	○	○
○	○	○	○
○	○	○	○
○	○	○	○
○	○	○	○
○	○	○	○

Number of seconds: ____

Number of errors: ____

You may have noticed that, rather than using images of modern weapons, this race-weapons IAT used pictures of weapons from past centuries: axes, swords, cannons, and pistols. We did this deliberately, so as to undermine the race stereotype by setting aside the kinds of weapons that are stereotypically associated with present-day urban crime. The weapons chosen for this test actually have strong historical associations with European cultures, meaning that their use in this test might, if anything, favor a *White = weapons* association.

However, as data from many respondents show, 70 percent or more of the people who take this test have greater difficulty with Sheet B, which pairs *White* with *weapons,* than with Sheet A, which pairs *Black* with *weapons.* Analyses of more than eighty thousand race-weapons IATs completed at implicit.harvard.edu yielded three important results:

First, the automatic *Black = weapons* association is much stronger among all groups who took the test—White, Asian, Hispanic, and even African American—than is suggested by surveys that asked questions about this association. Second, the size of this automatic stereotype varies noticeably by groups—it is largest in Whites and Asians, next largest in Hispanics, and smallest in African Americans. But even African Americans show a modest *Black = weapons* stereotype.

Third, comparing the results of the two kinds of tests—reflective self-report and automatic stereotype—reveals another interesting fact about who carries the stereotype. The higher the education level, the lower the endorsement of the association between Blacks and weapons on the reflective self-report answers. However, on the test of automatic stereotypes, the IAT, education level matters not a whit. Those with greatest education carry as strong an implicit *Black = weapons* stereotype as do those with least education. From images and stories in which men with dark skin have been associated with violence, it would seem that we all, irrespective of our conscious beliefs, have a lack of immunity, and everybody, irrespective of education level, is infected by those beliefs.

Black men are well aware that those around them associate them with violence, often including other Black Americans themselves, who carry the stigmatizing belief to a lesser extent than Whites and Asians. They experience it every day, whether they are walking down a street, trying to hail a cab, entering a store, applying for a job, for housing, for a loan. Many have developed explicit strategies to signal that they are harmless. A poignant example comes from the journalist Brent Staples, who confesses to whistling popular pieces of classical music in public places to reassure passersby, to create an alternative *Vivaldi* = *harmless* association— that those who whistle Vivaldi are surely unlikely to also mug you.[5]

In terms of "guilt by association," a *Black* = *weapons* stereotype is particularly consequential when it plays out in the interaction between citizens and law enforcement. Although it is difficult to say conclusively how great a role race plays in the mistaken shooting of Black men, we do know that Black men experience the effects of such mistakes significantly more often than White men. Every so often, one case becomes emblematic of the tragic consequences of the problem, and one that has acquired that standing in recent years is the shooting of Amadou Diallo.

Diallo was a twenty-three-year-old Guinean immigrant of very limited means who sold videos on the sidewalks of New York City and was saving up for the dream of enrolling in college. One early morning in February 1999, a car carrying four White plainclothes police officers rolled past Diallo's apartment building in the Bronx as he was standing near the door. The officers, who were members of the NYPD's Street Crime Unit, mistook the young man for a serial rapist they were seeking. As the officers approached Diallo a series of errors stemming from the officers' blindspots created the conditions for tragedy. As Diallo reached for his wallet, presumably to show the officers some identification, officer Sean Carroll mistakenly perceived this as an attack and yelled "gun" to alert his partners, one of whom then tripped, causing the others to believe that he had been shot. Panic-stricken, the officers fired off forty-one shots in the next few seconds, nearly half of which sprayed Diallo's body.

At least two of the errors in judgment here deserve our attention. First, it is well known that people recognize faces from their own racial/ethnic group more easily than other-race faces. White Americans, for example, are not as able to distinguish between the faces of Black Americans as they are the faces of White Americans.[6] In the Bronx tragedy, we can speculate that this perceptual difficulty may have played a role in the officers' mistaking Diallo for a dangerous serial rapist.[7]

Second, an automatically operating *Black = weapons* stereotype may have played a role in the officer's mistaking Diallo's wallet for a gun.[8] Several experiments support the idea that Black men carrying harmless objects such as cell phones are indeed more likely to be shot at mistakenly.[9] These experiments, motivated by cases such as Diallo's, show more incontrovertibly than any single real event can, the probability of hidden stereotypes driving life-or-death decisions.[10]

For us, the ordinariness of the errors that emerge from blindspots is striking, because they require no malign intent and yet impose costs. Adrienne Rich, in her poem "Midnight Salvage," said it better than we can:[11]

> *lucky I am I hit nobody old or young*
> *killed nobody left no trace*
> *practiced in life as I am*

Practiced in life we all are, and it is such practice that readily provides the "pictures in our heads" that spur us on to the mistaken actions we take, all the while believing that we are the good ones.

THE COST OF THE STEREOTYPE
THAT AMERICAN = WHITE

CLAUDE STEELE, a psychologist at Stanford University, has spoken about the "burden of suspicion" that certain individuals in every society carry around because they belong to a group whose status in society is suspect. That burden can be crushing: Witness another, milder tragedy in the case of Wen Ho Lee, a nuclear scientist of Taiwanese origin, a U.S. citizen who worked at the Los Alamos National Laboratory in New Mexico. In 1999, Lee was accused of having turned over U.S. nuclear secrets to sources in the People's Republic of China. In short order, Lee was fired from his job and a grand jury issued fifty-nine indictments against him involving deceit, espionage, misleading the U.S. government, contacts with the Chinese government, and seeking employment abroad. Lee spent nine months in prison, all the while asserting his innocence.

In the remarkable series of events that followed, the case against Lee unraveled, beginning with FBI agent Robert Messemer admitting to giving false testimony, and the judge who had denied Lee bail apologizing to him for his incarceration and misidentification. In 2006, a federal court awarded Lee $1.6 million in his suit against the U.S. government for invasion of privacy.[12]

The central question the case raises is just how a series of decisions emanating from the blindspots of good people may have led to Lee's indictment in the first place. Was Lee's being Chinese a risk factor he carried, as he might a gene for a disease? Would the events have unfolded in the same manner had he instead been a scientist at Los Alamos of European origin with the same last name—say, Robert E. Lee? The bald conclusion Wen Ho Lee's story suggests is that he carried a burden of suspicion by sheer dint of ethnicity.

Stereotypes are hard to pin down because so often they are put into play without any feeling of personal animus or vengeance. There is no doubt that the conscious motive of the reporters at *The New York Times* who worked to break the story was their desire to do their job effectively. The main motive of the FBI agent who gave false testimony was most likely a desire to protect the country. But stereotypes generate their own compelling mental evidence, even if that evidence is incorrect. In turn the data generated by our minds can provide justification for a rush to report, the acceptability of lying, and the pragmatic decision to detain a suspect indefinitely.

Stereotypes do not take special effort to acquire. Quite the opposite—they are acquired effortlessly, and take special effort to discount.[13] Discounting stereotypes is not easy, because of the value of the general mental processes into which stereotypic thinking is embedded. The same mental abilities that allow us to perceive and categorize appropriately, that are necessary for us to learn and understand, and that make us successful at detecting and recognizing, are also the abilities that can lead us astray. Yet if we were to think of our minds as courtrooms in which trials are held to decide on guilt and innocence, one of the downsides of stereotypes is that they compromise due process. By relying on them, our minds indict before a prosecutor arrives on the scene.[14]

The case of Wen Ho Lee led us to research a particular stereotype of Asian Americans—that they are perceived as foreigners in their own country. The term *citizenship* has clear and precise meaning legally, and the concept is simple enough to be broadly known and shared. We know that two individuals, one with European grandparents, the other with Chinese grandparents, who were both born and raised in the United States, are equally American. The question is this: Irrespective of the conscious acknowledgment of the legal parity between the two and the knowledge that they both retain U.S. passports, do we think of them as equally American?

Thierry Devos, a postdoctoral scholar at Yale University when the Wen Ho Lee story first emerged, created an IAT measure of an *Asian = foreign* stereotype. The test used images of students' faces to represent the groups *Asian* and *White,* making it clear that both the Asians and Whites were born and raised in the United States, and measured associations to symbols that represented *American* and *foreign,* using pictures of monuments, currencies, and maps.

The results of the Devos IAT showed that both White and Asian American respondents were more adept at associating White Americans than Asian Americans with American symbols such as a dollar bill or a map of the United States. Though the association was not as strong in Asian Americans themselves, they too more readily associated their own group with *foreign* more than with *American*. This result is reminiscent of what we observed in the *Black = weapons* test. Yes, members of the group that is suspect tend to show lower negative stereotypes, but they are not exempt from carrying them. There is an obvious implication of this result for policymakers, who must consider the overall level of harm that a group encounters, and also consider how a civilized society should cope with built-in disadvantage.

To test just how bizarre such automatic associations can be, Devos next chose well-known Asian Americans such as Connie Chung, Michael Chang, and Kristi Yamaguchi, pairing them with well-known Europeans such as Hugh Grant, Gérard Depardieu, and Katarina Witt. He then tested the association of these famous Asian Americans and White foreigners with the concept *American*. Again, the same type of result was obtained. It was easier for test takers to associate White foreigners such as Hugh Grant than Asian Americans such as Connie Chung with the concept *American*. Even as his study subjects took the test, they seemed to be aware that their minds were revealing stereotypes that were opposed not just to their reflective beliefs but to the facts. This test result is a strong contender for our Most Ridiculous Mindbug Prize!

In the weeks and months following the election of Barack Obama, a group that came to be known as the "birthers" formed and grew sufficiently in size to generate media attention. Quite simply, the birthers believe that Barack Obama is not American-born and therefore not legally fit to be president. It is easy to set such folks aside and label them as the lunatic fringe. But we suggest the uncomfortable possibility that at some automatic level, a larger number of us are similar to the birthers, to the extent that we possess the *American* = *White* stereotype. The difference between birthers and non-birthers lies instead in their conscious beliefs. In voting for Obama, non-birthers demonstrate their ability to set aside the automatic association of *American* = *White* and allow their conscious thought to dictate their behavior.

In discussing Devos's test, we are often told that the stronger

American = White association arises from the legitimate fact that White Americans came to the United States before Asian Americans did and are therefore regarded as being more legitimately American. Fair enough. But if that's the case, it should be a no-brainer as to who ought to be considered more American: Native Americans or European Americans. Predict your response! The test is available at implicit.harvard.edu.

SELF-DEFEATING STEREOTYPES

WHEN WE HEAR the standard admonition "Don't stereotype!" we assume that the stereotyper is referring in a pejorative way to a group other than her or his own—and certainly that the stereotyper is typecasting somebody other than herself or himself. Yet we have noted the idea that often people show evidence of automatic negative stereotypes about their own groups. Earlier in this chapter, we reported that Black Americans themselves hold the *Black = weapon* stereotype and that Asian Americans themselves hold the *American = White* stereotype, even though they reject such beliefs consciously. These results are consistent with demonstrations of *stereotype threat,* a concept introduced by Claude Steele to describe the phenomenon that when those who are members of a negatively stereotyped group—women in the domain of math, Black Americans and the poor on achievement tests in general—are even subtly reminded of their group membership, they underperform on these tests.[15] There is strong evidence for this result from dozens of experiments, and we turn to the self-defeating nature of stereotypes next.

THE GENDER–CAREER TEST

IN MANY SOCIETIES of the world, women and men have occupied and often continue to occupy different spheres, with women dominating the world of the home and men dominating the world of work. But we are also witness to a major change in this arrangement: the entry of women into the workforce in large numbers. In February 2010, for the first time in U.S. history, the Labor Department announced that the number of women in the ranks of non-farm payroll employees had overtaken that of men—64.2 million women to 63.4 million men.[16]

Despite the fact that a massive cultural and economic change has resulted in 50 percent of the workforce in the United States now being female, there has been much less of a change in who occupies the role of primary caregiver at home. As a colleague once said, "It's not that my husband can't make lunch; it's that he can't imagine lunch!" Her tongue-in-cheek observation was meant to suggest that even though both she and her husband were equally invested professionally, and he did perform necessary domestic duties, there remained a palpable difference in their investments in matters of the home. So even though the workplace is now populated by as many women as men, we suspect that stereotypes remain present because of the strong and dominating presence of women in the home sphere and the strong and dominating position of men in the highest status positions at work.

For those of us who believe that the *female* = *home* and *male* = *career* associations are not in *our* minds, the gender-career IAT on the next two pages may be informative. As before, you can take the test in either order, completing Sheet A or Sheet B first. If you'd prefer to complete this test online or on a mobile device, please go to bit.ly/SY5lF4. Here are the four categories in the test.

> Female: *she, her, woman, women, girl*
> Male: *he, him, his, man, men, boy*
> Home: *garden, laundry, kitchen, marriage, children, home*
> Career: *office, job, profession, briefcase, manager, salary*

Timing yourself and going as fast as possible, classify each word as either male- or female-associated by marking the circle to either the right or left of it, while also checking off "home" or "career," as directed on the page. For full instructions on taking and scoring IAT tests, see the first test in Chapter 3.

A

For **FEMALE** words and **family** words mark in the circle to the left. For everything else (_MALE_ words and career words) mark in the circle to the right. Start at top left, go from top to bottom doing all items in order, then do the second column. At bottom right, record the elapsed time in seconds.

FEMALE or family	MALE or career	FEMALE or family	MALE or career
◯ SHE ◯		◯ WOMEN ◯	
◯ garden ◯		◯ home ◯	
◯ HER ◯		◯ MAN ◯	
◯ office ◯		◯ manager ◯	
◯ HE ◯		◯ MEN ◯	
◯ laundry ◯		◯ salary ◯	
◯ GIRL ◯		◯ SHE ◯	
◯ job ◯		◯ office ◯	
◯ HIM ◯		◯ BOY ◯	
◯ profession ◯		◯ garden ◯	
◯ HIS ◯		◯ HIM ◯	
◯ briefcase ◯		◯ marriage ◯	
◯ WOMAN ◯		◯ WOMAN ◯	
◯ kitchen ◯		◯ children ◯	

Number of seconds: _____

Number of errors: _____

B

For **FEMALE** words and <u>**career**</u> words mark in the circle to the left. For everything else (<u>MALE</u> words and <u>family</u> words) mark in the circle to the right. Start at top left, go from top to bottom doing all items in order, then do the second column. At bottom right, record the elapsed time in seconds.

FEMALE or career		MALE or family		FEMALE or career		MALE or family	
◯	SHE	◯		◯	WOMEN	◯	
◯	garden	◯		◯	home	◯	
◯	HER	◯		◯	MAN	◯	
◯	office	◯		◯	manager	◯	
◯	HE	◯		◯	MEN	◯	
◯	laundry	◯		◯	salary	◯	
◯	GIRL	◯		◯	SHE	◯	
◯	job	◯		◯	office	◯	
◯	HIM	◯		◯	BOY	◯	
◯	profession	◯		◯	garden	◯	
◯	HIS	◯		◯	HIM	◯	
◯	briefcase	◯		◯	marriage	◯	
◯	WOMAN	◯		◯	WOMAN	◯	
◯	kitchen	◯		◯	children	◯	

Number of seconds: _____

Number of errors: _____

The gender-career IAT was designed to answer a question about a familiar automatic stereotype: Do we make *male* = *career* and *female* = *family* associations more strongly than the reverse associations? If you are like the majority of test takers, you will have completed Sheet A, which has the traditional pairings of female with family and male with career, more quickly and with fewer errors than Sheet B, which asks you to link female with career concepts, and male with family concepts. This result isn't especially surprising. After all, as discussed above, men still dominate in the world of work, and women still dominate domestic life.

The data from the gender-career IAT show that about 75 percent of male respondents display the automatic gender stereotype of *male* = *work* and *female* = *family*. Leading them by a little, 80 percent of women show the same automatic stereotype![17] Mahzarin, who never imagined a life without a career outside the home, never has been without one as an adult, and is largely free of domestic responsibilities, regularly shows the gender stereotype that the majority of women do—she's a lot quicker to associate *male* with *career*, even when the profession named is her own chosen career of university professor. As with her performance on the race-attitude IAT, when asked about her score, Mahzarin will report that she has "flunked" this test because its score deviates from her aspiration to be unbiased in these associations, however automatic they may be.

Those in search of a silver lining to this rather discouraging news can find reason for optimism in the data from various age groups of test takers, for on this test, the effect of age is quite clear. Decade by decade, the younger the test takers are, the weaker is this automatic gender bias. The optimism comes from the recognition that with the *male* = *career* association growing ever fainter among the young, perhaps we will see its complete disappearance in the future.[18] But if the constancy of many other stereotypes and attitudes across age groups is any indication, that day may be further off than we realize.[19]

GENDER AND ACHIEVEMENT

LAURIE RUDMAN, a psychologist at Rutgers University, has asked if the presence of implicit gender stereotypes about romance and home, achievement and career, has consequences for the women who hold them. She tested the possibility that part of the problem might lie in the minds of women themselves, put there by the fairy-tale fantasies they have consumed throughout their lives about love and marriage. Rudman speculated that for women, such fantasies may lead them to believe that they will find their access to power and achievement through the success of a male partner, the Prince Charming figure who swoops down and "rescues" them from their helplessness.[20]

Rudman gave women an IAT test of various automatic stereotypes, measuring the relative strengths of *romantic partner = fantasy hero* and *romantic partner = regular guy.* She also obtained a measure of these women's aspirations for high-status occupations and economic rewards (income), and of the strength of their commitment to the education required to reach those goals. She found that the more strongly women associated the idea of a romantic partner with the idea of Prince Charming, the less they aspired to status and power themselves. The findings led her to conclude that "associating romantic partners with chivalry and heroism may curtail women's direct pursuit of power" and that these may be "the psychological processes that may nonconsciously inhibit women from competing with men for status and prestige."[21]

Interestingly, then, there are automatic or unconscious stereotypes in women's own minds that impose a cost on their access to status and prestige. In this case the damage is compounded by views such as "But that's what women *themselves* really want"—the idea being that renouncing power and prestige should not be seen as a cost borne by women because it's a choice they have freely made.

Accordingly, we sought to evaluate a clearly demonstrable cost of this gender stereotype in lost wages. The question was posed: *Do you care if your boss is male or female?* and respondents, young professionals looking for their first jobs, gave a resounding no as their answer. Their responses identified other aspects of the job that would be important to them, such as salary, location, and the boss's personality. But whether they would directly report to a male or female manager was—so they insisted—not part of their job-evaluation equation.

Eugene Caruso and Doby Rahnev, students at Harvard at the time, used a technique called *conjoint analysis* to test this assessment directly.[22] The data showed that in opposition to the job seekers' statement "I have no preference for a male or female boss," subjects' answers tilted in a systematic way toward jobs with male bosses. On jobs with average salary of $42,500, these presumably savvy respondents showed themselves willing to take a salary penalty averaging $3,400 in order to work with a male supervisor. That is, they preferred lower-pay jobs with male bosses over higher-pay jobs with female bosses.

Remarkably, male and female respondents were equally willing to give up a chunk of salary for the pleasure of having a male boss, even though they had sworn to having no such preference. Both men and women were willing to lose several thousand dollars by making this choice. Now, if the job seekers were consciously seeking a male boss and chose him even if the salary was lower, the result would have meant something entirely different. But the self-undermining bias sat in their blindspot and remained undetected, a bias they presumably would have opted to avoid had they been aware of the patterns of their choices.

In another study that tested whether such self-defeating costs are paid in situations involving other hidden biases, Caruso and Rahnev asked respondents to select from a series of candidates the person they thought would be the strongest teammate in a quiz competition. Now, results showed that respondents took account of relevant features such as IQ score, education level, and past competitive experience, but also factored in their potential teammate's body weight. Surprisingly, respondents traded nine honest-to-goodness IQ points for a partner who was thinner than the smarter alternative![23] It doesn't occur to us to consciously attend to body weight when it comes to judging intelligence or merit. But apparently we do this automatically, and irrationally, self-defeatingly so.

If the number of people who choose to take a given IAT test on the Project Implicit website is any measure, our stereotypes about weight have substantial impact on us. Interestingly, more people choose to know about their weight bias than any other test on the website except the one on race, showing the importance the issue body image has in our minds.

Self-defeating consequences such as the ones we have been describing are psychologically intriguing, because they run counter to the assumption that people will always act in their own self-interest. John Jost, a psychologist at New York University, has suggested that, contrary to that expectation, people in fact are willing to sacrifice their self-interest for the sake of maintaining the existing social order. His experiments have shown that we do cognitive and emotional work to justify the hierarchies that make up the status quo, even when that means imposing costs on ourselves as well as on the groups to which we belong. Because automatic stereotypes often work to perpetuate the prevailing system, no matter what its flaws, we see Jost's research as further evidence of the self-undermining nature of automatic stereotypes.[24]

Jost has gathered an array of evidence to show that members of disadvantaged groups play a perplexing role in maintaining their own disadvantage through their acceptance of self-undermining stereotypes. Examples of system justification are found in the poor who believe themselves to be unintelligent and therefore less deserving of resources; Asian Americans who believe that they may be good with numbers but should stay out of leadership roles in public life; women who believe that they are not suited to high-paying jobs and so don't apply for them or negotiate appropriately; and men who believe that they don't have the talent for caregiving jobs and consequently stay away from parenting or careers that could be gratifying.

MATH = MALE, ME = FEMALE, THEREFORE MATH ≠ ME

PURSUING OUR INTEREST in the role of stereotypes in important life choices, we worked with our collaborator Brian Nosek to test the power of the implicit *math = male* and *science = male* stereotypes among college men and women.[25] Using multiple IATs, we measured the speed and errors made in associating the categories *male* and *female* with science concepts such as *geometry, math, chemistry,* and *Einstein* and with humanities concepts such as *literature, arts, drama,* and *Shakespeare*. The women who had stronger *math = male* stereotypes were also less likely to prefer mathematics and less likely to associate themselves with math than were those with weaker stereotypes. Moreover, the strength of the *math = male* stereotype predicted SAT math performance among women—the stronger the stereotype, the lower their math test scores.

Nosek and his University of Virginia collaborator Fred Smyth also did large-scale tests of more than a hundred thousand college students and college graduates, which yielded a wealth of information.[26] They found that women who hold the strongest *science = male* stereotypes are least likely to major in science, while men who hold the strongest *science = male* stereotypes are the most likely to do so. In this study, the gender-science stereotype turns out to predict women's choice of science majors significantly better than do either consciously expressed gender-math/science stereotypes or even, remarkably enough, math SAT scores.

All of this tells us that stereotypes, especially automatic stereotypes, don't just engage the neurons in our heads and the thoughts in our minds and remain there. They have impact on behavior such as the intellectual pursuits we select—a decision that in turn may influence what career path we chart for ourselves, the happiness we derive from it, and the contributions we make by the end of our lives.

Nobody seriously questions the idea that stereotypes influence behavior; but the discussion can get pretty fierce when the conversation turns to the accuracy of stereotypes and their origins. On January 14, 2005, a public controversy regarding gender and math erupted in Cambridge, Massachusetts, and soon went viral, attracting attention from remote parts of the world. Harvard University's president, Larry Summers, offered the view that one of three reasons for women lagging behind in mathematics might be an innate lack of ability in mathematics. A heated national debate ensued because others thought differently. They claimed that too often we look at existing differences in achievement between groups and use them as evidence for assuming they exist because of differences in ability.[27] Such a naturalistic fallacy, it has been argued, can make what "is" seem to be what "ought to be." Although more than two thousand editorials and news reports were written worldwide about the Summers debacle, the debate left no clear winner.

No single piece of evidence can be decisive in response to a complex issue such as this one, whether it concerns gender and math, race and athletic ability, ethnicity and musical ability, or any other noticeable group difference in aptitude and achievement. However, it is possible to assess whether there are any relevant data that are incontrovertible—anything that, irrespective of our opinions, we would agree on.

We know that some group differences remain fairly stable over time even as environments change, suggesting at least the possibility of a clear genetic basis for the difference. Autism and related mental disabilities are an example.[28] Among those afflicted by the disease, boys outnumbered girls by a ratio of about 4:1 in the 1940s, and while much has been made of the fact that the number of diagnosed cases of autism has exploded in recent times, the sex ratio itself has persisted to the present day. However, other gender differences have diminished precipitously over relatively short periods of time. As it happens, the gender difference in math performance is one such example. The preponderance of boys with high SAT math scores has gone from a 10.7:1 ratio favoring boys in the 1980s to 2.8:1 in the 1990s.[29] In other words, the ratio favoring boys was nearly four times as large a mere decade earlier. Such a rapid closing of the gap between groups that used to be strikingly different should be surprising to those who favor a largely genetic explanation for gender differences in math ability, because genetically based differences cannot be reduced so dramatically in such a short period of time.

Here's another fact: Some countries show large gender differences, others show smaller differences, and yet others show no differences at all.[30] If gender differences in mathematical ability are largely the result of genetic causes, one would be hard-pressed to explain why such differences vary so much across societies; gender differences should be more universally observed.

Finally, working again alongside our colleague Brian Nosek and a collection of other researchers around the world, we took advantage of having data on IAT-measured gender-science stereotypes from thirty-four countries. In those data we found that the stronger the *science = male* stereotype in a given country, the larger the national gender difference in eighth-grade boys' and girls' mathematics and science achievement. That is, in countries for which the IAT gender-science stereotype data showed stronger *science = male* associations, boys outperformed girls to a greater extent than in countries where this automatic stereotype was weaker.[31]

Because what used to be large gender differences in mathematical ability have shrunk rapidly in recent years, because they vary greatly from country to country, and because the national strength of gender-math stereotypes is related to national gender-math performance, the belief that male-female differences in math represent innate variations in ability has taken a beating. Rest assured, however, that the genetic explanation remains alive if weakened, even as women enter science and engineering programs in numbers close to or equal to men. This will be an interesting stereotype to monitor, because it is conceivable that in the not-too-distant future the idea that once upon a time such a stereotype existed might seem quaint.

7

Us and Them

HOWEVER DEARLY WE LOVE DR. SEUSS, HIS WERE NOT THE SUB-tlest of allegories. One of our favorites, *The Sneetches,* offers a powerful message about prejudice in delightful rhymed verse. The Sneetches are yellow ducklike birds who come in two varieties—those who have a green star on their bellies and those who don't.

The Star-Bellies consider themselves naturally superior and refuse to have anything to do with the starless, never inviting them to their picnics or parties; the Plain-Bellies seem to have internalized their inferior status and mope around, envying the Star-Bellies cavorting on the beach. As in most societies, the class system in the land of the Sneetches is stable—until the arrival one day of an entrepreneur named Sylvester McMonkey McBean, who makes their peaceful hierarchy go, well, belly up.

McBean invites the Plain-Bellies to avail themselves of his ingenious invention, a Star-On machine, which adorns them with the much-coveted star—for a small fee, of course. When the Plain-Bellies pop out of his machine they are plain no more, and soon the number of newly starred Sneetches grows exponentially, infuriating the original Star-Bellies, who can no longer tell in-group from out-group. What to do about the dilution of their stock? Well,

McBean has just the solution: His still newer invention, Star-Off, can remove the now-cheapened symbol to distinguish the May- flower Star-Bellies, as we may think of them, from *les nouvelles étoiles*—for a slightly larger fee, of course. In the ensuing madness of class warfare, stars are repeatedly stamped in and out, driving all the Sneetches, star and plain, to financial ruin:

> *Until neither the Plain nor the Star-Bellies knew*
> *Whether this one was that one . . . or that one was this one*
> *Or which one was what one . . . or what one was who.*

In the Dr. Seuss story, McBean exits laughing and rich, con- vinced that the Sneetches will never learn. But he is wrong, for by the end of the book they do come to understand that, with or with- out stars, "Sneetches are Sneetches."

Would that human society were as enlightened. True, we have evolved to be social animals with both positive and negative traits, demonstrating strong tendencies for cooperation and altruism as well as conflict and violence.[1] But as our long, bloody history of violence against others of our species shows, we seem to be quite willing to pay a high price for the right to group-based warfare, with group boundaries constructed along arbitrary demarcations of religion, race, and geography and requiring little more than dis- tinctive stigmata and status as cues. We plot, scheme, and plan in- tergroup violence, all of which suggest highly conscious and reflective acts of hostility. But even here, we will see the hand of automatic feelings and beliefs emerging from blindspots as igniters and stokers of intergroup conflict.

STAMPING IN

WHEN WE WANT to understand anything, be it the seemingly mag- ical abilities of music or math or things more pernicious such as the growth of a cancer, we must try to get to the moment of its begin- ning. The origins of things, such as the moment when a single cell changes, can teach us much about their nature, and this is a primary reason scientists look at developmentally rudimentary forms of life to grasp the nature of their fully formed state. The infants and children of a species become quite interesting for this purpose, because in them we might see the unvarnished and immature form of the behavior, and this may give insight into why an organism grows the way it does, and turns into the thing we know and recognize in its more mature forms.

Konrad Lorenz, the mid-twentieth-century Austrian ethologist, was fascinated with ducklings and other young birds whose attachment behavior revealed a choreographed interplay between nature and nurture. In his work with ducks, Lorenz discovered the phenomenon of filial imprinting. When ducklings, goslings, and chicks first hatch, they instinctually follow the first moving object they encounter. Normally this will be the biological mother. Lorenz's intervention into their lives gave us one of the more memorable images in behavioral science: a happy gaggle of greylag geese single-mindedly trailing him (and not their mother) wherever he went. The young birds had "imprinted" upon the scientist, or rather upon his wading boots, because the shoes, rather than the birds' own mother, had been the first moving objects they saw immediately after birth.

What Lorenz had discovered was a built-in mechanism that predisposed the newborn to bond and identify with a potential caregiver—usually, of course, its mother. The term *imprinting* is the English word that best captures Lorenz's German phrase, *Prägung,* which is literally translated as "stamping in." The phenomenon Lorenz observed did indeed seem stamped in, so long as it occurred during a critical period, in this case shortly after birth. And so it proved to be with his greylags, who continued to prefer Lorenz to their fellow geese even after they grew up, so powerful was their early attachment.

Of course we ask how young birds imprinted on galoshes or a wheelbarrow (it can even be a yellow Volkswagen) illuminate the path to understanding group identity in humans. Imprinting is a chapter in a greater tale of evolutionary adaptation. It is "smart" in the sense in which such adaptations generally are, because of the survival value it confers. In this case, imprinting helps the animal to survive by ensuring that it attaches itself very early to a protective caregiver (the odds being very good that a wheelbarrow or Konrad Lorenz will not usually interfere with the way the process plays out in nature). Imprinting is also "dumb" in the sense in which such adaptations often are. These fowl would follow a live hand grenade were it to waddle before them shortly after they hatched! Although attachment is generally inevitable, the particular object to which an animal forms an attachment is not necessarily the mother (as we've just seen) but rather whatever is offered up by the environment and reinforced with repeated exposure.

Lorenz initially believed that imprinting was permanent, and specific to the critical period (about fourteen to sixteen hours after hatching). While recent imprinting research attributes greater flexibility and less irreversibility to the process, the fact that it occurs is unquestioned.[2] And it can occur not only in response to visual stimuli presented to the eyes of a hatchling but also in response to auditory stimuli that are experienced even prior to birth. Here's how a study done more than forty years ago demonstrated this: A 200 Hz tone, which sounds like a G below a piano's middle C, was repeatedly played in the presence of one group of pre-hatched chicks, while other eggs were not exposed to the tone. Upon hatching, the two sets of chicks were put in the presence of a speaker playing a 200 Hz tone and another one playing a 2,000 Hz tone, about three and a half octaves higher. Those who had been prenatally familiarized with the 200 Hz sound ran toward the speaker playing that tone, whereas those who hadn't heard it displayed no preference one way or another.[3]

A "preparedness" to favor the familiar is a fundamental property of all animals—including humans—and it is a powerful determinant of attachment, attraction, and love. What, then, does this tell us about members of our own species in their early years and beyond? What do we know about the tendency of infants and children to form attachments that in turn cause them to divide those they encounter into the familiar "us" and the foreign "them," and to bond and identify along those lines?

Certainly we know that, once formed, the identities humans take on play a powerful role in their lives, dictating not just our love for kith, kin, and even sports teams but our lack of warmth toward those who are not only foreign, but even just a little bit different. Consider, as just one of many examples, religion, a group identity for which countless people over the centuries and into today have given their lives, out of the belief that their own religion is the true one—this despite the fact that the religion one is typically identified with is a matter of circumstance; a person with the same genes would likely end up Jewish if born in Israel, Muslim in Saudi Arabia, or Hindu in India.

But when do those identities become fixed? Or do they? Ethologists are still trying to understand when and how the imprinting occurs, and when and to what extent it becomes permanent. Imprinting in birds and other animals does provide a mirror of what happens in our species. That said, it's an oversimplified reflection, for imprinting doesn't occur in quite the same way in human babies as it does in other animals. This is partly because humans enter the world in relatively less mature form than goslings or chicks, for example, with brains that still have a lot of growth to achieve, and with very limited motor skills as well. The fact that human brains are so unformed at birth means that they are more malleable for a longer period of time than are those of other species.[4] Thus the behavioral patterns humans acquire, including those involved in identity formation, have less rigidity or permanence compared to other species, a finding that has many implications for our research on prejudice. We take away from this work two conclusions: We are similar to many other species, including waterfowl, in the way we form attachments, and we are different from other species in the flexibility the process affords.

INFANTS

BABIES, we know, can tell familiar from strange: After birth, they can distinguish tones, melodies, and stories they heard while still in the womb from ones they hear for the first time after birth. Babies even a few days or weeks old can tell the voice of their mother from that of a stranger, and they prefer to look at their mother's face compared with that of a stranger. If their primary caregiver is female, they prefer to look at female rather than male faces. By three months of age they stare longer at a face from their own racial group than at one from a less familiar racial group. We know infants do not display this capacity for race discrimination at birth, so it is clear that they acquire the preference, but they do so quite quickly after birth. Like the chicks responding to prenatally familiarized tones, human babies appear to enter the world "prepared" to form preferences, including complex social ones. And familiarity always seems to be the basis for the preferences they express. Babies will always tend to gravitate to sensory information they have been exposed to before, preferring it to sights, sounds, and other sensory inputs that are unfamiliar and strange.[5]

Once familiarity is achieved, it facilitates new learning on the foundation of what is already in place. For example, babies whose familiar caregiver is female are able to more easily distinguish one female face from another than one male face from another.[6] This ability to perceptually discriminate between two or more members of a familiar category extends to the social category of race: By nine months of age infants are better able to tell two own-race faces apart compared to two other-race faces. But the facility at recognizing faces in our own group has a flip side and may be the basis of a curious mindbug we know well in our adult selves—the perception that members of groups other than our own look (and even behave) "alike." Thus many White Americans may find that all East Asians look so similar to one another that they can't tell them apart. The failure to discriminate within an unfamiliar category is such a well-documented phenomenon that it has a name in the psychological literature: the *out-group homogeneity effect*.[7]

But there's marvelous evidence of flexibility in this skill as well. As we already saw, White infants are less likely to be able to discriminate between individual Black or Asian faces. However, two French developmental psychologists showed that we can enhance out-group sensitivity by exposing the infant to a mere three instances of out-group faces (Asian faces in the case of the White infants). Even such a trivial intervention appears sufficient to "extend the power of face processing."[8] What we now understand is that the child's mind is primed to lock into a familiarity-based racial preference, yet also open to new input that can expand the repertory of preferences.

In studying babies' preferences, researchers have had to develop yardsticks by which to measure behaviors, since of course babies can't talk. One such yardstick is the length of time a baby spends looking at one thing versus another. But such measurements still need to be interpreted in order to accurately tell us what is going on in the infant's mind, which is not an easy task. For example, if a baby is presented with several female faces in a row and then a male face and the baby looks longer at the new male face, this tells us that the baby "knows" that male and female are different, but it doesn't necessarily tell us what the baby likes or prefers.[9]

What commands the baby's attention in this situation may simply be a matter of novelty, not preference. And if both male and female faces are presented simultaneously and the baby looks longer at one of the faces than the other, again we can't say with any assurance why that might be. Is the one that is looked at longer "preferred" in some sense, or is there something other than liking that elicits the additional attention?

Limited as it was as a source of information about infant preferences, the duration of time a baby devoted to looking at something was until recently one of the few pieces of evidence we had. But newer measures allow us to more confidently assess a real preference in the form of a choice on the part of older infants who are able to grasp objects, significantly opening up the repertoire of possible behaviors that can be measured. In a series of studies, Liz Spelke and her students at Harvard University measured which of two people a baby will take a toy from.[10] In one study designed by Katie Kinzler, now a professor at the University of Chicago, American and French infants barely ten months old were offered two equally attractive toys, one from an adult speaking English, the other from an adult speaking French. Using this simple measure, the researchers showed that American babies reached more often for the toy offered by the English-speaker, while French babies showed exactly the opposite preference. Like the chicks we described, they too prefer familiar sounds.

These language and accent preference studies confirm that the tendency to prefer members of one's own group emerges early in infancy and is in large part based on familiarity. Such an orientation, which no doubt has survival value in that it serves to align the child with those who are like her and therefore more likely to offer safety, is a clear sign that even in these early months, babies do not occupy socially neutral space. Distinguishing between "like us" and "not like us," they first express very simple forms of preference, such as accepting an object from one person rather than another. But to the rapidly developing brain of the infant, which is acquiring new stores of knowledge at an exponential rate, each such interaction is a building block, reinforcing the foundation on which a more fully formed social being will one day stand. The name we give to this foundation is *identity,* and unique as each individual is, identity is deeply bound to the characteristics that are true of "us" as a group and differentiated from "them."

YOUNG CHILDREN

AT DIFFERENT POINTS in development, a child comes to know that she is, for example, female, Irish, middle-class, brown-eyed, and athletic. One of our colleagues noticed early in childhood that any mention that she had eight siblings always elicited the same question from acquaintances: "Are you Catholic?" She cites this experience as a precursor to her interest in intergroup matters.[11] Those who have easily recognizable regional accents doubtless will have had many "Are you from _____?" experiences of this type. Some group identities develop only gradually and are freely chosen. For example, identifying yourself as *athlete* or *scholar* may happen only after multiple experiences over time have made it clear that this is a group you belong in because the activity that is the basis for the group's shared identity is something you're really good at. Other divisions into "us" and "them" may emerge quite abruptly, and without any choice in the matter. An African American colleague recalls that when she was a toddler another child asked if she could lick her because she was so obviously made out of chocolate. Her instant discovery of the difference between herself and the other child came as a true revelation.

Surface differences—the star on the belly, the color of the skin, the sound of the voice—spur the beginnings of the ability to recognize similarity and difference. But once language comes into play, the sheer force of words can rapidly "stamp in" the meaning of group identities.

The use of language to establish identity was nicely demonstrated in a recent study led by Andy Baron at Harvard University. In his study, three- to five-year-olds were shown pictures of two groups of cartoon characters, one colored purple, the other red. One group did *rotten things* such as break toys and cause car crashes, while the other did *nice things* such as help others. If the children merely saw these differently colored and differently behaving characters, they didn't seem to assign them a group identity. But if they were given names for the two groups ("These are the Nifs," "These are the Lups") they quickly figured out who were the good guys and who were the bad guys. In other words, at that age, the differences in the appearance of the two sets of characters (purple versus red) were not automatically seen as cues to group membership. But once the groups had names, the children became aware of the differences between them and understood that they belonged in different categories.[12] This is the beginning of stereotyping.

Gender is a strong basis for identifying oneself as a member of a group, *male* and *female* being among the earliest social category distinctions that children make.[13] In one recent study, three-year-old boys and girls were seated, one by one, in front of a video monitor and shown the faces of a boy and a girl, each paired with a novel object they had never seen. The boy in the video said: "My name is Ben. I like spoodles. Spoodles are my favorite thing to eat!" The girl in the video said: "My name is Betsy. I like blickets. Blickets are my favorite thing to eat!" Next an experimenter would ask the child watching the video: "Tell me, what would you like to eat? Spoodles or blickets?"

Kristin Shutts performed these and other similar experiments to observe the influence of group membership in shaping a young child's preferences. If the blicket- or spoodle-eater's group identity as male or female (and in other iterations of the experiment, as Black or White, old or young) didn't matter to the child watching the video, then the child should select blickets or spoodles randomly. Instead Kristin found, in the gender experiment, that boys chose the item Ben (rather than Betsy) picked 65 percent of the time. Girls chose the item Betsy (rather than Ben) picked even more robustly—85 percent of the time. Yet the reason for this group-based preference was outside the child's awareness. When asked why they might have chosen the spoodle or blicket, children's typical answer was "I don't know"; the next most typical answer was "Because I like it!"

Shutts's study suggests that seemingly free choices in young children are in fact strongly influenced by the choices made by somebody else in their gender "club." Other clubs to which the children felt they belonged, such as those based on age, seemed to dictate their choices as well.

How to interpret this evidence—whether to be heartened or disheartened by it—is a separate question. Is it good or not so good that even so early in life a match between "me" and "her" determines liking for food, toys, and clothing? The answer, of course, depends on the degree to which we value individual freedom and choice. To those who regard gender-based mimicry (or other group-influenced forms of behavior) as natural and appropriate, the necessary foundation for learning the repertoire of behaviors that grease the wheels of the social engine, this is a fine method for acquiring the conditioning that keeps society working in traditional ways. On the other hand, to those who cherish the idea that each person should be free to follow a unique path, one that is not determined by membership in a group, the "matching" result should be worrisome. The downside comes from the recognition that blind, automatic imitation constrains such choices, which keep individuals and their social groups from achieving to the limits of their potential.

While conducting her research, Shutts noticed something of interest: Never did the parents accompanying a child seem bothered by their child's repeated preference for the object offered by a same-sex kid. In fact, they seemed reassured by such sex-based mimicry. Parents were far less sanguine, however, when they observed a race match in choices—when a White child asked for the same toy or food selected by another White child rather than a Black child, the parents seemed embarrassed. (Remember, this study was conducted in Massachusetts, in the politically liberal climate of the "People's Republic of Cambridge," where parents strive almost as hard to create racially nonbiased behavior in their children as they do to get them into the proper school.)

This contrast between influence by shared gender and by shared race is interesting—identity-influenced choices aren't all equal. We not only accept some, such as gender matching, but are relieved to see that our children have them; others, such as race matching, may, depending upon the cultural and social context, meet with dismay (and attempts to explain away the results). Yet both are equally important in shaping preferences and choices that can determine opportunities and achievements in adulthood.

A TERRORIST IS A TERRORIST IS A TERRORIST?

IT'S SOBERING to realize the many ways in which racial identity affects our interactions with others. Think back to the example of Brent Staples trying to head off worry about him (Staples is Black) among those who stroll the same streets by whistling Vivaldi. The "us"/"them" dichotomy that involves race can cut both ways, actually, with both Blacks and Whites having a tendency to be more fearful of those unlike themselves. In a study conducted in the laboratory of Elizabeth Phelps at New York University, researchers showed White and Black Americans photos of two faces, one Black and one White. They conditioned their study subjects to fear both faces by delivering to a finger a painful but tolerable electric shock (at a shock intensity chosen by the subjects themselves) whenever either face appeared on a computer screen.[14] Students of psychology will recognize this procedure to be a standard way to produce Pavlovian or classical conditioning. Just as expected, the researchers were able to "condition" the subjects to a fear response, as evidenced by the fact that more sweat was measured from their palms when they saw the shock-associated faces than when they were shown two faces unassociated with shock.

The researchers wanted to explore how long this fear response would last if they continued to show the subjects photos of the shock-associated faces but ceased delivering the shocks. They also investigated whether the study subjects' own race would have any effect on what is known, in the language of classical conditioning methods, as the ease or difficulty of "extinguishing" the fear response.

The researchers found that White Americans showed faster extinguishing of fear toward a White face than a Black face, and

Black Americans showed the opposite effect, being faster to recover from their fear of the Black face. This means that while we may fear people from both races depending on circumstances (the administering of shock in an experiment, the actions of a person in real life), both Whites and Blacks recover from their fear more quickly if the race of the person who inspired it is the same as their own.

If we extrapolate from this finding, it seems plausible to believe that the persistence of negative racial associations will play out in all kinds of social and professional settings. Imagine a Black manager who has had a bad experience with a White employee; he may find that his dislike or disapproval of this employee persists long after the event that inspired it, even if absolutely nothing else occurs to reinforce the negative feeling. Or, as a commentator on the study from the Phelps lab noted, the result suggests that an act of terrorism committed by a member of the in-group may be forgotten faster than a similarly reprehensible act perpetrated by a member of a foreign group.[15]

While the persistence of such negative reactions may once have had a survival value, this is yet another instance of a hardwired response that has lost its relevance. In the modern world, where friendships, collaborations, businesses, and entire economies span the globe in a highly networked web of interdependence, the ability to create alliances that bypass boundaries of race, nationality, and culture can have bearing on our well-being, our prosperity, our productivity—and perhaps even our survival.

THE MINIMAL GROUP

It's EASY to see that our racial identity goes deep, just as our gender identity does. But it turns out that the group identities we form can be based on almost laughably negligible differences. In 1970, the British psychologist Henri Tajfel made one of the most significant discoveries in social psychology.[16] Interested in understanding how group identities lead to discrimination—in this case, the relatively greater giving of resources to one's own group and taking away from another's group—he and his students conducted a simple experiment. They created the most minimal of group identities simply by telling people that they were either "overestimators" or "underestimators" by nature. What did they seemingly over- or underestimate? The number of dots in a random pattern—that's all.

In fact, they didn't even do that: unbeknownst to them, the participants in the study were labeled "underestimators" or "overestimators" at random. To further guarantee that no real basis existed for either camaraderie or conflict, the experimenters made sure that there was no interaction among members within a group or between groups. In effect, subjects were given only participant identification numbers of those who had ostensibly scored similarly to or differently from them on a computer task, making these among the flimsiest of group identities ever created.

Yet although the basis of difference was absolutely meaningless, Tajfel found that the two groups proceeded to discriminate in allocating resources, giving more to members of their own group.[17] (This makes the basis for color wars at camp look profound by comparison.)

Even we who teach about it year after year are continually amazed by what Tajfel discovered about the dynamics of minimal group identities—as, it turns out, was Tajfel himself. His results showed that group identity abhors a vacuum. Create an arbitrary connection between a person and a group and provide the mere suggestion that there are others who lack this connection to self, and the psychology of "us" and "them" rushes in to fill the void. Lines are drawn, whether or not the basis for the groups makes any sense, and discrimination follows.

The first of these "minimal group" studies showed that not only did group members assign more resources to their own minimal group, even when they would gain nothing personally from it, but, even more surprisingly, they were willing for their group to pay a cost in resources in order to maximize the difference between "us" and "them." That's even harder to explain, adding self-defeat to mere collective selfishness.[18]

In the years since this discovery, hundreds of experiments have been conducted to advance understanding of the various facets of social identity. A thriving community is engaged in understanding how the individual person comes to be so easily and integrally tied to the social group.[19] Our own interest took the form of observing the neural responses elicited by those who are either similar to or different from us.

DO NEURONS CARE ABOUT "US" VERSUS "THEM"?

THE RAPID ADVANCE of brain-imaging technology has had a significant impact on the neuroscience of social cognition, allowing researchers to see how the brain distinguishes us and them, and how it represents the minds of others more generally. In one such study Jason Mitchell at Harvard University showed face photos of two young men, John and Mark, and asked Harvard undergraduates to form impressions of them, based on the photos and the text that accompanied each. Here is what the students read about the two men:

> John considers himself a typical college student. While John respects religion, his politics are relatively left of center. He still can't quite believe that George Bush managed to become president. In addition to his academic interests, John keeps himself busy at college with a variety of extracurricular activities; for example, over the last year, he has participated in intramurals for his college and helped with college committees. After graduation, he plans to take a year or two off before returning to graduate school. John would ultimately like to have the kind of career where the work is fulfilling and rewarding.

Mark has considered himself a fundamentalist Christian for the past four years. He attends church every Sunday, in addition to several prayer services on his Midwestern college campus. Because of his religious convictions, Mark is a strong supporter of the Republican Party. He feels strongly about the Republican Party's social platform. In fact, during the last election, Mark was a very active member of the United Republican Brethren group on campus, which helped raise money for the Bush campaign through a variety of faith-based fund-raising events. After college, he hopes to be able to settle down and start a family. Mark hopes to have the kind of career that would allow his future wife to stay at home and have a large family.

Having read these two descriptions, the students answered dozens of questions about John and Mark while lying in the bore of a magnet that used functional MRI to allow their brains to be imaged. Here are two typical questions out of the many they were asked:

How likely, do you think, is John looking forward to going home for Thanksgiving?
How likely, do you think, is Mark to think that European films are generally better than Hollywood films?

To most of us, it would seem sensible to assume that the neurons recruited to answer the questions about John would be the same ones figuring out the answers about Mark. Yet as the brain activation observed in this study showed, that was not the case.[20]

The brain, it turns out, engages two different clusters of neurons in thinking about other people, and which cluster gets activated depends on the degree to which one identifies with those others. In this case the participants, mainly liberal East Coast students, tended to identify more with John than with Mark (measured by a test administered to them earlier). In those who identified with John, thinking about him led to the recruitment of sets of neurons in the ventral region of the medial pre-frontal cortex (mPFC). Among that group, thinking about Mark led to recruitment of a different set of neurons, located in the dorsal region of the mPFC.

The separation of these two areas within roughly the same brain region does not appear to be arbitrary. From previous research at Dartmouth University, we know that the ventral mPFC is more engaged when we think about our own selves than when we think about others.[21] The Mitchell study at Harvard suggests that, by extension, we engage the same region of the brain when we try to anticipate what somebody who is similar to ourselves would do. Psychologists call this recruitment of the brain regions associated with ourselves a *simulation* of the mind of the other person. But apparently we recruit that particular area of the brain in thinking about someone else only if we identify with that person.

Because we are not aware of tapping into different areas of the brain depending on whom we are thinking about and how much we identify with that person, this result has some potentially disturbing implications of the same sort we discussed when speaking about the constraints of group membership on children's ability to achieve their potential. Think, for example, about a judge. She must routinely make decisions about other people, some similar to herself, others quite different. How can she take into account the ways in which her judgment may be affected by the different neural processes activated by thinking about, say, a professional woman experiencing marital difficulties (similar to herself), and a professional man in similar circumstances (not similar to herself)?

Because there is no physical sensation whatsoever to let her know that different brain regions are being invoked depending on whom it is she's thinking about, she cannot possibly be aware of how this selective neural activation may influence her decisions. For example, might a custody decision involving the aforementioned professional woman and man be affected by her identification with one and not the other? It seems plausible to think it might.

CARLA'S HAND

HENRI TAJFEL, the psychologist who investigated the phenomenon of "minimal group" identities, became interested in the psychology of prejudice because of his experiences in World War II. Born Jewish in Poland, he lost all of the members of his immediate family in the Holocaust, and after the war abandoned his work in chemistry to study psychology. Although his original interest in prejudice was inspired by the genocidal anti-Semitism of the Nazis, he understood that "us" and "them" identities can be forged on the basis of the flimsiest of criteria, and that the allocation of resources to members of one's own group at the expense of others can take a much subtler form than it did under Hitler, yet still exact a high price on those who are discriminated against.

The issue of the allocation of resources depending on membership in an in-group comes into vivid relief in the story of a former colleague of Mahzarin's. Carla Kaplan was an assistant professor of American literature at Yale in the late 1980s, a serious young scholar in her late twenties who looked even younger than her actual age. Carla was also a dedicated quilter. While working with patches of cloth, she could be transported to faraway places of pattern and color, oblivious to all but the world she was creating.

One evening, while she was washing a crystal bowl in her kitchen, it accidentally slipped from her hands. As she tried to catch the bowl, it hit the sink and broke, and the jagged edge slit her hand from mid-palm to wrist. Blood splashed all over the floor, and her boyfriend hastily improvised a bandage before rushing her out the door to drive her to the emergency room of the university affiliated Yale–New Haven Hospital.

At the ER, Carla's boyfriend made it clear to the resident physician on duty that Carla's quilting was very important to her and that he feared the injury might impair the fine motor control she needed for this activity she loved so much. The doctor seemed to understand this concern and expressed confidence that all would be well if they could just "stitch it up quickly."

As the doctor prepared Carla's hand for the stitches, a student volunteer who had been working nearby recognized Carla and exclaimed, "Professor Kaplan! What are you doing here?" and this sentence seemed to stop the doctor in his tracks. "Professor?" he asked. "You're a professor at Yale?" Within seconds Carla found herself on a gurney, being escorted to the hospital's surgery department. The best hand surgeon in Connecticut was called in, and a team worked for hours to restore Carla's hand to perfection. The good news is that Carla regained full use of her hand and can type, quilt, or do anything else with the same fine motor control she had before.

It may not be obvious, but can you spot the "us"/"them" discrimination in Carla's ER visit? Since Mahzarin first heard the story, it has stuck with her as tellingly emblematic of the complexities of hidden bias in everyday life. The act of discrimination here is not easy to spot because it was an act not of hurting but of *helping,* triggered when the doctor registered "Yale professor." Those two words catalyzed recognition of a group identity shared by doctor and patient, transforming the bloody-handed quilter into a fellow member of the Yale in-group, someone who suddenly qualified for elite care.

Recently, when we wrote to Carla to confirm the story, she elaborated: "Suddenly, they were calling in one of the most renowned hand specialists in New England. A complete 180-degree turnaround. My being a quilter meant nothing to them in terms of doing the needed nerve repair on my right thumb. But being Yale faculty got me that expensive and complex surgery."

Perhaps the future of Carla's hand never would have been in any doubt had Carla been Carl, who arrived at the hospital in a rumpled tweed jacket with a pipe sticking out of his pocket. No student volunteer would have been needed to trigger the in-group identification in that case. It is only when we view Carla's story from a distance that the compromising of ethical standards becomes apparent in the decision to treat a Yale professor with greater care than a mere quilter. Viewed from up close, to most observers the action of the doctor would have seemed praiseworthy because a valued patient received good care. If there is a radical suggestion here, it is that intergroup discrimination is less and less likely to involve explicit acts of aggression toward the out-group and more likely to involve everyday acts of helping the in-group.

Carla the quilter was discriminated against by a failure to take appropriate action. Look at some of the results we describe in Appendix 1—the discoveries from a raft of experiments done in the 1970s that studied helping behavior. Those studies showed that White Americans consistently received more help than Black Americans. The only harm done to Black Americans in those studies was the consequence of inaction—the absence of helping. This left them without advantages that were received by the White Americans who were, by contrast, helped. We can call this *hidden discrimination,* in the same way that the discrimination displayed in the story of Carla's hand surgery is hidden. Discrimination is hard to perceive because it does not present itself in obvious comparisons, where we must decide in a single moment whether to help one or the other. These behaviors happen in sequence, allowing the fact that one was helped and the other not to remain in our blindspot. Actually, the "us" versus "them" bias involved in Carla's story is hidden in at least four ways, two of them along the lines of what we have been defining all along as hidden bias—that is, it's hidden from the person who possesses it.

First, it was hidden from the emergency room resident himself in the sense that he was almost certainly unaware of having implicit attitudes that favored members of one group (Yale professors) over others (artisans). Second—and, again, this is a matter of its being hidden from the doctor himself—the fact that he was not doing anything explicitly harmful would have made it hard for him to see that in choosing the better of two helpful options to pursue for Carla the Yale professor, he was expressing a bias.

The third way in which the bias was hidden was that no one in the situation was hurt by the doctor's action. Carla, the only person who was affected, was *helped* by the revelation of her identity as a Yale professor. Finally, there was no easily identifiable disadvantaged group in the situation. If pressed to say what group was being discriminated against, we would have to define it as consisting simply of "all those who would not get the same special care."

The importance of Carla's story is that by capturing not just acts of commission but acts of omission, we expand our sense of how hidden bias operates. It also allows us to see that the people responsible for such acts of omission are, like the doctor who is the main actor in this story, by and large good people who believe that helping is admirable. So far as we can tell, the doctor was a responsible and caring professional who had no conscious intention to discriminate against Carla the quilter. Nevertheless, he did discriminate and the harm that could have been done to Carla's hand had she not been recognized as a member of the in-group is a real one.

The lesson from Carla's story is that discrimination of even the most apparently well-intentioned kind—helping members of the in-group—has significant impact on both those who are not part of the in-group *and* those who are. As psychologists, we have learned that if we study hidden bias by the traditional method of looking for expressions of negativity or hostility directed against out-groups, if we measure it by counting the number of out-group churches or mosques that are burned down, we may fail to see the far more pervasive ways in which hidden biases maintain the status quo, depriving those on the bottom rungs of society of the resources available to the more privileged by birth and status. It won't be surprising, then, that the Star-Bellies will always get more of the good stuff than the Plain-Bellies.

Receiving the benefits of being in the in-group tends to remain invisible for the most part. And this is perhaps why members of the dominant or majority groups are often genuinely stunned when the benefits they receive are pointed out. Blindspots hide both discriminations and privileges, so neither the discriminators nor the targets of discrimination, neither those who do the privileging nor the privileged, are aware. No small wonder that any attempt to consciously level the playing field meets with such resistance.

8

Outsmarting the Machine

THE PSYCHOLOGY DEPARTMENT AT UNIVERSITY OF WASHINGTON offers an excellent service that is a very welcome by-product of the digital age—creating electronic documents from old books. Tony recently requested an electronic version of a chapter from a long-cherished forty-year-old book. When the electronic file arrived, he discovered that each of the even-numbered pages had lost the last letter or two from the right-hand side of every line of text. Tony drew the problem to the attention of the department administrator to request a correction. It came back later that day—same problem. He sent it back once again, expressing some consternation that the problem was still there. Surely this was something that could be easily fixed! When it returned the third time, all the pages had been properly reproduced.

Curious about what had happened, Tony stopped at the administrator's office to find out what the problem had been. The answer: An "intelligent" feature of the copier had "thought" that the margins of all the pages of the chapter should have the same area. However, because the electronic version was made from a book in which margins of even-numbered and odd-numbered pages were different, the text of all even-numbered pages was positioned more to the right than that of the odd-numbered pages. The eventual fix: Create a paper copy on which even-numbered and odd-numbered pages had similar margins and then use that as the basis for the electronic version.

The administrator who figured this out made a telling observation: "The trick is to outsmart the machine." This idea of outsmarting the machine captures the essence of what we would like to do to meet a much bigger challenge: enable the human brain to outsmart the mindbugs that reside within it.[1] Can we use our reflective, analytic minds to devise techniques that will allow us to override unintended results of our automatic, reflexive patterns of thought? In other words, can we outsmart the machinery of our own hidden biases?

THE MUSICIANS' GUIDE TO
OUTSMARTING A GENDER MINDBUG

IN 1970, fewer than 10 percent of the instrumentalists in America's major symphony orchestras were women, and women made up less than 20 percent of new hires. Not many considered this a cause for concern. As most people understood it, nature had favored men more than women with whatever it is that makes for musical virtuosity. The evidence for this had to be immediately obvious to anyone who could reel off the names of the world's top instrumental virtuosos—Sviatoslav Richter, David Oistrakh, Vladimir Horowitz, Pablo Casals, Mstislav Rostropovich, Yehudi Menuhin, Jascha Heifetz, Sergei Rachmaninoff, Glenn Gould, and Fritz Kreisler—all men.[2]

Or maybe not. Another way of looking at male dominance in instrumental virtuosity is that it is less a gift of nature to men than a gift of culture that recognizes, encourages, and promotes male talent. But this thought had occurred to very few until about forty years ago, when feminism became a cultural force in the United States and allowed such disparities to be noticed and questioned.

Was the Boston Symphony really selecting the best talent when it sought to recruit the best available trombonist? If not, how could the symphony determine whether a blindspot was preventing its selection of the best musicians?

By long tradition, orchestra applicants competed for positions by performing before an audition committee—experts selected mostly from the orchestra's musicians. Starting in the 1970s, several major American symphony orchestras experimented with a new procedure that involved interposing a screen between the auditioning instrumentalists and the committee, leaving the applicants audible but not visible to the judges. The adoption of this procedure was not prompted by any suspicion that women were being discriminated against. Rather, it was suspected that selections might be biased in favor of the students of a relatively small group of renowned teachers.

The next twenty years provided interesting evidence. After the adoption of blind auditions, the proportion of women hired by major symphony orchestras doubled—from 20 percent to 40 percent. In retrospect it is easy to see that a *virtuoso = male* stereotype was an invalid but potent mindbug, undermining the orchestra's ability to select the most talented musicians. Two things stand out about the introduction of blind auditions for orchestra hiring. First is that they did the experiment at all; few experts are able to have sufficient distrust of their own abilities to actually put themselves to a test. Second, the fix was simple and cheap—a piece of cloth. Outsmarting this particular mindbug required awareness, a desire to improve, and a method for improving. It did not need to be complicated or costly.[3]

THE SEARCH FOR MORE
MINDBUG-OUTSMARTING SOLUTIONS

THERE IS NO DOUBT that the blind audition was an inspired and effective solution for outsmarting the *virtuoso = male* stereotype mindbug in orchestra hiring. So let's consider similar strategies that could work in other situations. For example, high school and college teachers can often grade students' essays without knowing the student author's identity, and any kind of test that is done in written form can be graded without the grader knowing who is being graded.

Unfortunately, the blinding strategy is not possible in most work situations that involve hiring decisions or performance evaluations. Job applicants provide résumés from which names might be removed, but much other information that might reveal gender information would of necessity remain. For example, knowing that an applicant captained a women's soccer team gives it away, as will the pronouns found repeatedly in letters of recommendation even after obscuring first names.

And, of course, it would be very difficult if not impossible to forgo personal interviews with applicants in the great majority of hiring situations. When it comes to evaluating the work of employees, there is typically no way to prevent supervisors from knowing the identities of those they must evaluate. Likewise, the blinding strategy can't be extended to most other situations in which mindbugs can produce discrimination, such as in health care, criminal justice, and the search for housing, all of which generally involve face-to-face interactions. Doctors cannot treat patients without seeing them, nor can judges and juries be expected to decide about anonymous, invisible defendants. And although, in a digital world, one can learn a great deal about available apartments or homes without a personal visit, ultimately one cannot rent or purchase without being fully identified to the seller or renter. Technology has made obtaining demographic information about almost anyone easier now than ever before. Electronic searches now make it almost trivially easy to obtain personal information when one has a person's name.

CAN MINDBUGS BE EXTERMINATED?

INSTEAD OF TRYING to outsmart mindbugs, why not deal with them the way computer programmers deal with computer program bugs? Just identify them and get rid of them. Unfortunately, effective methods for removing the mindbugs that contribute to hidden biases have yet to be convincingly established.

We've experienced a roller-coaster ride in our own understanding of the ease or difficulty of destroying mindbugs. When the IAT was new in the late 1990s, Mahzarin and Tony took some of the tests numerous times. As disappointing as it was to discover that the tests revealed associations that we preferred not to have, it was even more disappointing to observe that our results for these tests changed little over time, as we took them repeatedly. Awareness of the hidden biases did not seem to help us to eradicate them. At least, we could not see shifts in our continued taking of the test. Those early experiences with the IAT led us to think that the kinds of mindbugs measured by the IAT might be resistant to change.

At about the same time that we were becoming discouraged about eradicating our own hidden biases, other researchers were starting to experiment with procedures that they had devised with the aim of weakening, possibly even eliminating, IAT-measured mindbugs. One of the first of these researchers was Nilanjana (Buju) Dasgupta, who worked with both of us during the early stages of her career in the late 1990s.

Buju devised an innovative laboratory experiment using the face images of twenty well-known Americans. The experiment investigated whether results of the Race IAT would show reduced automatic White preference for subjects who started the experiment with a task that involved exposure to images of ten famous, highly esteemed Black Americans—among them Martin Luther King Jr., Colin Powell, Michael Jordan, Denzel Washington, and Bill Cosby. Given two alternative descriptions of each person, both quite positive but one correct and one incorrect, Buju's subjects were asked to select the correct identification for each. For example, Colin Powell's photo required a choice between "former chairman of the Joint Chiefs of Staff for the U.S. Department of Defense" (correct) and "U.S. ambassador to the United Nations." Interspersed with the ten Black Americans' pictures were those of ten infamous White Americans, including serial murderers Jeffrey Dahmer, Ted Bundy, Charles Manson, and Ted Kaczynski, and mass murderer Timothy McVeigh. The ten White images were also accompanied by a choice between two labels, both extremely negative. For Kaczynski, for example, the choice was between "the Unabomber who injured and killed using letter bombs" (correct) and "convicted pedophile." After choosing a description for all twenty pictures twice—to ensure good exposure to each—subjects completed the Race IAT.

Having become skeptical about the possibility for change on the basis of observing the intractability of his own IAT scores, Tony was doubtful enough about the prospects for success of Buju's procedure that he put $5 on the line—which he promptly lost, but with no regrets. The student research subjects who viewed the pictures of ten admirable Black Americans and ten despicable White Americans did indeed show weaker IAT-measured *White = good* associations than did those who had completed a comparison procedure involving an initial exposure to either admirable White Americans or pictures of flowers and insects.

Buju followed this experiment with a parallel one in which subjects viewed ten admirable elderly people, including Mother Teresa, Walter Cronkite, Eleanor Roosevelt, and Albert Einstein. The result was similar. Those who saw the admirable elders showed weaker IAT-measured *young = good* associations than did subjects who instead saw pictures of admirable young people. These results immediately changed our thinking about the malleability of IAT-measured hidden biases and about the prospects for exterminating mindbugs.[4]

At about the same time that Buju did her experiment, researchers in several other laboratories were similarly finding results that encouraged belief that implicit attitudes or stereotypes could be modified with relatively simple procedures. At the University of Colorado, for example, Irene Blair had college men and women do a brief imagination exercise, asking them to "take a few minutes to imagine what a strong woman is like, why she is considered strong, what she is capable of doing, and what kinds of hobbies and activities she enjoys." That simple mental exercise effectively weakened an IAT-measured *male = strong* stereotype. This became evident by comparing the experimental subjects' IAT measures of that association with those of subjects who engaged in alternative mental exercises.[5]

Among the attractive aspects of being in our science at this time is the opportunity to have one's mind routinely changed by research evidence. This was one such moment. Our initial belief that it might take long periods of hard work to change existing associations needed revision. The data were showing that hidden-bias mindbugs could be weakened by relatively minimal interventions. Perhaps repeated applications of the types of modest interventions that were used in these laboratory studies *would* provide a means of eradicating mindbugs.

We are often asked what steps we have taken to reduce our own hidden biases. Mahzarin came up with one. Inspired by the accumulation of results indicating malleability, and hoping that it would dislodge some of her own mindbugs, she created a screensaver for her computer that displays images of a diverse array of humanity. She assumes that these images may do little more than keep her alerted to the actual range of diversity in the world, as opposed to that of the more limited set of humans she encounters in her daily experience. She also favored images that represent counterstereotypes. Short bald men who are senior executives is one of her favorite counterstereotyping images. Another is a drawing from a *New Yorker* magazine cover, of a construction worker with hard hat on, breast-feeding her baby. Her aim is to build up associations counter to the stereotypic ones that are strengthened in the rest of her daily life through observation and media exposures.

More than a decade after Buju's study, experiments similar to hers continue to produce similar findings. As promising as these consistent results are, we must set a high standard for concluding that our science understands how to dismantle the hidden-bias machinery. Alas, there has not yet been a convincing (to us) demonstration that interventions of the types investigated in research of the last decade will produce durable changes. The experiment that has most successfully shown durable change in the strength of an IAT-measured association is a study of the effects of a three-week therapy program to reduce a spider phobia, which resulted in a phobia reduction measured one month after completion of the program.[6]

We now suspect that the changes observed in the studies by Dasgupta, Blair, and others were ones that we should understand as *elastic* changes. Like stretched rubber bands, the associations modified in these experiments likely soon return to their earlier configuration. Such elastic changes can be consequential, but they will require reapplication prior to each occasion on which one wishes them to be in effect. Such suppression of mindbugs can be useful, but it is not the equivalent of eradication.

There are some other encouraging findings. Buju Dasgupta found a strengthening of *female = leader* and *female = math* associations in women college students after they had received sustained exposure via their college courses to women faculty members. Women who had taken more courses from women faculty showed the greatest weakening of these stereotypes. In an as yet unpublished study conducted at the University of Wisconsin, Patricia Devine tested a multiple-component training procedure that was aimed at reducing IAT-measured White racial preference. She found reductions that were observed up to six weeks after the training procedure. This promising work notwithstanding, we have come to regard mindbugs as dauntingly persistent.[7]

At least for the time being, it appears necessary to find work-arounds for mindbugs—so we come back to the strategy of trying to outsmart the machine. That possibility of outsmarting, rather than eradicating, has served well in many other places, especially in dealing with incurable diseases. For malaria, for example, out-smarting strategies include preventive strategies, such as the use of mosquito nets and the sterilization of disease-bearing mosquitoes; for HIV, outsmarting strategies include the use of condoms to prevent sexual transmission and, perhaps most ingeniously, a variety of antiretroviral drugs.

OUTSMARTING MINDBUGS BY BYPASSING THEM: THE NO-BRAINER SOLUTION

WE MET JOAN A. in Chapter 6. Her physician, Dr. M., had thought that Joan, at age forty-eight, had no reason for concern about her cardiovascular health. His judgment was based partly on valid medical knowledge that middle-aged women are less at risk for heart disease than are middle-aged men and also on his knowledge of her body weight (low) and her level of athletic activity (high). When at Joan's insistence he ordered a test of her blood cholesterol levels, Dr. M. discovered that—contrary to his probabilistic expectations—Joan's cholesterol levels were high enough to call for some treatment.

The episode with Joan A. and Dr. M. took place about twenty-five years ago, at a time when there was less awareness of women's risk for heart disease than there is today. It is now understood that, despite women's risk level being generally lower than men's, the risk is still significant enough to warrant screening, even if the woman in question is lean and athletic. As a result, the medical profession has adopted a different approach to cholesterol testing. Guidelines promulgated by the National Heart, Lung, and Blood Institute (NHLBI) now advise that everyone over age twenty have blood cholesterol levels checked at least once every five years. Of course, the NHLBI guideline is just that—a guideline, not a requirement. In day-to-day practice, some physicians no doubt still make recommendations for cholesterol testing that are based on the *female = low cardiac risk* stereotype. But doctors who choose to follow the latest guidelines no longer need to make *any* judgment about a given middle-aged woman's likelihood of having a heart attack. The recommendation for periodic testing becomes a no-brainer: by using the guideline, the doctor does not need to take into account any personal knowledge of the relative risks for men and women, eliminating the possibility of inappropriately applying a stereotype.

It is easy to recognize that the *female = low cardiac risk* stereotype is a mindbug that one would want to outsmart. However, there are other situations in which we may have difficulty persuading ourselves that a stereotype should be outwitted. For example, recently the happy owner of a few American Staffordshire terriers sought Tony's help in designing an information campaign to overcome a negative stereotype of his pets. You may be puzzled until you learn that these dogs are widely known as pit bulls.

In the United States, pit bulls account for perhaps 1 or 2 percent of all registered dogs but (according to various sources) are responsible for more than 25 percent of reported dog bites and for a similarly high proportion of fatalities that result from dog bites. Seattle, Washington, recently became a focus of attention among pit bull opponents after a Seattle resident and bite victim launched an anti–pit bull website. Perhaps typical of other cities, in Seattle about half of the dogs who are euthanized in animal shelters are identified as pit bulls. It was to try to counter the stereotypes about these dogs and to prevent such widespread euthanasia that the Staffordshire terrier owner asked Tony for advice.[8]

Do you have a stereotype of *pit bull = vicious*? And if so, should you try to change your view of pit bulls and modify your behavior accordingly? We can help you find your answers by replacing these questions with three others, the first two of which we can answer for you. (1) Are pit bulls, on average, more vicious than other types of dogs? This can get a yes response, meaning that the stereotype has some validity, even though this deserves to be qualified by the claims of pit bull advocates that aggressiveness in the breed is often the result either of deliberate training or of inhumane treatment. (2) Are *all* pit bulls vicious? Certainly not, so this gets a no. Many pit bulls are well-loved pets who play gently and safely with children as well as with other pets, including kittens. (3) The question you'll have to answer for yourself is this: On first encounter with an unfamiliar pit bull, should you react to it by assuming that it will be vicious?

When you have your answer to that last question, consider the three parallel questions about middle-aged women in relation to the risk of heart disease. (1) Are middle-aged women less likely to have heart attacks than middle-aged men? This needs a yes response—the stereotype has some validity. (2) Are all middle-aged women unlikely to have heart attacks? Certainly not—large numbers of middle-aged women have heart attacks. (3) On encountering a middle-aged woman, should a doctor assume that she has no risk for heart disease? As we already know, the answer to the third question, now codified in NHLBI guidelines that call for periodic cholesterol testing for anyone over age twenty, is no.

We are dwelling on this pit bull example because we expect it to be challenging to many readers. Readers may have difficulty discovering any no-brainer solution (parallel to the NHLBI guideline for cholesterol testing) that can allow them to respond the same way to pit bulls as to all other breeds. We expect many readers to resist our suggestion that the two situations, of middle-aged women and pit bulls, are parallel. Many, we expect, will think that there are good reasons to treat pit bulls differently than other breeds.

We intend to leave the challenge of such parallels open for discussion. For our own part, we can argue it both ways. The case for parallel treatment of the two categories is straightforward—both cases reflect operations of stereotypes that are not justifiably treated as characterizing all individual members of the category. The case for nonparallel treatment of the two categories can be made by arguing that the *pit bull* = *vicious* association is actually more than a stereotype—rather, it may be an association of such great validity that viciousness should be treated as an essential property of pit bulls, much as *poisonous* is treated as an essential property of all rattlesnakes. The problem with this argument is that we know with certainty that viciousness is *not* an essential property of pit bulls—there is no evidence that viciousness characterizes more than some minority of pit bulls.

The best we can do in stating a defensible justification for treating pit bulls differently than other dog breeds is in terms of fear—"I want nothing to do with pit bulls for the very good reason that I'm scared to death when I see one." Seen this way, one's response to pit bulls has more the nature of a phobia than a stereotype. The significance of labeling this as a phobia rather than a stereotype is that the cause of aversion is seen to be a property of the person responding to the dog, rather than a property of the dog. However, we expect that pit bull advocates will find the phobia justification to be dubious.

In an alternate world there might be an easily administered test for canine aggressiveness that, when passed, would result in nonaggressive dogs wearing visible indicators of their test result, somewhat like the way doctors wear stethoscopes around their necks as status markers. This alternate world is not totally removed from present reality, because tests do exist for dogs' aggressiveness. However, the most valid of those tests require trained personnel and standardized test situations, and at present it is not practical to administer them routinely.[9]

Applying a guideline to eliminate a yes-or-no judgment from the decision to administer a test works to bypass a mindbug in the situation of Joan A., Dr. M., and cholesterol testing, but it is impractical for dealing with the abstractly parallel situation of pit bull stereotypes. More generally, the successful method of outwitting one mindbug has limited ability to deal with others. More methods are needed. In the next several years, we anticipate a wave of new research on machine-outsmarting methods.

OUTSMARTING MINDBUGS THE NUMERICAL WAY

TESTING, WHEN DONE WELL—as is possible for blood cholesterol or canine aggressiveness—has the desirable property of producing numerical scores. It is easy to see testing as a cure-all. It is tempting to assume that judgments expressed in numbers guarantee objectivity and bias-free treatment. However, by themselves, numbers do not guarantee freedom either from hidden bias mindbugs or from more deliberate bias. This may never have been more apparent than in the figure-skating competition at the 2002 Winter Olympics in Salt Lake City, when numerical scores provided by the nine-judge panel provoked an international scandal.

International figure-skating competitions use a complex scoring system that requires each judge to make many numerical judgments of the components of a skating performance. These judgments are sorted into two basic categories: technical merit and presentation. Long regarded as being susceptible to bias, the scoring system for international figure skating fell into total disrepute after the judges in Salt Lake City awarded the gold medal in the pairs competition to a Russian pair who—as was thought by almost all observers at the skating venue and on television—had clearly been outperformed by a Canadian pair.

Shortly after the competition, a French member of the judging panel was reported to have admitted to colluding with another judge by agreeing to support the Russian pair in exchange for that judge's support of a French skater in another event. Less than a week after the competition, officials of the International Olympic Committee and the International Skating Union (which presides over international ice-skating competitions) decided that a second gold medal should be awarded to the Canadian pair—an action that acknowledged that the numerical system was compromised, but which was also seen by many as an insufficient response.

In the wake of the 2002 scandal, the International Skating Union overhauled its judging system, presumably aiming to achieve greater objectivity. However, after having been in operation for several years, the new system appears to offer no more than a partial improvement. By tying scores for spins and jumps to videotaped evidence of successful completion, the new system came close to eliminating subjectivity and bias in "technical components." However, the replacement for the presentation scoring, newly labeled "program components," remained largely subjective and therefore susceptible to bias. And, of course, the use of numbers did nothing to prevent vote trading and other deliberate forms of corruption.[10]

HIDDEN BIASES OF GOOD PEOPLE: UNDERSTANDING IN-GROUP FAVORITISM

THE "GOOD PEOPLE" of this book's title are people who, along with their other good traits, have no conscious race preferences. But even though they regard themselves as egalitarian, they nevertheless obtain an "automatic White preference" result on the Race IAT. This, as we know, is no small group. Among the more than 1.5 million White Americans who have taken the Race IAT on the Internet, about 40 percent show this pattern of having explicit egalitarian beliefs accompanied by the automatic White preference result of the Race IAT.

Social psychologists Samuel Gaertner and Jack Dovidio have focused a sustained research program on a subset of Americans whom they describe as "aversive racists." These are White Americans who earnestly describe themselves as egalitarian but, nevertheless, display subtle forms of race discrimination, such as by being more ready to offer help to Whites than to Blacks. The "aversive" piece of the "aversive racism" label captures Gaertner and Dovidio's assumption that, for these White egalitarians, interracial interactions often provoke anxiety and discomfort, which can prompt avoidance or withdrawal rather than interracial engagement.

Even though we embrace Gaertner and Dovidio's theoretical understanding of aversive racism, we may want to choose a different label. (Appendix 1 has a fuller treatment of the labeling issue in regard to race.) Our reason here is similar to our reason for concluding that it is unwarranted to attach a "racist" label to the many people who show an automatic White preference on the IAT. A possible alternative label for people who display Gaertner and Dovidio's aversive racist syndrome is "uncomfortable egalitarians."

We have some observations about these uncomfortable egalitarians. First, there are a lot of them, and we are entirely serious in including ourselves among them. Our present best estimate is that they comprise 40 percent or more of White Americans and Asian Americans, perhaps a bit smaller fraction of Latino Americans, and a substantially smaller but not at all negligible proportion of African Americans.

Second, their differential behavior toward White and Black Americans can well be responsible for a substantial portion of the disadvantage experienced by Black Americans (Appendix 2 has more detail on this). Third—and perhaps most needing explanation—is that uncomfortable egalitarians are extremely unlikely to notice that their differential behavior toward Whites and Blacks contributes in any way to the disadvantages experienced by Black Americans.

It may seem a long leap from the story of the doctor who took care of Carla's hand in Chapter 7 to the understanding of uncomfortable egalitarians. However, the connection is actually close and provides insight into why uncomfortable egalitarians have no awareness that they are doing anything discriminatory. Uncomfortable egalitarians may be the prototypical "good people" who have hidden biases. They see themselves as helpful, but it turns out that their helpfulness is selective, caused in part by their discomfort in interracial interactions. Their discriminatory behavior consists of being selectively ready or able to help only or mostly those who are like them, those in their circle of friends and acquaintances—in other words, those in the groups for which they have automatic preferences.

In telling the story of Carla's hand in Chapter 7, we mentioned that the doctor—whose behavior was altered when he discovered an in-group connection to Carla—could not possibly have regarded his subsequent extra helpful behavior as contributing in any way to age, gender, race, or social class disparities in health care. He would have been aware only that he was going the "extra mile" to help a patient—clearly a good thing of the type that doctors do all the time. Like the doctor, uncomfortable egalitarians will remain unaware that their comfort and helpfulness in interactions with in-group members is not matched by similar levels of comfort and helpfulness toward out-group members.

Readers may wonder why we label the differentially directed helping of uncomfortable egalitarians as discrimination. How can we justify calling the act of helping an in-group member an act of discrimination? The answer requires distinguishing among a few different types of in-groups.

If you are a parent, no one (certainly not us) will accuse you of discriminating when you help your children by giving them meals, clothing, a secure home, and even some help with their schoolwork, even though you provide none of that help to the neighbors' children. Likewise, no one will accuse you of discriminating if you donate a kidney to a sibling rather than to a stranger.

Now put yourself in the role of a hiring manager who gives a job to someone who is a college classmate or a friend from church. In doing this, you will likely reject other applications, possibly including that of a more qualified person whom you don't know personally and who may be of a different nationality, religion, race, or ethnicity. Legally, that is discrimination. If you are a doctor serving on a hospital transplant committee, you would likewise be seen as discriminating if, on the list of candidate transplant recipients, you

place someone of your own religion ahead of a more qualified recipient who happens to be of a different religion. If you are a school
administrator, you would be seen as discriminating if you promote
a teacher of your own race while not promoting a teacher of another race who has an equivalent or superior performance record.

The examples in the last two paragraphs were the easy ones.
More challenging are situations falling between those that are obviously not discrimination (such as parental helpfulness toward children) and those that obviously are (such as nepotistic hiring).
Consider the following example of a perfectly noble action that can
have the unintended effect of increasing an existing societal advantage of your own group.

Suppose that you are a White American and contribute money
to worthwhile charitable organizations that primarily serve needy
people who happen to be primarily White Americans. Without
your consciously planning it, your gifts are adding to the advantages of an already advantaged demographic category. Even though
you are certainly not violating any civil rights law, your actions will
contribute to the relative advantages of White Americans and,
thereby, to the relative disadvantages of others. To the extent that
many others act in the same way that you do, the cumulative effects can be very substantial.

Another challenging example: Suppose that you are a bank
manager and inform a fellow manager that one of the loan applications being received by the bank is from a personal friend, a relative, or a former school classmate, and that you would appreciate its
receiving "careful attention." Or suppose that you are a university
faculty member and are asked to write a letter of recommendation
to the university's admissions office on behalf of a friend's son or
daughter. (We have been asked to do that.)

These situations are ones that divide the world into those who
have connections—by virtue of money, social class, profession, or
some other elite identification that is unequally distributed—and
those who don't. In using those connections, one's good actions can

have the side effect of increasing the relative advantages of those who are already advantaged.

The transforming effect that our research has had on our own understanding of discrimination has gradually brought us to the point of believing that selective helping of the type we are now describing—helping that is nicely captured by a familiar term, *in-group favoritism*—may be the largest contributing factor to the relative disadvantages experienced by Black Americans and other already disadvantaged groups. Yes, some people do actively intend harm to members of these groups, and their harmful actions do indeed contribute substantially to these groups' disadvantages. But we also know that these overtly prejudiced people are only a minority of Americans, quite likely a small minority.

In a society in which the ability to help falls more to Whites than to Blacks and in which in-group favoritism is the norm, ordinary acts of helping will necessarily contribute to White advantage. The cumulative effects of in-group favoritism are what sociologist Robert K. Merton had in mind when he described the "Matthew effect" as being the result of acts by which "the rich get richer at a rate that makes the poor become relatively poorer."[11]

If you are an egalitarian who wishes to be helpful in a way that contributes to a level societal playing field, what can you do to avoid the Matthew effect? Here's an unusual example of just such an action. After a good friend of ours heard us explain how acts of altruism may have unintended effects of increasing the existing advantage of those who are already relatively well off, she pondered the implications of a sizable monetary donation that she was about to make to her college. Although by long tradition her college was racially integrated and nondiscriminating, it was also true that it had substantially more White than Black students, so her gift ultimately would have the effect of increasing White advantage—which was not at all her intention.

At first she asked herself if, under the circumstances, she should make the gift at all. She resolved the dilemma imaginatively (even if expensively) by carrying through on her intention to donate to her college while also contributing an equal amount to the United Negro College Fund. Interestingly, she neither outsmarted nor eliminated the mindbug that prompted in-group favoritism—she merely neutralized it.

CAN SELF-UNDERMINING MINDBUGS BE UNDONE?

MOST WOMEN do not endorse the stereotype that men are naturally better at having careers or that they have superior abilities in science, mathematics, or music. Because women do not endorse these stereotypes, the gender-career IAT (which we hope you tried in Chapter 6) has been an eye-opener for many women. Upon trying it, they may discover that they have automatic associations of exactly this type—strong *female = family* and *male = career* associations. One might think that a *male = career* association would affect women's careers primarily because men in powerful positions may draw on that association to obstruct women's progress in outside-the-home professions. But that's not the only possible influence, and it may not be the most important influence.

Automatic gender stereotypes have recently been found to have the possibility of adversely affecting women's careers when they are self-directed. Women are at risk of applying automatic gender stereotypes to themselves. *Female = family* and *male = career* mindbugs can constitute a subtle and sustained influence on women by becoming an unrecognized source of discomfort in their pursuit of full-time careers or in their nonpursuit of child rearing.

Other possibly self-undermining mindbugs include the *old = infirm* stereotype that has been implicated as a factor impairing the health of elderly people, and race stereotypes that associate Asians or Whites more than Blacks and Latinos with academic achievement. (We described these in Chapter 5.) The latter set of stereotypes is widely believed to be an influence that guides Blacks and Latinos away from academic pursuits.[12]

We do not yet know how to go about either eliminating or outsmarting self-directed mindbugs. However, they may prove modifiable by exposure to role models—this was found in Dasgupta's study of women college students whose *male* = *math* stereotype was weakened when they took math courses taught by female faculty members. At the University of Washington, our faculty colleague Sapna Cheryan has demonstrated situational interventions that (at least temporarily) strengthen women's associations of female gender with the possibility of computer science careers. Her method is surprisingly simple—it involves adding typically feminine decor to computer science classrooms.[13]

Mass media are potentially rich sources of counterstereotypic role models. Media exposures to attractive, healthy, and vital elders, for example, may help counter mindbugs triggered by automatic *old* = *infirm* associations. This reasoning could be the inspiration for the frequent appearance of attractive, sixtyish male and female movie stars on the cover of the American Association of Retired Persons magazine in recent years. A quarter century of national media exposure to Oprah Winfrey, followed by Barack Obama's election as president of the United States, may have occupied enough American media space to be contributing to alterations of African Americans' stereotypes of their own race.

That said, there is no reason to doubt that the mindbugs we direct toward ourselves are every bit as durable as those we direct toward others. The challenge of overcoming self-undermining stereotype mindbugs brought to mind an eighteenth-century poem by the Scottish writer Robert Burns, whose inspiration was a different kind of bug. After watching a head louse wandering through the folds of a bonnet atop the head of a well-to-do lady seated in front of him in church, Burns penned "To a Louse," ending with the well-known verses in which he imagined what would happen if the fine lady could see herself as he was seeing her or, more generally, what would happen if we all could see ourselves as we appeared to others.

O wad some Pow'r the giftie gie us
To see oursels as ithers see us!
It wad frae mony a blunder free us,
An' foolish notion!
What airs in dress an' gait wad lea'e us,
An' ev'n devotion!

As it happens, the mindbugs we have been writing about, when they are stereotypes of our own groups, *do* cause us to see ourselves as others see us—even if this seeing happens without our being aware of it. When it takes the form of applying societal stereotypes to ourselves, "seeing ourselves as others see us" is remarkable in that it shows no signs of bringing the benefits that Burns assumed should result (freedom from blunders, foolish notions, and airs in dress and gait).

Recognition of the potential damage from self-applying cultural stereotypes provided us the inspiration to rewrite Burns's lines. Our rewrite (in modern English rather than Burns's Scottish) proclaims the value of *not* seeing ourselves as others see us.

To a Mindbug

Oh would some power deign to free us
From seeing ourselves as others see us!
What errors in dress and gait would leave us,
And limitation;
What aims and plans might come to please us,
And aspiration!

MINDBUGS, BLINDSPOTS, MACHINES, AND GOOD PEOPLE

WE BEGAN THIS BOOK by introducing the idea of a mindbug, which we borrowed from computer scientist Kurt VanLehn's name for mental arithmetic habits that could malfunction when applied in situations they weren't intended for. We extended VanLehn's notion far beyond arithmetic to include a wide array of mental automatisms that could cause undesired and unintended results. Although the automatisms that produce mindbugs function well in their most appropriate circumstances, they can fail when used in tasks that require thoughtful (conscious) attention.

In our preface, we used the retinal blind spot as a metaphor that likened hidden biases to a very ordinary gap in vision. An even better-known blind spot provides another useful metaphor. This is one that is well known to automobile drivers—the gap in side-view mirrors' coverage of areas on either side of the car. A new device that may soon be widely available uses radar that can signal when approaching vehicles are in the side-view mirrors' blind spots. When the sensor detects something, the driver is alerted to enter a state of heightened caution to avoid accidental collision.

As a means of sensing mental associations that reside in the blindspot that houses hidden biases, the IAT shares properties with the new automotive device. IAT measures likewise can provide warnings that prompt caution for those who wish to avoid unintended discrimination. Although it is not now possible, it is conceivable that a future descendant of the IAT might operate in real time, looking into the blindspot and generating warnings when an important judgment might be unintentionally contaminated by hidden bias.

At present, the strategies available to avoid unintended discrimination resulting from hidden biases are less easily described than are the methods for avoiding collisions with vehicles that enter side-view mirrors' blind spots. But there are a few good weapons against hidden biases. The blinding method that worked to dramatically increase women's success in symphony orchestra auditions is a known successful strategy that remains underused in many circumstances in which it can work. Another underutilized strategy is the "no-brainer" solution of developing evidence-based guidelines to eliminate discretion from judgments that might otherwise afford opportunity for hidden-bias mindbugs to operate. When faithfully applied, intelligently developed guidelines will leave little room for hidden biases.

We expect the next several years to produce a steady accumulation of research on methods to eradicate or outsmart mindbugs. Although we (presently) lack optimism about fully eradicating mindbugs, we are not similarly pessimistic about prospects for research to develop and refine methods for outsmarting mindbugs.

Among the situations for which effective mindbug-outsmarting strategies do not yet exist, most troublesome are the many routine, daily social interactions in which automatic in-group preferences unintentionally put out-group members at a disadvantage. The "good people" of this book's title likely include many who want to identify the situations in which hidden bias mindbugs operate to be prepared to outsmart them.

It may require some thought.

APPENDIX 1

Are Americans Racist?

Racism isn't that big a deal anymore. No sensible person supports it. Nobody of
importance preaches it. It's rapidly becoming an ugly memory.

—TONY SNOW
(soon to be press secretary to President George W. Bush), October 2002

I am constantly surprised by how much I hear racism talked about and how
little I actually see it.

—DINESH D'SOUZA,
What's So Great About America?

AMERICANS BORN SINCE 1960 MAY HAVE DIFFICULTY COMPREHEND-
ing that in the forty years prior to 1930, lynchings of Black Americans averaged between fifty and a hundred per year.[1] They may
know that before the Civil Rights Act of 1964, many states had
laws permitting or requiring segregation of Blacks from Whites in
public places such as schools, buses, hotels, and restaurants. But
that world may seem unimaginably remote. The quotes from Snow
and D'Souza reflect dramatic changes that have occurred in the
last fifty years, and with an African American president having
been elected in the United States, their statements might seem to
be appropriate final words on the subject of American racism.

But many scientists regard Snow's and D'Souza's statements as
capturing only a surface appearance. This appendix looks at nearly
a century of scientific studies of racial attitudes. That history will

provide a basis for understanding why many scientists now believe that, rather than disappearing, Americans' race prejudices have merely metamorphosed into harder-to-see forms. While milder in appearance than what came before, these evolved forms of prejudice may remain potent as sources of race discrimination.

WIDESPREAD OVERT RACISM BEFORE 1950

THE EARLIEST SCIENTIFIC STUDIES of discrimination in the United States documented prejudices against just about every ethnic and racial group in the country. Sociologist Emory Bogardus was the first to study prejudicial attitudes scientifically. In the early 1920s he asked Americans to say how close they were willing to be to members of forty "races"—almost all of which were groups that present-day Americans refer to as "nationalities" or "ethnicities" rather than as "races." The groups named in Figure 1—Greeks,

According to my first feeling reactions I would willingly admit members of each race (as a class, and not the best I have known, nor the worst members) to one or more of the classifications under which I have placed a cross (X).

	To close kinship by marriage	To my club as a personal chum	To my street as my neighbor	To employment in my occupation, in my country	To citizenship in my country	As visitor only to my country	Would exclude from my country
Mexicans	—	—	—	—	—	—	—
Greeks	—	—	—	—	—	—	—
Negroes	—	—	—	—	—	—	—

Figure 1: Bogardus's measure of social distance for three groups

Mexicans, and Negroes—were just three of the forty groups that Bogardus asked about in the first study using his newly created Social Distance Scale. Considerably more than half of Bogardus's 1,725 respondents indicated that they did not welcome the prospect of even the most distant form of contact with Greeks, Mexicans, or Negroes. They preferred that members of those groups not even visit the United States.

A few years later, psychologist Louis L. Thurstone created a "nationality preferences" measure, which he tested on 239 White male undergraduate students at the University of Chicago. Figure 2 shows one version of the question that was put to Thurstone's subjects. However, instead of being asked to indicate preferences among just the four pairs of nationalities shown in Figure 2, Thurstone's subjects were asked to indicate this type of preference for all 210 possible pairs of the twenty-one nationalities that he studied. Using mathematical analysis of each subject's 210 judgments, Thurstone was able to measure attitudes toward each of the twenty-one groups.

This is an experimental study of attitudes toward races and nationalities. You are asked merely to underline the one nationality, or race, of each pair that you would rather associate with. For example, the first pair is:

Greek — Mexican

If, in general, you prefer to associate with Greeks rather than with Mexicans, underline Greek. If you prefer, in general, to associate with Mexicans, underline Mexican. If you find it difficult to decide for any pair, simply underline one of them anyway. If two nationalities are about equally well liked, they will have about the same number of underlinings in all of the papers. Be sure to underline one of each pair even if you have to make a sort of guess.

American — Hindu

Englishman — Swede

Negro — Turk

Figure 2: Four of the 210 judgments used in Thurstone's 1928 study of nationality preferences

Because twenty of the forty "races" that Bogardus studied were also among Thurstone's twenty-one "nationalities," it was straightforward to construct a picture (Figure 3) that shows how closely the two methods agreed in what they revealed about racial attitudes.

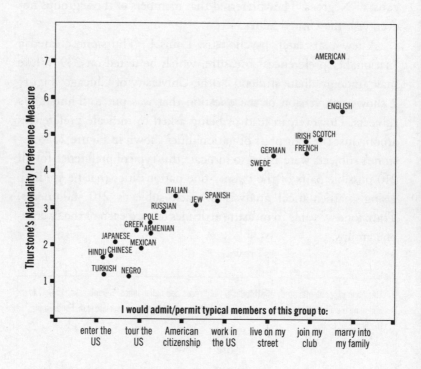

Figure 3: Comparison of Bogardus's and Thurstone's findings

In the upper right of Figure 3 is *American*. Most of Bogardus's respondents were ready to welcome Americans to "marry into my family," the closest relationship that he asked about. In close alignment with this finding, almost all of Thurstone's respondents judged that they preferred Americans over all of the other nineteen groups.

At the lower left of Figure 3 is *Turkish*. To get as low a score as

Turks received, most of Thurstone's student subjects must have said that they preferred every other group to Turks. Bogardus's subjects were similarly extreme—most of them wanted Turks to be excluded from the United States. For Thurstone's subjects, *Negro* received an even lower preference score than *Turkish,* while on Bogardus's measure there were four groups—Japanese, Chinese, Turkish, and Hindu—that were more readily nominated for exclusion from the United States than were Negroes. Perhaps this difference indicated only that Bogardus's subjects knew that "Negroes" were already well established in the United States, so keeping them out would require the extreme measure of deporting them rather than just denying them entry.

The degree to which Bogardus's and Thurstone's findings converged can be seen in the nearly straight line running from the points at lower left to those at upper right in Figure 3. The two researchers' different procedures can therefore be seen as having tapped essentially the same psychological phenomenon—a mental attribute that social psychologists of the 1930s were just beginning to refer to as "attitudes" toward the various groups—and the two researchers arrived at similar assessments of those attitudes.

One irrefutable conclusion to be drawn from this simple graph is that attitudes toward the less-liked groups were extreme in their negativity. For example, a majority of Bogardus's respondents did not welcome members of more than half of the twenty groups as either coworkers or as neighbors.

The negativity of pre-1950 Americans' race attitudes became even more apparent after 1929 when E. D. Hinckley introduced another measure, his Attitude Toward the Negro scale, which asked subjects to agree or disagree with thirty-two statements about African Americans. Six of those statements appear in Figure 4.

Consider Statement 1: "The educated Negro is less of a burden on the courts and is less likely to become a dependent or a defective than the educated White man." Most present-day Americans will consider the language of this statement objectionable enough that it would be difficult for them to express either agreement or disagreement. Hinckley's subjects, however, had no reluctance about responding. Their frequent endorsement of Statement 1 was interpreted as a sign of a favorable attitude toward Black Americans.

Now consider statement 6: "The feeble-mindedness of the Negro limits him to a social level just a little above that of the higher animals." This statement (like quite a few others from Hinckley's study that are not shown here) may be so offensive to present-day Americans that their response to any survey that included it might be either to tear up the survey form or to request that the researcher who devised it be fired.

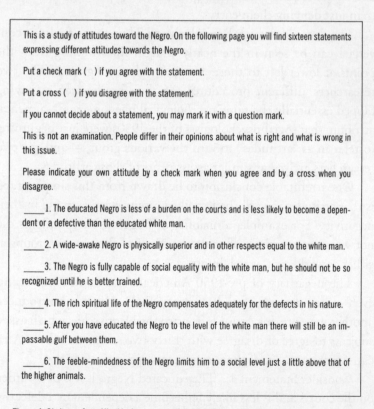

This is a study of attitudes toward the Negro. On the following page you will find sixteen statements expressing different attitudes towards the Negro.

Put a check mark (　) if you agree with the statement.

Put a cross (　) if you disagree with the statement.

If you cannot decide about a statement, you may mark it with a question mark.

This is not an examination. People differ in their opinions about what is right and what is wrong in this issue.

Please indicate your own attitude by a check mark when you agree and by a cross when you disagree.

_____1. The educated Negro is less of a burden on the courts and is less likely to become a dependent or a defective than the educated white man.

_____2. A wide-awake Negro is physically superior and in other respects equal to the white man.

_____3. The Negro is fully capable of social equality with the white man, but he should not be so recognized until he is better trained.

_____4. The rich spiritual life of the Negro compensates adequately for the defects in his nature.

_____5. After you have educated the Negro to the level of the white man there will still be an impassable gulf between them.

_____6. The feeble-mindedness of the Negro limits him to a social level just a little above that of the higher animals.

Figure 4: Six items from Hinckley's measure of Attitude Toward the Negro

The results of the Bogardus, Thurstone, and Hinckley studies made it clear that Americans of the first several decades of the twentieth century were very ready to openly express strong racial prejudice. Indeed, in the cultural climate of early twentieth-century America, it may have been as politically incorrect to express tolerance as it is to express intolerance in early twenty-first-century America.[2]

EVOLUTION OF RACIAL ATTITUDES, 1950–2000

As THE SCIENCE of survey research developed in the second half of the twentieth century, researchers continued to refine the question-asking techniques of the preceding decades to document Americans' racial attitudes. They focused increasingly on Black-White relations, which became the most intensely studied form of prejudice—a status that it retains to the present day. To enable tracking of changes in racial and other attitudes over time, researchers administered surveys in which the same questions were repeated every few years. Q1 and Q2 below are examples of questions that were repeatedly used in surveys over four decades between 1960 and 2000. The changes in response over those decades tell a story similar to what many other studies in the late twentieth century showed.

Q1. Do you think White students and Black students should go to the same schools or to separate schools?

Q2. Do you think that White people have a right to keep Blacks out of their neighborhoods if they want, and Blacks should respect that right?

Figure 5 shows four decades of results for White Americans' answers to Q1 and Q2. In the early 1960s only about 60 percent of White Americans favored racially integrated schools. By 1995 that support had grown to nearly 100 percent—after which the question was removed from surveys because it was no longer informative. White Americans' endorsement of residential integration of

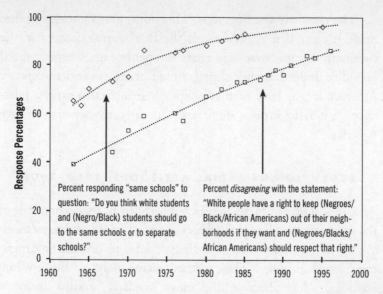

Figure 5: White Americans' increasing rejection of segregation (1963–1996)
Data source: Schuman, H., Steeh, C., Bobo, L., and Krysan, M. (1997) Racial attitudes in America. Cambridge,
Mass.: Harvard University Press. Table 3.5A.

housing showed a similarly sharp rise over time, increasing from less than 40 percent in the early 1960s to more than 80 percent in the 1990s.

Q3 and Q4, just below, are two other questions that were regularly repeated in surveys of Americans' race attitudes. These questions asked about the appropriateness of government assistance to Black Americans.

Q3. Do you think that the government in Washington should make every possible effort to improve the social and economic position of Blacks and other minority groups?

Q4. Do you think that Blacks have been discriminated against for so long that the government has a special obligation to help improve their living standards?

One might expect these two questions to provide evidence of the same increasingly favorable attitudes toward Black Americans that

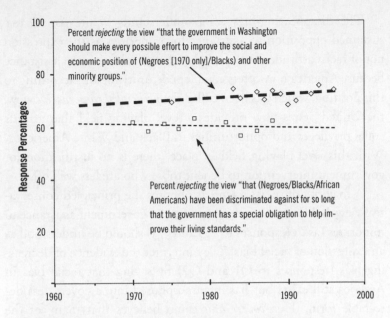

Figure 6: *White Americans' steady rejection of government help to minorities (1970–1996)*
Data source: Schuman, H., Steeh, C., Bobo, L., and Krysan, M. (1997) Racial attitudes in America. Cambridge,
Mass.: Harvard University Press. Tables 3.1A and 3.1B.

were revealed by the time trends for Q1 and Q2 in Figure 5. But, as
Figure 6 shows, across three decades the time trends for Q3 and Q4
are flat. The top line shows gradually increasing opposition to government assistance to African Americans. The lower line shows that
majority opposition to assistance to African Americans remained
stable over the decades during which the question was asked.[3]

What does it mean that between 1960 and 2000 White Americans expressed consistent opposition to government assistance to
minorities at the same time that they were expressing steadily increasing support for racial integration? Scientists have disagreed in
interpreting these juxtaposed trends. One camp, guided mainly by
the responses to questions such as Q1 and Q2, believes that Americans' racial biases have largely disappeared. The other camp, persuaded more by responses to questions such as Q3 and Q4,
concludes that Americans' racial biases persist, but in altered form.

The disappearing-bias camp understands White Americans' sustained opposition to assistance for minorities as the expression not of racist attitudes but of a belief that Blacks need no assistance because America now offers equal opportunity for all. According to this position, which has been called the *principled conservative* view, the United States now provides a level playing field that affords equal privileges and opportunities to Black and White Americans. With this level playing field in place, there is no justification for government intervention to benefit those who are less well off.[4]

A majority of social scientists opposes the principled conservative view, holding that wide opposition to government assistance to minorities (as in responses to Q3 and Q4) should be understood as an expression of racial bias. They interpret the evidence of decreasing bias (responses to Q1 and Q2) by saying that racial bias in America still exists but has metamorphosed into a covert, less detectable form. This *covert bias* camp believes that many of the Americans who express egalitarian views in public continue to quietly harbor, in private, racial biases that remain potent sources of discrimination.

More than a decade into the twenty-first century, the debate between these two camps has persisted unresolved for about thirty years. A recent study that was designed to settle this long-standing disagreement asked 1,077 White Americans to respond to a survey including two questions about government assistance. Each survey respondent answered both questions. Half of them got this question first, which asked about assistance to women:

> *Some people say that because of past discrimination, women should be given preference in hiring and promotion. Others say that such preference in hiring and promotion of women is wrong because it discriminates against men. What about your opinion— are you for or against preferential hiring and promotion of women?*

The other half of the respondents got the following question first. It was the same as the question above, with the exception of four words ("women" changed three times to "Blacks"; "men" changed once to "Whites"):

> *Some people say that because of past discrimination, Blacks should be given preference in hiring and promotion. Others say that such preference in hiring and promotion of Blacks is wrong because it discriminates against Whites. What about your opinion—are you for or against preferential hiring and promotion of Blacks?*

The study's results showed that White respondents were less opposed to preferential hiring when it benefited women than when it benefited Blacks. From this finding the authors concluded in favor of the covert bias view: "The finding that people are more opposed to affirmative action programs for Blacks versus women is one of the most compelling indicators that race remains a factor driving opposition to affirmative action."

Although this interpretation has some justification, it is not the only possible interpretation. Many of the survey's respondents opposed government assistance for *both* women and Blacks, which appears consistent with the principled conservative position. Also, because the question about assistance to Blacks did not mention the gender of potential Black beneficiaries of hiring preference, the survey's respondents may have assumed that this question was asking mainly about Black men. If so, part of their opposition to preferential hiring could have been due to opposition to preferential hiring for men of *any* race.

The bottom line is that after considering the results of this interesting study, we have to conclude that both interpretations of survey respondents' unchanging answers (across three decades) to questions about government assistance to Blacks—the covert bias view and the principled conservative view—seem viable. And because these two interpretations do not actually contradict or exclude each other, it may be most reasonable to believe that each is partly correct. In other words, those who oppose government assistance plausibly include some who are racially biased, some who are principled conservatives, and some who are both.[5]

"UNOBTRUSIVE" RESEARCH METHODS

BECAUSE OF the difficulties of drawing conclusions from studies based on question-asking methods, researchers in the 1970s began to develop alternative methods that had roots in two famous experiments from the 1930s.

In 1934, Richard LaPiere reported the results of an ingenious study for which his main piece of research equipment was an automobile. Between 1930 and 1932, accompanied by a Chinese couple, LaPiere toured the southwestern United States, where the trio stopped to request accommodations at 251 hotels, motels, campgrounds, and restaurants. They received the accommodations they sought in 250 of their 251 attempts, being denied only once.

Approximately six months after each visit, LaPiere sent a letter to proprietors of each of the 251 establishments, asking for a response to this question: "Will you accept members of the Chinese race as guests in your establishment?" Surprisingly, more than 90 percent of the answers he received stated that they would not. This was puzzling. Why were answers to the mailed inquiry so consistently negative, while face-to-face responses to the three travelers were so uniformly positive?

Any interpretation of LaPiere's study is complicated by a few details of his methods. For one, the person who answered each establishment's follow-up letter was not always the same person from whom the traveling trio had received accommodations. Even more important, LaPiere's Chinese traveling companions were young, polite, and middle-class, none of which was necessarily assumed by the person who answered the mailed inquiry. These complications notwithstanding, the unarguably important scientific takeaway from LaPiere's study was the value of using behavior observation in addition to using question-asking methods.

Mamie and Kenneth Clark, two African American psychologists who were interested in the way Black children internalized racism, reported a stunning series of experiments that came to be known as the "doll studies." These started with work done by Mamie (Phipps) Clark while she was a graduate student at Howard University in the late 1930s. The Clarks' experiments showed that when young Black children ages three to seven were offered a choice between playing with a Black doll or a White doll, two-thirds of them chose the White doll. These studies later became famous to law scholars because of their role in the U.S. Supreme Court's 1954 decision in the *Brown v. Board of Education* case—the decision that declared racial segregation of public schools to be unconstitutional. The Supreme Court drew on the Clarks' findings in concluding, in the words of Chief Justice Earl Warren, that race segregation "generates a feeling of inferiority . . . that may affect the children's hearts and minds in a way unlikely ever to be undone."[6]

What the studies by LaPiere and the Clarks had in common was that neither the proprietors visited by LaPiere's peripatetic trio nor the small children who made doll choices in the Clarks' studies had any awareness that their actions in offering accommodations or choosing among dolls were being recorded, let alone being used to infer racial attitudes. These were the first *unobtrusive-method* studies. But that name for the method did not appear until the late 1960s. And it was not until the 1970s that two forces prompted researchers studying discrimination to conclude that unobtrusive methods were attractive. One force was the expansion of scientific interest in prejudice, propelled by the tense and sometimes violently confrontational race relations of the 1960s. The other was a growing discovery of problems with question-asking methods. Social psychologists were becoming increasingly aware of the tendency of research subjects to fall prey to impression management—the desire to present themselves in ways that would be looked upon favorably by others (see Chapter 2).

The first researchers to develop new unobtrusive methods for studying racial bias in the 1970s wanted to see whether Whites would help Blacks with the same frequency with which they would help other Whites. Further, they wanted to observe this when research participants had no inkling that anyone was observing whether or not they would help. Social psychologists Samuel Gaertner and Leonard Bickman invented a "wrong number" technique to see how a sampling of residents of Brooklyn, New York, would respond to calls from Blacks and Whites seeking help. The help seekers trained by Gaertner and Bickman called 1,109 Brooklyn residents, 569 White and 540 Black. (Because of the sharp racial segregation of Brooklyn's neighborhoods circa 1970, the researchers knew with near certainty whether each call would be received by a White or a Black resident. The callers themselves were also easily identified by race on the basis of racially characteristic speech accents.)

All calls began with the caller saying, "Hello . . . Ralph's Garage? This is George Williams. . . . Listen, I'm stuck out here on the parkway . . . and I'm wondering if you'd be able to come out here and take a look at my car." After being informed that he had not reached Ralph's Garage and after apologizing for his mistake, the caller (indicating some distress with his predicament) said that he had used his last coin in a pay phone, immediately following which he made the critical request: "Do you think you could do me the favor of calling the garage and letting them know where I am . . . ? I'll give you the number. . . . They know me over there."

The result: White call recipients discriminated by race—they were less likely to help Black callers (53 percent) than White callers (65 percent). For any single call recipient who did not help a Black caller, that nonhelping could have been race discrimination, but it could also have been caused by other factors—such as mishearing the phone number for Ralph's Garage, failing to make an accurate note of the number, or forgetting it. Problems caused by this necessary uncertainty were overcome by assigning all call recipients at random to receive the call from either a Black or White caller. This use of randomization is an essential ingredient of experimental methods, and it is what makes experimental findings convincing. It helped also that three later repetitions of Gaertner and Bickman's experiment reproduced their findings, each confirming that the caller's race was critical. In each of these follow-ups, Black callers received significantly less help than White callers.

Another innovative study that used unobtrusive measures began with researchers preparing stamped, addressed, and (importantly) unsealed envelopes, each containing a completed application to graduate school. These envelopes were placed in airport telephone booths, where they would inevitably be discovered by travelers. Only data from White travelers were considered. When 604 of these White travelers found and (naturally) looked at the envelopes' contents, they could not avoid seeing a photograph that showed the applicant's White or Black face. A note in the envelope, which asked "Dad" to mail the envelope, made it appear that the applicant's father had lost the letter before mailing it. Again, race was critical in determining helping. The letter was more likely to be mailed when the applicant's photograph was White (45 percent) than when it was Black (37 percent). As an interesting additional finding, the researchers found that more attractive photos (of both races) led to more help.

Dozens of other experiments in the 1970s tested the amount of help that Black and White help seekers would receive from White potential helpers who did not know that they were being observed. The sought help consisted mostly of minor favors, such as picking up a box of dropped pencils, providing change for a quarter, or donating money to a Salvation Army stand attendant during the Christmas season. In a few experiments the help was more substantial, such as helping a Black or White person who had fallen in a subway car or who was standing alone on the roadside next to a disabled car.

When in 1980 social psychologists Faye Crosby, Stephanie Bromley, and Leonard Saxe reviewed a large collection of these unobtrusive-measure studies, they concluded that the findings of race discrimination in these studies disagreed with what was expected based on previous studies that had used question-asking methods to assess race prejudice: "Discriminatory behavior is more prevalent in the . . . unobtrusive studies than we might expect on the basis of survey data." Crosby and her colleagues also found that race bias was more evident in "remote" interactions, when the help giver and recipient were not face-to-face. That conclusion very nicely made contact with LaPiere's observation forty years earlier that discrimination against travelers was expressed only in the remote situation of answering a letter that asked whether Chinese travelers would be welcomed.

The lost-letter and other unobtrusive-measure studies of the 1970s had the character of *Candid Camera*–type snapshots of behavior in natural settings, and they definitely strengthened scientific belief that racial bias remained a potent force, albeit in a covert form that appeared very different from the open racism expressed in the early twentieth century. After 1980, this type of research waned as researchers became increasingly reluctant to observe people who were unaware of being observed. Nevertheless, unobtrusive-measure studies still appear occasionally and they continue to reveal race discrimination in the form of reduced helping.[7]

ANSWERING THE QUESTION

THE QUESTION WE HAVE in mind is the one in the title of this appendix: *Are Americans racist?* The strongest case that America is no longer racist is made by results of surveys that use questions such as Q1 and Q2, shown in Figure 5. These questions and others that ask about attitudes toward segregation have shown changes spanning four decades, by the end of which Americans were expressing very little support for racial segregation. Another observation supporting the conclusion that American society is not presently racist is the extent to which egalitarian principles have been adopted in American laws and institutions. In addition to the existence of federal legislation outlawing all forms of racial discrimination in public life, it is now effectively a requirement for any large organization—business, government agency, school, hospital, or charitable institution—to have a publicly stated policy that describes its efforts to be egalitarian both in the treatment of employees and in the provision of services to clients.

Egalitarian principles also now appear routinely in informal public discourse. The years since passage of America's major civil rights laws in the 1960s have seen the introduction of strong social pressures—often disparagingly labeled "political correctness"—that effectively prohibit spoken or written expressions of prejudices or stereotypes. The present-day power of political correctness is suggested by a recent list of famous people who made remarks that were taken to indicate their racial or ethnic bigotry, setting in motion barrages of negative publicity that no doubt were damaging in themselves but also often resulted in the people being fired from prominent positions: radio host Don Imus (April 2007), Nobel Prize–winning biologist James Watson (October 2007), actor Mel Gibson (July 2010), radio talk show host Laura Schlessinger ("Dr. Laura," August 2010), TV news anchor Rick Sanchez (October 2010), and radio news analyst Juan Williams (October 2010).

Two incidents deserve mention outside this list of prominent people embarrassed by racially or ethnically insensitive or inflammatory speech. After a November 2006 anti-Black tirade in response to audience hecklers during his nightclub comedy routine, Michael Richards (portrayer of Cosmo Kramer on the long-running television comedy series *Seinfeld*) used a television appearance several days later to make a very public and self-critical apology. In July 2010, a high official in the U.S. Department of Agriculture, Shirley Sherrod, was fired for remarks that were almost immediately shown to have been misleadingly edited by political opponents to appear racist. A few days later, Sherrod received very public apologies from those who fired her. Although she was offered her job back, she did not return to it.

These unambiguous examples of America's rejection of racism notwithstanding, compelling bodies of research provide evidence of remaining prejudice and discrimination (detailed further in Appendix 2). Even the 2008 election of Barack Obama, which many interpreted as proof that America had at last become "postracial," contained its own clear indications that potent racial influences persist in American politics. If Obama had been obliged to rely only on the White American electorate, he would have lost in a landslide—exit polls revealed that Obama lost the White vote by 12 percent. That 12 percent deficit was noticeably larger than the 8 percent deficit in Obama's White vote predicted by pre-election polls. The surprisingly large 4-percentage-point discrepancy between forecasts and the actual vote was itself an indication that racial factors were involved in the way people described their voting intentions to pollsters.[8]

Although racially discriminatory attitudes persist in American society, it is a mistake to characterize modern America as racist—at least not in the way that the label of "racism" has long been understood. Most Americans—a large majority—advocate racial equality. Although some Americans who oppose government assistance to African Americans and other minorities likely do so as an expression of either implicit or explicit racial bias, others base this policy stance on egalitarian principles, believing—in line with the two quotes that opened this appendix—that America has already achieved racial equality.

At the same time, it is all too clear that any portrait of America as a postracial society provides, at best, a poor likeness. The unobtrusive-measure studies clearly indicate otherwise, and many social scientists have interpreted White Americans' opposition to assistance for minorities—as shown in Figure 6—as indicating the persistence of racial bias in a covert form that is quite different from the racism that was so openly professed in the early twentieth century.

We view America's persisting racial bias as a strong undercurrent, composed of two types of hidden biases. What may be the lesser type consists of biases that are recognized and espoused by their possessors but deliberately suppressed from public expression, plausibly in response to the pressures of political correctness and impression management. In our view, the stronger portion of the hidden undercurrent of biases consists of those that remain outwardly unexpressed for the simple reason that their possessors are unaware of possessing them. These are biases in the form of associative knowledge that can be measured by the IAT, as described in Chapter 3. Collectively, these two types of hidden bias plausibly contribute more to discrimination in America than does the overt prejudice of an ever-decreasing minority of Americans—a minority that remains content to openly express racial and ethnic dislikes.

APPENDIX 2

Race, Disadvantage, and Discrimination

THIS BOOK DEALS WITH MANY TARGETS OF BIAS, INCLUDING women, gays, religious and ethnic groups, the elderly, and the overweight. But we have given most attention to race discrimination—not only because of the societal importance of race discrimination in the United States but also because it has received more scientific research attention than any other form of bias. We continue that attention in this appendix, which focuses on two important questions for which much scientific knowledge has accumulated.

First, we ask what is known scientifically about the extent to which there exists, in the United States, the widely desired "level playing field" on which Black and White have equal footing. (Not to be coy about this, we conclude that the playing field is far from level.) Second, we ask a considerably more difficult and controversial question about what light scientific research has been able to shed on the causes of existing Black disadvantage. Our aim is to generate a list of conclusions that are widely regarded as being confidently established in scientific research.

A LIST OF CONCLUSIONS

As a start, we constructed an initial list of ten conclusions about White-Black race relations that we thought might receive wide acceptance as scientifically established. Knowing, however, that our own acceptance of those conclusions might not be generally shared, we contacted about two dozen social scientist colleagues, whom we asked to tell us which of our ten conclusions they regarded as accepted and which they regarded as controversial.

The list that we ended up with retained only seven conclusions that were regarded as established by all or most of the colleagues we asked. The first of our final list of seven conclusions seems almost universally accepted. There is no scientific opposition.

CONCLUSION 1: BLACK DISADVANTAGE EXISTS

Relative to White Americans, Black Americans experience disadvantages—meaning inferior outcomes—on almost every economically significant dimension. This includes earnings, education, housing, employment, status in the criminal justice system, and health, all of which are detailed later in this appendix.

Conclusion 1 is deliberately silent on possible explanations for Black disadvantage. We have a path to travel before we can express any confidence in our knowledge of the causes of Black disadvantage.

Group-Responsible Theories of Black Disadvantage

Theories about the causes of Black disadvantage can be sorted into two categories. One set of theories credits Black Americans themselves with full responsibility for the disadvantages they experience. We call these the "group-responsible" theories. The other set is "others-responsible" theories, which place the entire responsibility elsewhere. The difference between these two types of theory is critical when one contemplates formulating policy for how American society can best deal with the existence of Black disadvantage.

Policies designed to deal with disadvantaged groups often reflect a "responsibility principle"—the idea that those responsible for creating a problem should be responsible for fixing it. This principle is set deeply into our psyches, having roots in earliest childhood. If young Suzie breaks her brother's favorite toy, she knows that she is expected to apologize and, if possible, to undo or correct the damage—if not by fixing the toy, then perhaps by offering her crying brother a prized possession of her own. Although Mahzarin and Tony grew up in countries halfway around the globe from each other, like most children we were both brought up to understand that when we caused damage, even when we believed that we had not intended harm—as when Mahzarin urged her sister to do a headstand right after dinner—we had responsibility for the cleanup.

There are at least two kinds of group-responsible theories. The *biological* form of the theory assumes that race-associated genes endow Black Americans with strong predispositions toward violence and perhaps with weak dispositions toward productive work. The *cultural* form of group-responsible theory holds that it is Black American culture that draws Black Americans toward the pursuit of criminal careers and away from opportunities for self-improvement.[1]

Some occurrences of Black disadvantage are not easily placed into either the group-responsible or the others-responsible camp. Imagine a hypothetical business—we'll call it FairPlay Inc. Examination of FairPlay's personnel records shows that, on average, its Black employees receive noticeably less pay than do its White employees. This is undeniably a disadvantage. Company records also show that, on hiring, FairPlay's Black employees are typically assigned to lower-skilled jobs than their White counterparts. When questioned about the possibility that they are discriminating, FairPlay's executives point out that their Black and White employees differ in educational qualifications. They assert confidently that all of FairPlay's staff are being paid appropriately and placed appropriately in positions in consideration of both their qualifications and their contributions to products and services.

The FairPlay scenario is an interesting one. Although Black employees at FairPlay are undoubtedly at a disadvantage, if FairPlay's policies do not apply differently, in either statement or practice, to White and Black employees, FairPlay is *not* discriminating. Their managers are presumably not discriminating in hiring decisions, job assignments, performance evaluations, pay increases, or promotions. The higher average pay and position of FairPlay's White employees can be attributed entirely to the White employees having stronger educational credentials. If FairPlay were sued for discriminating against its employees, American courts likely would dismiss the suit as lacking in merit. The disadvantage at FairPlay would be attributed to societal factors operating outside the employment setting, for which FairPlay would not be held legally responsible.

Discrimination: Others-Responsible Theories of Black Disadvantage

There are several theories of discrimination that identify various "others" as culprits responsible for Black disadvantage. In the longest-established of these theories, Black disadvantage is the result of deliberate, overt race discrimination. A very different type of others-responsible theory credits discrimination to people who have no intention to discriminate and no awareness of doing so—their discriminatory actions can be explained as the operation of hidden bias. Institutional discrimination is a third type of others-responsible theory, crediting Black disadvantage to structural or regulatory characteristics of society's major institutions—government, schools, courts, hospitals, and corporations.

In America, institutional discrimination as a cause of Black disadvantage is undeniable historical fact. Documented forms of institutional discrimination include the now-defunct Jim Crow laws that, until the 1960s, segregated Blacks from Whites in schools, in restrooms, at drinking fountains, and on public transportation. America's civil rights laws of the 1960s mandated the end of blatant forms of institutional discrimination in the United States. But that does not mean that institutional discrimination ceased to exist—

only its most blatant forms are gone. As just one set of examples of what remains, in the 2000 and 2004 U.S. presidential elections, American news media provided many reports of discriminatory acts at polling places. For example, on Election Day precinct workers sometimes vigilantly applied voter qualification laws to Black voters while not giving equal scrutiny to the credentials of White voters. The selective enforcement of voting rights laws might be understood as an act of overt discrimination that is expressed through institutional structures and procedures.[2]

The Role of New Measures of Discrimination

Appendix 1 described the 1970s burst of unobtrusive-measure experiments that revealed race discrimination in the behavior of people who had been approached for help by either Blacks or Whites and who did not know that their helpfulness was being observed by researchers. The help seekers in those studies included stranded motorists trying to contact a service station, college students whose applications to graduate school had been left in a phone booth by their fathers, passersby requesting change for a quarter, Salvation Army volunteers seeking small cash donations, and experimenters who pretended to accidentally drop a box of pencils. Because those who were approached were assigned at random to either a Black help seeker or a White help seeker, it was implausible that any factor other than the race of the help seeker was responsible for what the studies revealed: Whites consistently gave less assistance to Blacks than to other Whites.

The disadvantages suffered by Black Americans in the many unobtrusive-measure experiments were modest—often no more than the withholding of relatively minor forms of help. At about the same time that those experiments were being done, other studies were beginning to use similar methods to discover the impact of race on outcomes with much greater economic impact. Housing discrimination was the first highly consequential area to receive this research scrutiny.

HOUSING

In the 1950s, informal versions of what later came to be called an *audit* method were deployed to examine possible discrimination against Black and Hispanic Americans in their search for housing. Although legislation had given all Americans the right to rent or purchase any homes they could afford, there were many anecdotal reports of Black and Hispanic home buyers or renters being discriminated against. They might be told that the apartment or house they were interested in had been rented or sold, even while a White investigator posing as a potential renter or buyer would learn on a follow-up visit that it was still available.

In the rigorous audit method that developed from those early efforts, researchers did not wait to learn that minority clients had been turned down by rental or real estate agents. Instead, pairs of White and minority testers, selected and trained to appear similar on all characteristics other than race or ethnicity, were dispatched separately to visit each renter or seller, to determine the availability of advertised housing. The order in which the two testers in each pair contacted each renter or seller was randomized so that White and minority testers were equally often the first of the pair to seek the advertised housing.[3]

The U.S. Department of Housing and Urban Development conducted the first national audit study of housing discrimination in 1977. Another two national audits followed in 1989 and 2000. These three are the most important of what is now a large set of housing discrimination audits, almost all of which documented discrimination against Black and Hispanic renters and home buyers.

The same housing audit studies also documented that Black and Hispanic buyers were at a disadvantage in obtaining mortgage loans. Black and Hispanic home buyers might be denied a mortgage or be required to pay higher mortgage interest rates than Whites for otherwise similar loans. An added problem for minority buyers is that they might encounter greater difficulty purchasing insurance for a home they wished to buy, effectively making it impossible for them to buy homes in White residential areas.

Difficulties encountered by Blacks and Hispanics in obtaining insurance or loans were sometimes the consequence of deliberate policies of banks and insurance companies to maintain racial homogeneity of neighborhoods—a now-illegal practice known as redlining. The 2000 national housing audit concluded, "Housing discrimination raises the costs [to minorities] of the search for housing, creates barriers to homeownership and housing choice, and contributes to the perpetuation of racial and ethnic segregation."

Each of the three national housing audit studies was designed to produce a *net estimate* of discrimination, which is a comparison of the number of times the White tester was favored to the number of times that the minority tester in the pair was favored. A positive net estimate percentage indicates the favoring of White over minority testers. For the 1989 audit, the net estimates showed that White apartment seekers were favored 13 percent more often than Blacks, and White home buyers were favored 17 percent more often than Blacks. Both of these figures were lower in the 2000 audit—8 percent for both apartments and homes—but it is too soon to interpret the lower 2000 values confidently as evidence for a sustained trend of reduced housing discrimination.[4]

HIRING

There has not yet been a national employment audit, but there have been numerous regional audits that utilized rigorous methods. Hiring audits use matched pairs of White and minority job applicants, similar to the matched pairs used in housing audits. They also use net estimates of discrimination and have typically found discrimination against both Black and Hispanic job applicants. As in housing audits, the quality matching of the paired job seekers' prepared credentials ensures that they are equally qualified on objective criteria that can be gleaned from those credentials, leaving race or ethnicity as the only plausible explanation for net discrimination. In summarizing the results of these employment audit studies, economist Marc Bendick found that they revealed average net estimates of 16 percent favoring White over Black job applicants and 14 percent favoring White over Hispanic applicants.

Two recent hiring audit experiments provided still more evidence for the role played by race in hiring decisions. One was by economists Marianne Bertrand and Sendhil Mullainathan. Responding to a large number of newspaper help-wanted advertisements in Boston and Chicago, the researchers submitted two separately mailed résumés that were equally strong on all relevant qualifications. The only thing that they systematically varied in the 2,435 pairs of mailed résumés was the first name of the job applicant. In each pair, one applicant had a name—such as Aisha, Ebony, Darnell, or Hakim—that suggested a Black American identity. The other had a name that seemed typically White American, such as Kristen, Meredith, Neil, or Todd. Bertrand and Mullainathan then just waited for the phone to ring. For the White-named applicants, the callback rate was 9.7 percent, compared to only 6.5 percent for Black-named applicants. The authors concluded, "A White applicant should expect on average one callback for every 10 ads she or he applies to; on the other hand, an African American applicant would need to apply to about 15 different ads to achieve the same result."

Sociologist Devah Pager reported surprising findings from a hiring audit study she did in Milwaukee, Wisconsin. Pager arranged for paired testers to apply in person for jobs that required no experience and only a high school education. After completing an application at the employment site, White applicants were more than twice as likely as matched Black applicants to be called back for an interview. The surprising finding was one that went beyond anything previously reported in audit studies: White applicants who described themselves as having a criminal record received more callback invitations (17 percent) than did otherwise comparable Black applicants who did *not* have a criminal record (14 percent). The 17 percent callback rate for Whites with criminal records could also be compared with the much lower 5 percent callback rate for otherwise matched Black applicants with criminal records.[5]

HEALTH CARE

The Institute of Medicine (IOM), a branch of the United States National Academy of Sciences, was asked by Congress to examine the role of race and other demographic factors in American health care. Their 2002 report, titled *Unequal Treatment,* reviewed about six hundred studies in which medical diagnoses, treatments, and health outcomes were examined in relation to the age, sex, and race of patients. The IOM's conclusion: Black Americans and other minority groups suffered health care disparities that resulted in their receiving less effective medical care than did White Americans. These disparities occurred even when minority and White patients were matched on socioeconomic status and when they were known to have the same insurance coverage.

In the IOM study, health care disparities were found in treatments for heart disease, kidney disease, cancer, and HIV/AIDS. Members of minority groups received fewer routine screenings, less medication for pain, less surgery, less dialysis, and fewer organ transplants. Minorities also received less-preferred treatments. Diabetes provided a particularly disturbing example, given the disproportionately high rates of diabetes among minorities and the seriousness of diabetic complications. For example, minorities were more likely to suffer limb amputations that could have been avoided by earlier diagnosis of diabetes or by more vigilant preventive care.

Unequal Treatment's Finding 4-1 declared that implicit bias was a plausible cause, even if not a conclusively established one, of health care disparities:

The committee finds strong but circumstantial evidence for the role of bias, stereotyping, prejudice, and clinical uncertainty from a range of sources, including studies of social cognition and "implicit" stereotyping, but urges more research to identify how and when these processes occur.[6]

It is not easy to do the "studies of social cognition" that the IOM report urged. Medical institutions, like many other large organizations, are reluctant to expose themselves to investigations that might reveal bias. Nevertheless, some pioneering studies have used IAT measures of implicit bias in health care settings. Although there are still too few such studies to allow strong conclusions, the available findings have shown that IAT-measured race attitudes of physicians *do* predict the quality of the medical care they provide. Doctors who displayed stronger automatic White preference on the IAT made cardiac treatment decisions that favored White patients relative to Blacks. In two other studies, Black patients of physicians who had stronger White preference perceived their physicians as being less helpful.[7]

CRIMINAL JUSTICE

A 2006 study by the U.S. Department of Justice (DOJ) reported that 40 percent of the American prison population was Black. That 40 percent figure is hugely out of proportion to the percentage of Blacks in the U.S. population at the time—about 12 percent. Among prison inmates, the percentage of Black inmates incarcerated for violent crimes is higher than the corresponding percentage for White inmates (27 percent versus 22 percent), and there is a similar pattern for drug offenses (31 percent versus 19 percent). We cannot confidently say how much of the difference in imprisonment rates is due to different rates of crime commission by the races (a group-responsible explanation) or, alternatively, to race-discriminatory treatment by the criminal justice system (an others-responsible explanation). Nevertheless, some conclusions about group-responsible versus others-responsible causes can be drawn from studies that have examined the role played by race in such police activities as stopping, searching, and arresting motorists.

A 2006 DOJ report summarized results of a survey of 76,910 drivers age sixteen or older. Those results included:

- About 9 percent of drivers age sixteen or older reported having been stopped by police. This percentage was approximately the same for White, Black, and Hispanic drivers.
- About half of the stops were for speeding. After being stopped for speeding, Black drivers (78 percent) and Hispanic drivers (85 percent) were noticeably more likely than White drivers (70 percent) to be ticketed.
- Among young male drivers who were stopped, Black drivers (22 percent) and Hispanic drivers (17 percent) were noticeably more likely than White drivers (8 percent) to be searched.

Although the frequencies of being stopped for speeding were found to be similar for Whites, Blacks, and Hispanics, what happened afterward was not, with Blacks and Hispanics more likely than Whites both to receive speeding tickets and to have their cars searched. Among male drivers under age twenty-four, fewer Black (58 percent) than Hispanic (81 percent) or White (also 81 percent) drivers regarded the reason for their stop as legitimate.

The DOJ report in which these statistics appeared was remarkably devoid of any conclusion about discrimination. In the only two paragraphs of the report in which the word *profiling* appeared, the report stated that there was no way to determine whether the higher rates of ticketing and searching Black and Hispanic drivers represented discriminatory bias.

However, in a 1994 study of the New Jersey State Police, psychologist John Lamberth was less reluctant to declare that traffic stop data revealed discrimination. Lamberth found that Black drivers on the New Jersey Turnpike were much more likely than White drivers to be stopped and searched by the state police. In court testimony based on his study, Lamberth concluded that "the magnitude of the disparities lends overwhelming support to the assertion of discriminatory policy."

Our understanding of implicit bias leads us to favor a modified version of Lamberth's conclusion. Although it is plausible that some New Jersey State Police officers may have engaged in deliberate discrimination—perhaps because of either a personal policy of profiling or a profiling policy that was encouraged by their supervisors—it is also possible that the police were acting out of implicit bias. Without any conscious intent, the officers' hidden biases (implicit race attitudes or stereotypes) could have contributed to their stopping Black drivers more frequently than White drivers.[8]

MORE AUDITS

Americans buy many cars. The purchase price of a car is a significant expense for anyone but the very wealthy. It is an especially large expenditure for those with relatively low incomes who work at jobs that are unreachable by public transportation. To investigate possible discrimination in costs of automobiles, Yale economist and law professor Ian Ayres trained White and Black testers, some male and some female, to present themselves as equally qualified for an automobile purchase. Ayres's testers visited automobile showrooms in search of specific automobile models. Their finding: Prices quoted to Black testers were consistently several hundred dollars higher than those quoted to White testers for the same model.

Extending his interest to monetary transactions with much smaller dollar values, Ayres obtained the cooperation of New Haven, Connecticut, taxi drivers, whom he asked to keep records of their fares and tips. Ayres and his colleagues found that Black taxi drivers' tips averaged 33 percent lower than those received by White drivers.

A study of restaurant tipping by Cornell University psychologist Michael Lynn observed a similar race difference—Black waiters received tips 18 percent lower than those received by White waiters. Both Ayres's and Lynn's studies had an additional interesting twist. Both of them found that White customers were not the only ones to give smaller tips to Black cab drivers or waiters than to White ones. Black customers also did.[9]

CONCLUSION 2: THE DISADVANTAGE EXPERIENCED BY BLACK AMERICANS IS AT LEAST PARTLY DUE TO RACE DISCRIMINATION

The many experiments done with matched pairs of Black and White testers call for a conclusion that goes beyond our already stated first conclusion, that Black disadvantage exists. The further conclusion—one demanded by the great weight of evidence—is indisputable: Some portion of Black disadvantage is attributable to the way people respond to Blacks just because they are Black.

Given the variety and weight of supporting evidence, it may appear that we have been remarkably slow to reach this conclusion. However, we see this caution as an appropriate strategy, given our goal of limiting conclusions *only* to ones for which there is strong consensus among social scientists. The large volume of research, along with the consistency of the findings of that research, makes the conclusion inescapable not only to us but also to almost all those who are familiar with the evidence. These research studies have employed a variety of methods, especially including randomized experiments, which are the most powerful scientific techniques available to draw conclusions about causes and to rule out alternative explanations.

We have *not* concluded that Blacks and Whites are, in general, equally qualified for housing, jobs, or loans. Nor have we concluded that Blacks and Whites are equally law-abiding. (It is possible that Black Americans are more law-abiding than White Americans or vice versa.) We have also declined to draw any conclusions about whether Black and White taxi drivers or waiters provide the same quality of service. Again, it is possible the two groups provide comparable service, but it is also possible that one or the other group provides superior service.

We are silent about these group-responsible explanations because the available research provides no decisive evidence. The research *has* provided decisive evidence on the outcomes to be expected when sound research methods rule out possible causes other than race, as has been done rigorously both in the audit studies and in the unobtrusive-measure experiments. Those studies have found that when random assignment and controls for causes other than race were in use, disadvantages to Blacks were consistently observed. The only plausible explanation for these repeatedly observed disadvantages is discrimination on the basis of race.[10]

But Is It Important?

All the findings of race discrimination described in this appendix merit serious consideration because they achieved the widely accepted standard of obtaining statistical significance. This standard, also known as the ".05 level," means that there is only a small probability (5 percent at most) of the finding having been obtained by chance if there really is no effect of race. But achieving the .05 level does not by itself mean that a finding is important.

To determine whether statistical significance translates to importance—meaning practical significance—one needs to know three things. First, does the finding involve an outcome that reasonable people would agree is consequential? Second, can it affect the same person repeatedly? Third, does it affect many people?

CONSEQUENTIAL OUTCOMES

Sending an innocent person to prison or failing to provide treatment that would prevent an avoidable limb amputation are without doubt consequential outcomes. So yes, in some of the studies described above the outcomes are ones that are obviously consequential.

However, some of the forms of discrimination examined in the research involved more minor consequences. Nevertheless, more minor consequences can be important if they are repeatedly encountered or if they happen to many people.

REPEATED SMALL EFFECTS

Consider an athletic practice routine that improves the athlete's performance by 1/100 of 1 percent per day. That is so small an improvement that there would be no way to detect it statistically in any study that lasted only a few days or even a few weeks. In a ten-second run by a world-class 100-meter sprinter, that improvement is 1/1,000th of a second—a millisecond, the time it takes to run a centimeter! Nevertheless, if this practice method is repeated with that same small benefit for two hundred days, the athlete's performance will have improved by two hundred milliseconds, which is two-tenths of a second. That is enough to be the difference between holding a world record and being an unnoticed also-ran. In the men's 100-meter race, 0.2 second is how long it takes to run 2 meters and also encompasses the summed differences among the men's 100-meter race's last six world records, extending back to 2002.

Many minor acts of discrimination can produce effects that are likewise too small to be noticed when they occur but which, if repeated many times, can accumulate in much the same way—only with negative effects, exacting a serious toll on the targets of the discrimination.[11]

Consider two groups of people, A and B, whom we follow through three years of professional education and three following years of employment. They all receive regular evaluations, such as by a supervisor who evaluates their work on a monthly basis. Assume also that each evaluation has a very high probability of success—99 percent—where success means continuing on their professional career path and failure means falling off that path. After six years of monthly evaluations, each with the same 99 percent probability of success, the overall survival is just under 50 percent, which seems reasonable as a six-year survival figure for demanding professional work.

To reveal what a very small difference between the evaluations of Groups A and B would mean, let us assume that Group A's predicted success rate is just 1 percent higher than Group B's. That translates to a predicted success rate of 99.5 percent for Group A and 98.5 percent for Group B. After six years of monthly evaluations, that tiny monthly difference will become huge. Elementary algebra is all that is needed to establish that Group A will end up with twice as many survivors (70 percent) as Group B (34 percent).[12]

This example may give some insight into why the percentages of minorities (and women) often drop off sharply over the course of the years between taking entry-level jobs and moving into the higher positions that can be reached only after extended service in an organization. The greater attrition of women and minorities could be the consequence of very small levels of differential treatment that are encountered repeatedly.

Another example of the consequences of repeated small effects: We might not worry much if a person is denied $10 because of discrimination. But if a person loses $10 per week over a forty-year career, that adds up to $70,000 (assuming 5 percent annual interest compounded monthly)—enough for a four-year college education at some public universities, a 20 percent down payment on a $350,000 home, or several new automobiles.

IMPACTS ON MANY PEOPLE

If small effects are experienced by many people, they can add up to something societally significant. We might not be very troubled about a single person being denied the opportunity to vote on one occasion due to discrimination, but if discrimination keeps many people from voting in an election, it can affect the outcome— especially if the contestants are closely matched.

As an example involving a more substantial impact that may affect many people, consider the possibility that discrimination is a partial contributor to the 10 percent difference in recent high school graduation rates for Whites (91 percent) and Blacks (81 percent) in the United States. For purposes of illustration, let us assume that discrimination is the cause of only one-tenth of this 10 percent Black-White difference. In other words, discrimination contributes 1 percent to the 10 percent White-Black difference in high school graduation rates. We can figure out what that 1 percent means when applied to the total American population. (To be clear: Neither we nor anyone else has data to say whether this 1 percent hypothesis about an effect of discrimination on high school graduation rates is accurate, too large, or too small.)

The U.S. Census Bureau reports that as of July 2009, there were 39.6 million Black Americans, 71.5 percent of whom— 28.3 million—were past high school age (18 or older). If the hypothetical figure of 1 percent is applied to these 28.3 million post-high-school-age Black Americans, that would mean that 283,000 of them would have been denied high school graduation because of discrimination. In other words, a relatively small effect of discrimination (10 percent of the difference in high school graduation rates) would have had very serious consequences for more than a quarter of a million Black Americans alive today.[13]

Expected Objections to Conclusion 2

Broad consensus among scientists on the nature of its supporting evidence notwithstanding, we expect Conclusion 2 to be controversial. Objections are likely to sound something like this: "If Person X doesn't want to hire a Black person (or rent to a Black person or give a Black person a mortgage loan), it has nothing to do with discriminating against someone who is Black. Rather, it has entirely to do with disqualifying characteristics that are more likely to be found in Black people than in White people." The objector may proceed to assert that, on average, Blacks have weaker job-relevant aptitudes, are less reliable in making monthly payments for rent or loan interest, and are less respectful of property. A final step in the argument might be: "If I had the opportunity to evaluate two people, one Black and one White, who were equal in job aptitude or in monthly-payment conscientiousness or in their respect for property, I would have no reason to prefer the White to the Black for hiring, renting, or giving a loan."

Many people are likely to use such reasoning to conclude, "I am color-blind when it comes to these choices. I do not discriminate." We can believe that this self-description is very often true. Nevertheless, three decades of experimental studies have established beyond doubt that when Black and White job or housing applicants are equally qualified on all attributes from which one might infer their relevant abilities and personal qualities, the White applicant receives a favorable outcome about twice as often as the Black applicant.

Consider those who have been in the role of real estate agent or potential employer in an audit study, facing one of the Black, White, or Hispanic matched testers dispatched by researchers to seek an apartment, home, or job. Those real estate agents and employers may honestly declare egalitarian values and assert that they are certain that they will be equally likely to choose a Black, White, or Hispanic when all are equally qualified. How, then, are we to explain the repeated finding in housing and employment audit studies that Blacks and Hispanics succeed noticeably less often in obtaining desired housing or jobs than do equally qualified Whites? In the following section we try to work further toward answering this question.

SEVEN CONCLUSIONS

THE CHALLENGE WE SET for this appendix was to state conclusions about American race relations that are regarded as valid by most social scientists. Here is the list, starting with the two already stated, and continuing with conclusions that have been developed previously in this book's chapters.

Conclusion 1: Black disadvantage exists. Compared to White Americans, Black Americans experience multiple consequential disadvantages—including, on average, less formal education, less satisfactory health care, less property ownership, less employment, less pay for the work they do, and higher rates of imprisonment.

Conclusion 2: The disadvantage experienced by Black Americans is at least partly due to race discrimination. The main business of this appendix has been to describe the broad range of evidence that establishes, beyond any doubt, that Black Americans experience race discrimination—disadvantage that is caused just by their being Black.

Conclusion 3: Social differentiation exists. Chapter 5 celebrated the mental virtuosity that allows humans to instantly sort people into highly distinctive categories—such as Black female Nigerian tap dancers or elderly White male Swedish furniture makers—and to immediately infer characteristics that they associate distinctly with these categories. Stereotyping is inseparable from this remarkably refined human ability to recognize and categorize human diversity.

Conclusion 4: Attitudes have both reflective and automatic forms. Attitudes are one's likes or dislikes for categories of people (lawyers, Muslims, Asians, babies, etc.). Chapter 4 described the sorting of attitudes into two types. Reflective or explicit attitudes are those that we are aware of having (for example, Mahzarin knows that she likes *Star Trek,* and Tony knows that he likes bebop), while automatic or implicit attitudes consist of associative knowledge for which we may lack awareness (for example, *old = bad,* shared by Tony, Mahzarin, and apparently 80 percent of everyone else). The two forms need not agree, which is a circumstance called dissociation. For example, explicit or reflective "I like elderly people" can exist in the same head with implicit *old = bad.*

Conclusion 5: People are often unaware of disagreement between the reflective and automatic forms of their own attitudes and stereo-types. The regularly observed disagreement between a person's IAT (implicit) results and survey question (explicit) results that can be observed when race attitudes are being assessed could mean that people deliberately misrepresent their views about race on question-naires. Although that must occasionally happen, we doubt it hap-pens much. Rather, we assume that in answering survey researchers' questions, most people try to respond accurately and honestly. However, they may also be unaware of having automatic attitudes that differ from their reflective attitudes.

Conclusion 6: Explicit bias is infrequent; implicit bias is perva-sive. Appendix 1 presented the evidence that early twenty-first-century Americans display low levels of explicit (overt) race prejudice in survey studies. This is a well-documented and striking reduction from the overt expressions of prejudice that were com-monplace in studies done fifty to seventy-five years previously. Even though present-day questionnaire studies show that most Ameri-cans now express egalitarian racial attitudes, uses of the IAT have revealed that approximately 75 percent of Americans display im-plicit (automatic) preference for White relative to Black. It is im-portant to understand that a race preference that is expressed only on the IAT is quite different from a personally endorsed racial at-titude. Nevertheless, as we saw in Chapter 3, implicit racial atti-tudes do have practical consequences, and this leads us to Conclusion 7.

Conclusion 7: Implicit race attitudes (automatic race preferences) contribute to discrimination against Black Americans. Of our seven conclusions, this is the only one that was not on the initial list for which we sought consensus from our colleagues. It was not there for a simple reason: As recently as four years ago, when we first circulated our list, no one—including ourselves—was aware of how extensive an accumulation of evidence there had been for Conclusion 7. But, as we described in Chapter 3, a sizable collec-tion of studies summarized in a 2009 journal publication made it clear that there now exists a substantial body of evidence that automatic White preference—as measured by the Race IAT—predicts discriminatory behavior even among people who fervently espouse egalitarian views. This evidence is far too substantial to ignore, and indeed, it has continued to accumulate steadily since early 2007 (the closing date for identifying studies that could be included in the 2009 meta-analytic review article).

Recent survey studies show that only 10 to 15 percent of Americans openly express prejudice against Black Americans. Yet as we have detailed in this appendix and in several chapters of the book, there is well-documented evidence of widespread acts of discrimination against Black Americans that have put them at a disadvantage in just about every economically significant domain of life. Although such discrimination could conceivably be due entirely to actions by the small minority of Americans who are overtly prejudiced, the evidence for the role played by implicit bias is too compelling for us to conclude that Black disadvantage is caused exclusively by explicit, overt prejudice. And, given the relatively small proportion of people who are overtly prejudiced and how clearly it is established that automatic race preference predicts discrimination, it is reasonable to conclude not only that implicit bias is a cause of Black disadvantage but also that it plausibly plays a greater role than does explicit bias in explaining the discrimination that contributes to Black disadvantage. Implicit bias may operate outside of awareness, hidden from those who have it, but the discrimination that it produces can be clearly visible to researchers, and almost certainly also clearly visible to those who are disadvantaged by it.[14]

ACKNOWLEDGMENTS

THE WRITING OF THIS BOOK HAS BENEFITED FROM THE IDEAS AND experiments of many people with whom we have worked during the past twenty-five years. No one is more central than Brian Nosek, who has been collaborator, steadfast colleague, and friend. His contributions to research on "implicit social cognition" (the technical name for our specialty) began upon his arrival as a graduate student at Yale in the summer of 1996 and continue to the present. With deepest gratitude and affection, we acknowledge his extensive contributions.

Since 1988, we have been the beneficiaries of partnerships with students and collaborators whose contributions have advanced understanding of this book's topics. Each has contributed pieces to a growing mosaic of the mind's operation outside conscious awareness: Richard Abrams, Scott Akalis, Bethany Albertson, Daniel Ames, Judy Andrews, Justin Angle, Jens Asendorpf, Rainer Banse, Yoav Bar-Anan, Andrew Baron, Irene Blair, Timothy Brock, Frederic Brunel, Huajian Cai, Susan Carey, Dana Carney (who suggested *Blindspot* as the title of this book), Siri Carpenter, Eugene Caruso, Daniel Chen, Eva Chen, Dolly Chugh, Emily Cogsdill, Juan Manual Contreras, Kathleen Cook, Lisa Cooper, Wil Cunningham, Dario Cvencek, Nilanjana (Buju) Dasgupta, Stanislas Dehaene, Thierry Devos, Christopher Dial, Claudiu Dimofte, Sean Draine, Ben Drury, Yarrow Dunham, Jeffrey Ebert, Shelly Farnham, Yuval Feldman, Christina Fong, Mark Forehand, Jerry Gillmore, Jack Glaser, Nicole Gleason, Stephanie Goodwin, Alex Green, Aiden Gregg, Elizabeth Haines, Curtis Hardin, Larisa Heiphetz, PJ Henry, Arnold Ho, Wilhelm Hofmann, Mary Lee Hummert, John Jost, Jerry Kang, Jocelyn Karlan, Kerry Kawakami, Do-Yeong Kim, Teri Kirby, Christoph Klauer, Mark Klinger, Chihiro Kobayashi, Linda Hamilton Krieger, Jennifer Kubota, Katie Lancaster, Kristin Lane, Keith Leavitt, Steven Lehr, Kristi Lemm, Dan Levin, Becca Levy, Eric Levy, Kristen Lindgren, Elizabeth Loftus, Dominika Maison, Steve McCullough, Jamaal McDell, Debbie McGhee, Paul Meinshausen, Deborah Mellott, Andrew Meltzoff, Jason Mitchell, Brandi Newell, Christelle Ngnoumen, Mark Oakes, Roisin O'Connor, Oludamini Ogunnaike, Kristina Olson, Andreas Olsson, Brian Ostafin, Marte Otten, Jaihyun Park, Lora Park, Andrew Perkins, Elizabeth Phelps, Jacqueline Pickrell, Brad Pinter, Andrew Poehlman, Doby Rahnev, Frederick Rivara, Alex Rothman, Laurie Rudman, Janice Sabin, Konrad Schnabel, Eric Schuh, Jordan Schwartz, Penelope Sheets, Alicia Shen, Kristin Shutts, Colin Smith, Kerry Spalding, Eric Spangenberg, Elizabeth Spelke, N. Sriram, Sameer Srivastava, Damian Stanley, Sabrina Sun, Jane Swanson, Christeine Terry, Brian Tietje, Eric Uhlmann, Piercarlo Valdesolo, Mark VandeKamp, Wendi Walsh, Greg Walton, Greg Willard, Caroline Wilmuth, Kaiyuan Xu, Susumu Yamaguchi, Vivian Zayas, and Talee Ziv.

As active audiences, a wide network of colleagues has helped to sharpen the ideas presented here. Our colleagues have provoked our thinking in discussions and correspondence, championed the work in various ways, or commented on our draft chapters, in some cases repeatedly. We are grateful beneficiaries of their engagement: Bob Abelson, Elliot Aronson, Visty Banaji, John Bargh, Ben Barres, Katherine Beckett, Marc Bendick, Mark Bennett, Danny Bernstein, Paul Bloom, Sam Bowles, Donal Carlston, Pam Casey, Sapna Cheryan, Nancy Cott, Robert Crowder, Jan DeHouwer, Patricia Devine, Ap Dijksterhuis, Ron Dotsch, Carol Dweck, Alice Eagly, Russell Fazio, Susan Fiske, Bill George, Daniel Gilbert, Malcolm Gladwell, Richard Gonzalez, Joshua Greene, David Hamilton, Jon Heron, Nancy Hopkins, Earl (Buz) Hunt, Shanto Iyengar, Larry Jacoby, Marcia Johnson, Christine Jolls, Lee Jussim, Cheryl Kaiser, John Kihlstrom, Meera Komarraju, Nancy Krieger, Jon Krosnick, John Lamberth, Ellen Langer, Larry Lessig, Jan Leu, Neil Macrae, William McGuire, Wendy Mendes, Philip Merikle, Walter Mischel, David Myers, Ken Nakayama, Maura O'Neill, Lee Osterhout, Thomas Pettigrew, Richard Petty, Steven Pinker, Scott Plous, Barbara Reskin, Dan-Olof Rooth, Peter Salovey, Laurie Santos, Giuseppe Sartori, Elaine Scarry, Frederick Schauer, David Schneider, Roger Shepard, Jeff Sherman, Jim Sherman, Yuichi Shoda, Jim Sidanius, Jane Simoni, Eliot Smith, Ron Smith, Claude Steele, Fritz Strack, Michael Tarr, Robert Trivers, Jim Uleman, Virginia Valian, Shankar Vedantam, Gifford Weary, Dan Wegner, Kip Williams, Karen Wynn, Richard Yalch, Robert Zajonc, and Michael Zárate.

The Radcliffe Institute for Advanced Study provided both of us a year in residence when it was most needed to establish the roots of the book (and a second year in residence to MRB). The Southern Poverty Law Center provided grant support early in the life of the website and many lessons on public outreach. Sabbaticals and monetary support were extended to MRB by Harvard University's Faculty of Arts and Sciences, Edmond J. Safra Center for the Study of Ethics, Institute for Quantitative Social Science, and Mind, Brain, Behavior Initiative. In addition, MRB also gratefully acknowledges support from the Bellagio Center of the Rockefeller Foundation, the Indian Institute for Advanced Study in Shimla, Russell Sage Foundation, Mind Science Institute, Wallace Foundation, and especially the Santa Fe Institute, which provided a haven for writing in the final stages of the book's completion.

Administrative staff and research assistants Sanden Averett, Christopher Dial, Michele Jacobs, William Kaplan (the observer of "outsmarting the machine"), Douglas Kalk, Jason McCoy, Tiffany Meites, Amanda Parsons, Elizabeth Rutherford, Roy Ruhling, and Shari Stout provided extraordinary support.

The Franklin Institute in Philadelphia, Le Laboratoire in Paris, the Museum of Natural History and Peabody Museum of Archaeology and Ethnology at Harvard, the Museum of Science and the Children's Museum in Boston, and the Exploratorium in San Francisco featured artistic renditions, stand-alone demonstrations of the IAT, or active data gathering and immediate sharing with visitors. In these locations as well as at our own website, visitors have provided us with the rewarding experience of observing their reactions as they confronted the hidden aspects of their own minds. Their curiosity and honesty have been an impetus to us to learn more, and they have our deepest admiration.

Several individuals have gone out of their way to support the work within universities, corporations, government agencies, and nonprofits, often in unexpected ways. They have made us see more directly than we ourselves could that these ideas have application to critical decisions that shape lives in the worlds of education, law, business, government, medicine, and any sphere where human beings make decisions about themselves and one another: Ian Ayres, Rohini Anand, Max Bazerman, Jeffrey Bewkes, Iris Bohnet, Sandra Bushby, Peter Cairo, Jim Carrier, Richard Cohen (the first to characterize implicit attitudes as "hidden biases"), Amy Edmonson, Mohamed El-Erian, Drew Faust, Pat Fili-Krushel, James Finberg, Hope Greenfield, Cintia Guimaraes, Lani Guinier, Jon Hanson, John Irwin, Mitchell Kapor, Freida Klein, Jennifer Lerner, Jay Light, Jim Lobsenz, Karen Mills, Amy Munichiello, Thomas Newkirk, Nitin Noria, Julie Oyegun, Eva Paterson, Lisa Quiroz, Judith Resnik, Louis Scenti, Susan Silbermann, Judith Singer, Michael Smith, Jim Turley, Alessandro Zanello, and Nina Zipser.

The National Science Foundation supported an initial five years of research, during which time we developed the Implicit Association Test (IAT); the National Institute of Mental Health supported the next eight years of this research. Yale University and University of Washington supported the 1998 launch of the website where the IAT was first made widely available as an educational demonstration. The website soon moved exclusively to Yale University, where Phil Long invested resources of the Yale Computing Center to realize our dream of web-based education and research. Starting in 2003, this Internet enterprise migrated to Harvard University, which has generously contributed to support the educational and research sites that continue to operate at implicit.harvard .edu.

In 2005, together with Brian Nosek, we established a not-for-profit corporation, Project Implicit, which has provided scientific support that also sustains the operation of the website, which presently resides at implicit.harvard.edu. Sean Draine created and developed software (Inquisit) that made it feasible to rapidly implement the IAT in hundreds of experiments. We recognize with gratitude his cheerful responses to our many requests for specialized procedures that allowed speedy improvement of experimental designs and made experiments easily transportable across laboratories for replication.

Toni Burbank at Random House first saw potential in these ideas and has special thanks from us. Our writing received in-depth advice from Roger Lewin and Beth Rashbaum, who found opportunities to help us write less academically. Will Murphy, our editor at Random House, demanded more from us than we considered necessary at the time, and we are grateful for his hand in the final shaping of the book. The publishing world witnessed changes as we went through successive drafts, making us aware of the expertise that publishers and editors commit to cultivating the interface of scientists with general audiences. Katinka Matson and John Brockman have our gratitude not only for representing us, but also for creating a forum for presenting science to the public that did not exist before they imagined it.

Over the years spent writing this book, three people provided unwavering moral and intellectual support: R. Bhaskar, Jean Greenwald, and Richard Hackman were unfailing in their support, and they will surely be glad not to have to inquire about our progress any further. They will also recognize tangible evidence of their influence in the ideas and even the words that constitute this book.

Our parents, Coomi and Rustom Banaji and Bernice and Bernard Greenwald, surely had blindspots when it came to us. Their aspirations for us, along with those of other members of our families—Papa Ayah; Bella Banaji Lodha and Nitin Lodha; Rukhshad Banaji and Nandita Shinkre Banaji; Leah, David, and Jonathan Greenwald; Emily Greenwald, Lauren Greenwald, and Joe Welsh; Eric Greenwald and Marjorie Clifton; Charlotte (Charlie), Julia, and Ben Welsh; Ann Alexander and Richard Khanlian—have sustained and nourished us.

The power of ideas cuts across age, gender, ethnicity, religion, culture, and nationality to bring minds together in the search for something larger than the limitations these categories typically afford. To each other we can simply say that we are fully aware of our good fortune in having found a kindred spirit in the other. It is not easy to imagine an alternative intellectual existence that could have been superior.

NOTES

1 Mindbugs

1   Kurt VanLehn, a computer scientist at Arizona State University, coined the term *mind bugs* to describe systematic errors that young children make when learning arithmetic. Asked to subtract 169 from 207, for example, beginners will frequently make carrying errors, resulting in an answer of 48 instead of 38. Such systematic errors are simply examples of glitches in the brain's software. (See VanLehn, 1990.) Arithmetic mindbugs cause children to stumble when learning to subtract. We use the term mindbugs to refer to a broad category of cognitive and social errors that are observed in children and adults, and that we assume have a basis in our evolutionary past as well as our cultural and individual histories. We have taken to so overusing the term *mindbugs* that we have turned it into both a single word and an entire chapter.

2   Living in a three-dimensional world, our ancestors had little need to evolve a visual mechanism for understanding the two-dimensional worlds they would themselves create by drawing on the walls of caves, on papyrus, and eventually on tablet personal computers—long after the evolution of the visual system had stabilized in a 3-D universe, sometime between 600 and 500 million years ago (Lamb, 2007). The legs of the tables tell us that the tabletops are surfaces in the horizontal plane, parallel with the floor. Our brains know from much experience, and perhaps even from innate wiring of our visual systems, that the vertical retinal size of a horizontal surface underestimates its extent in depth, so our unconscious inferences oblige by magnifying that dimension. This correction for foreshortening lengthens the long dimension of the tabletop on the left and the short dimension of the one on the right.

3   Even though it is quite true that being assured that the tabletops are identical doesn't render them identical to our mind, there is an odd experience, quite unpredicted, that one of us has experienced. After several hundred visualizations, Mahzarin does see the tables as more nearly the same than she did before. Now when she puts up a slide of the tables, she needs to check with others to make sure that they do indeed perceive them as dissimilar! Is this room for optimism about overcoming a mindbug—that perhaps even a mindbug so deeply ingrained may be correctable through repeated exposure to the correct answer?

[4]   Helmholtz, 1924.

[5]   Edward Adelson's checkershadow illusion and many others may be obtained by visiting web.mit.edu/persci/people/adelson.

[6]   Gallo, Roediger, & McDermott, 2001; Roediger & Gallo, 2002. You might argue, as a good critic would, that an error of this sort may not occur when the incident is a real one that has obvious and important consequences, such as witness reports of events like accidents, robberies, or murders. Unfortunately, this doesn't seem to be the case. Researchers have set up realistic enactments in which accidents and thefts are perpetrated in the course of natural life with tests of memory following the events. One of the more troubling aspects of this memory mindbug is the surprisingly weak correspondence between one's confidence in one's memory for the event and the accuracy of one's memory: Those who remember with the greatest confidence are not necessarily those who have the greatest accuracy. Unlike the memory experiment with insect-related terms, in which explicit instructions to memorize the list for later recall were given and memory was tested only a few minutes later, most real-life circumstances do not come with instructions to expect a test, nor does the test occur so soon. On top of that, the real world contains many more information contaminants that can trigger memory mindbugs.

[7]   Loftus & Palmer, 1974.

[8]   Innocence Project (www.innocenceproject.org/understand/Eyewitness-Misidentification .php); Garrett, 2011.

[9]   Tversky & Kahneman, 1973. If you find such studies interesting, you can explore further in Gilovich, Griffin, & Kahneman, 2002. Daniel Kahneman has also written a more popular book about the research he and his colleague Amos Tversky have done on thinking, which has had profound influence on the mind and decision sciences; see Kahneman, 2011.

[10] Ariely, 2009.

[11] Tversky & Kahneman, 1974.

[12] Marsat & Williams, 2009; Northcraft & Neale, 1987.

[13] The brain regions that are so far implicated in perceiving and understanding the minds of others are: the medial prefrontal cortex (mPFC), the posterior superior temporal sulcus (pSTS), and the adjacent temporoparietal junction (TPJ). See Frith, 2007.

[14] Reyes, Thompson, & Bower, 1980.

[15] This result was presented by Norbert Schwarz in a lecture given at Yale University (and confirmed via personal communication). For other such studies, see Schwarz, Bless, Strack, Klumpp, Rittenauer-Schatka, & Simons, 1991.

[16] Todorov, Mandisodza, Goren, & Hall, 2005. In this paper, the authors show that a one-second exposure to faces of each contestant in the 2004 Senate elections could predict the victor in an election much better than chance (68.8 percent).

[17] Susan Fiske has shown that two basic dimensions capture the way we think about social groups. First, we ask, how warm or cold are they, i.e., do we like them? Second, we ask, how competent or incompetent are they, i.e., how effectively can they act on their intentions? Fiske, Cuddy, & Glick, 2007.

[18] Most of these experiments have involved imaging the brain while people make simple predictions about people they have never met and know nothing much about. Mitchell et al., 2004; Mitchell et al., 2005a; Mitchell et al., 2005b.

[19] Bernard Madoff was convicted in June 2009 of having operated a massive Ponzi scheme that defrauded investors out of approximately $65 billion (Creswell & Thomas, 2009). In his analysis, Michael Shores suggests that group affinity was involved in the prevalence of Jews in the group that was defrauded (Shores, 2010).

[20] Powell, 2009.

[21] The mistaken shooting of Omar Edwards is not an isolated event. Both innocent Black citizens and Black policemen are mistakenly shot by police officers out of proportion to their numbers. And laboratory research evidence shows the higher likelihood of mistaken "firing" at Blacks than Whites in a video-game-like setting requiring rapid decisions in response to figures seen carrying either guns or harmless objects (Correll, Park, Judd, & Wittenbrink, 2002).

[22] Levy, Zonderman, Slade, & Ferrucci, 2009.

[23] Simon, 1983.

2 Shades of Truth

[1] The Dostoyevsky quote is from *Notes from Underground*, which is available in many translated editions.

[2] If you've got your own answer to Q7 *(How many drinks do you have per day?)*, you might want to evaluate it in terms of the drink-counting standards of medical research. A standard drink consists of 1.25 fl. oz. of 80 proof (40 percent alcohol) hard liquor, 5 fl. oz. of wine (12 percent alcohol), or 12 fl. oz. of beer (6 percent alcohol). It is difficult to miscount bottles of beer, but quite easy to pour more than 5 fl. oz. into a wineglass and even easier to pour twice the standard 1.25-fl.-oz. shot of 80-proof liquor into a glass in which you mix a cocktail. Strangely, these standard drinks differ in their pure (200 proof) alcohol equivalents—0.5 fl. oz. for 80-proof liquor, 0.6 fl. oz. for 24-proof wine, and 0.72 fl. oz. for 12-proof beer. The lesson is clear: If you wish to maximize self-dosage of alcohol while being scrupulously honest in the number of drinks you report to your doctor, drink beer.

[3] Evolutionary accounts of human deception can be found in books by Trivers (1985) and Smith (2004). Evidence showing rapid evolutionary change in human genes has been found in studies that have been made possible by the recent development of methods to describe the human genome. Although those studies have yet to focus on genes associated with behavioral traits, they have shown rapid change in genes associated with protection against sickle-cell anemia, post-weaning lactase production, and starch digestion (Allison, 1964; Enarrah et al., 2008; Perry et al., 2007). We thank Jon C. Herron, Robert Trivers, and Steven Pinker for pointing us to work on the pace of human evolution.

[4] Relevant to Q8, Abelson, Loftus, and Greenwald (1992) found that a surprisingly large number of registered voters reported, in response to a telephone-administered survey, that they had voted in an election that was held just a few days previously. But a later check of the official polling records revealed that many of them had not voted.

[5] The term impression management was introduced in an article by Tedeschi, Schlenker, and Bonoma (1971).

[6] There are many studies that report self-enhancing biases in self-reports of age, height, weight, income, education, and various health indicators (e.g., Rowland, 1990; Spencer, Appleby, Davey, & Key, 2002).

[7]   Another method for establishing honesty that is used by government agencies in screening potential employees who might need access to classified documents is the polygraph or "lie detector." Scientifically, it is well known that the polygraph is at best a weak device for distinguishing truth-telling from lying. This is why polygraph evidence is rejected by most courts (Saxe & Ben-Shakhar, 1999). Nevertheless, polygraphs have some effective use because of widespread public (mis)belief in their effectiveness. When the person hooked up to the polygraph accepts its efficacy as a lie detector, that person is much more likely to give truthful responses. This truth-eliciting function of the polygraph has been demonstrated in studies that used bogus contraptions portrayed as lie detectors to produce increased truthfulness in responding (see Jones & Sigall, 1971).

[8]   The study using Q14 and Q15 was by McConahay, Hardee, and Batts (1981). The history of question-asking methods in investigations of race bias is described in this book's Appendix 1.

3 Into the Blindspot

[1]   A small variation of the diamonds and spades versus clubs and hearts task turns out to be remarkably easy for experienced bridge players. Bridge players learn to group hearts and spades together as "major" suits—those two suits have greater point value than the "minor" suits of diamonds and clubs. This established knowledge gives bridge players an easy rule—minor suits left, major suits right—for sorting diamonds and clubs (not spades) to the left, and hearts and spades (not clubs) to the right. Try it. If you are a bridge player, it will be easy.

[2]   The concept of association has a long history in philosophy and psychology. It appeared in Aristotle's writings and was central to the writings of several eighteenth-century British philosophers, among them David Hume, John Locke, and John Stuart Mill. Association became a central concept in modern psychology with the work of behaviorist psychologists of the first half of the twentieth century, including Edward Lee Thorndike, Ivan Pavlov, John Watson, and Edwin Guthrie.

[3]   The order in which the two parts of the IAT are done *can* have a small effect. If you were just slightly slower on the second sheet, that could have been due to processing changed instructions for the second task. But research done more than fifteen years ago established that this "task order" effect could account for only a small amount of slowing on the second task.

[4]   The verse about flowers is from "The Crescent Moon" by Rabindranath Tagore. The verses about insects are from "What to Do When a Bug Climbs in Your Mouth," by Rick Walton.

[5]   The IAT was first published in an article by Tony together with two University of Washington graduate students, Debbie McGhee and Jordan Schwartz, who helped greatly with the experiments that were reported in the article (Greenwald, McGhee, & Schwartz, 1998). A few years before that first publication of the IAT, Brian Nosek arrived as a PhD student working in Mahzarin's laboratory at Yale. Brian was the primary force behind the September 1998 launch of the Internet demonstration site for the IAT, and ever since, he has guided that site's operation. Brian has also been a continuing fount of important research findings concerning the IAT, not to mention a treasure as a research collaborator and colleague.

[6]   The 75 percent figure for the proportion showing automatic White preference comes from the many people who have completed the Race IAT at the Project Implicit website. As large as this sample is, it is not a representative sample of the American population, so it is necessary to be cautious in declaring that the figure characterizes America as a whole. However, the 75 percent figure was found to apply—with only minor variations— to almost all demographic subgroups of those who have taken the Race IAT. The one striking exception is those who self-describe as either fully or partly African American— only about one-third of that group shows automatic White preference on the Race IAT.

[7]   As a method for combining findings across multiple studies, the value of meta-analysis has been most effectively established in drawing conclusions from collections of studies that evaluate effectiveness of medical therapies. The Michigan State study that provided the first "predictive validity" test of the Race IAT was by McConnell and Leibold (2001). The other predictive validity results briefly described in the text were from studies by Ziegert and Hanges (2005), Green et al. (2007), and Hugenberg and Bodenhausen (2003). The IAT meta-analysis appears in Greenwald, Poehlman, Uhlmann, and Banaji (2009).

    Soon after the development of the first IAT, additional IAT measures were rapidly developed, including ones to gauge automatic preferences for young relative to old, heterosexual relative to gay/lesbian, thin relative to fat, and (in Germany) German relative to Turkish ethnicity. The meta-analysis included thirty studies that used IAT measures of automatic preferences for social category contrasts other than Black-White race. These additional studies likewise supported the conclusion that IAT measures predicted discrimination. The demonstrations of predictive validity of the Race IAT from studies reported since the published meta-analysis were reported by Greenwald, Smith, Sriram, Bar-Anan, and Nosek (2009); Lynch (2010); and Penner et al. (2010).

[8]   The method for translating correlation numbers into practical judgment outcomes was first described by Rosenthal and Rubin (1982). It is no accident that the difference between 65 percent and 35 percent is .30, which is also the correlation number. If the predictive value of the credit-rating score was poorer—let's say it was at the conventional "small" value of .10—you could expect instead that only 55 percent of the top half of the credit scorers would pay enough to be profitable, compared to 45 percent for those in the bottom half (difference = .10). If the correlation were large (.50), the numbers would instead be 75 percent and 25 percent (difference = .50). This method of converting correlations to percentage expectations applies to a situation in which you can expect that half of those for whom you have scores on a predictor measure will produce the outcome that you seek to predict.

[9]   Since introduction of the Race IAT in 1998 we have received and answered many questions about its interpretation. The most frequent questions and their answers are available at the Internet site at which one can experience the IAT (implicit.harvard.edu/ implicit/demo/background/faqs.html). For current information on the validity of the IAT, visit faculty.washington.edu/agg/iat_validity.htm.

4 "Not That There's Anything Wrong with That!"

[1]   Nisbett & Wilson, 1977.

[2]   Zajonc, 1980.

[3]   Vedantam, 2005.

[4]   The activist, who had originally offered to be identified in the article, chose to withhold her name given her test result. The feelings evoked by the test's result are themselves of interest and we give fuller consideration to them later in the chapter.

[5]   Chesterton, 1908. The British writer and journalist commented on the difficulty of self-awareness by saying, "One may understand the cosmos, but never the ego; the self is more distant than any star."

[6]   Gladwell, 2007.

[7]   Festinger, 1957; also see Trivers, 2000. Today, we know that states of cognitive dissonance create predictable neural responses; in one study by van Veen et al. (2009), greater activation in the dorsal anterior cingulate and anterior insula (regions involved in resolving conflict that arises from competing responses) predicted how much a person's attitude changed. (In this study, as in many classic dissonance studies, participants are asked to tell another subject that an extremely boring task they themselves just completed was actually quite pleasant.)

[8]   Ayan, 2008.

[9]   Bargh, 1997.

[10]   Johnson, Kim, & Risse, 1985. The particular form of forgetting involved here is referred to as anterograde amnesia and involves damage to the brain's medial temporal lobe.

[11]   Lynch, 2010. The videos used in the study may be found at www.ehbonline.org/article/PIIS1090513809000683/addOns.

[12]   Nelson, 2002.

[13]   Nosek, Smyth, et al., 2007.

[14]   Analysis of data from Asian countries was motivated in part by the Western belief that Asians have greater respect for their elderly than do Americans or Europeans.

[15]   "When I'm Sixty-Four" is a song written by Paul McCartney when he was sixteen years old (credited as Lennon-McCartney, 1967, on the album *Sgt. Pepper's Lonely Hearts Club Band*).

[16]   Hummert, Garstka, et al., 2002.

[17]   The website originally appeared as www.implicit.yale.edu, when Mahzarin taught at Yale. In 2003 it migrated to Harvard. Both universities have identified with and supported the site in numerous ways for which we are duly grateful.

[18]   Attributed to Akutagawa, in his diaries.

[19]   "Racist Dawg" was the twentieth episode of Season 7 of *King of the Hill*.

5 *Homo Categoricus*

[1]   Walter Lippmann introduced "stereotype" in his 1922 book *Public Opinion*.

[2]   The earliest publication that we could identify as an experimental study of stereotypes was by Rice (1926). In a study of judgments made after his Dartmouth undergraduate student subjects viewed face photographs, Rice concluded that perceptions of face photographs were so influenced by stereotypes that errors in personnel judgments occurred.

The 2001 replication of the Princeton study (Katz & Braly, 1933) was by Madon et al. (2001). Although the change from 1933 to 2001 might in part be due to geographic or cultural differences between Princeton and the location of the 2001 study (Iowa), social psychologist and present-day Princeton professor Susan Fiske reports that current Princeton students also no longer credit racial and ethnic minorities with the negative qualities that their predecessors so freely assigned.

[3] Allport's statement about the importance of categories appears in his *Nature of Prejudice* (Allport, 1954). A collection of modern perspectives on Allport's contributions to understanding stereotypes and prejudice was published in a fiftieth-anniversary celebration of the book (Dovidio, Glick, & Rudman, 2005). A contemporary overview of scientific work on stereotypes is available in a comprehensive text by David Schneider (2004).

[4] The label for Feat 3—"leaping beyond the available information"—is borrowed from an influential essay by cognitive psychologist Jerome Bruner, "Going beyond the information given" (Bruner, 1957).

[5] The supposition that stereotypes captured by the methods of the 1933 Princeton study consist of traits characteristic of men (not women) of the various national groups was later tested and confirmed in research by social psychologists Alice Eagly and Mary Kite (1987).

[6] Many sources report that sex ratios in ducks, estimated by a variety of methods, show that males are in the majority (e.g., Brown, 1982).

[7] The use of "Ducks lay eggs" to illustrate the extent to which a statement that properly applies to "some" (ducks in this case) may be inappropriately applied to "most" is borrowed from illustrations used by cognitive psychologist Sam Glucksberg (Khemlani, Glucksberg, & Rubio Fernandez, 2007).

[8] The self-fulfilling prophecy aspect of stereotypes about the elderly has been described by Levy (2009). The self-fulfilling aspect of female and African American stereotypes has received attention in a large body of recent research on stereotype threat, especially by Claude Steele and his colleagues (Steele, Spencer, & Aronson, 2002).

6 The Hidden Costs of Stereotypes

[1] The strength of the obligatory nature of the riddle was brought home to us recently by a friend of Mahzarin's. Alice, as we'll call her, is a diversity trainer in a large multinational corporation. When she went in to conduct training with a senior partner, he gave her the doctor riddle we mentioned in Chapter 5. Alice was stumped when asked how it could be that a man had died in an accident and yet his surviving son's surgeon was claiming to be the boy's parent. Being resourceful, Alice began to think about how this could be possible; first she suggested that the surgeon could be the boy's biological father (rather than the adoptive father who had died in the accident). When told that was not the correct answer, Alice wondered if perhaps the surgeon was also a minister or priest and was using the term "my son" in that way. The fact that Alice didn't immediately see that the surgeon who said "He is my son" was a woman mortified her. To us, it is a highly instructive moment because it shows just how obligatory stereotypic interpretations can be. You can imagine the laughter that commenced her training of the partner in the craft of diversity.

[2]   Katz & Braly, 1933; Madon, Guyll, Aboufadel, Montiel, Smith, Palumbo, & Jussim, 2001.

[3]   Jacoby, Kelley, Brown, & Jasechko, 1989.

[4]   Zawitz & Strom, 2000.

[5]   Staples, 1986. This story of Staples lent itself to the title of a book by psychologist Claude Steele, who used it to speak about the power of stereotypes to shape performance (Steele, 2010). Here's the poignant comment by Staples: "And on late-evening constitutionals along streets less traveled by, I employ what has proved to be an excellent tension-reducing measure: I whistle melodies from Beethoven and Vivaldi and the more popular classical composers. Even steely New Yorkers hunching toward nighttime destinations seem to relax and occasionally they even join in the tune. Virtually everybody seems to sense that a mugger wouldn't be warbling bright, sunny selections from Vivaldi's *Four Seasons*. It is my equivalent to the cowbell that hikers wear when they know they are in bear country."

[6]   Meissner & Brigham, 2001.

[7]   In fact, Kurt Hugenberg and Galen Bodenhausen have shown that when Whites perceive racially ambiguous faces that are frowning versus smiling, they tend to perceive the former as more likely to be Black and the latter as more likely to be White. Interestingly, this bias is related to the IAT race bias: Those who have stronger anti-Black preferences are more likely to show the perceptual bias of judging faces based on expression (Hugenberg & Bodenhausen, 2003; Hugenberg & Bodenhausen, 2004).

[8]   There is the additional possibility that race stereotypes may make a seen object transfer hands. In 1945, Gordon Allport and Leo Postman conducted a study in which they presented an image of two subway travelers, one Black and the other White, with the White man holding a knife in his hand. A description of the article was transmitted to others, who then transmitted it to yet others. After six generations of such transmission, Allport and Postman reported a 50 percent switch in the knife from the White to the Black traveler. See Allport & Postman, 1947.

[9]   Correll, Park, Judd, & Wittenbrink, 2002. See also Greenwald, Oakes, & Hoffman, 2003; Payne, 2006.

[10]   The more recent shooting of a young Black man, Trayvon Martin, by a neighborhood vigilante hasn't yet gone to trial, but it also involves an error in which the shooter mistakenly assumed that Martin was dangerous when in fact he was unarmed (and later discovered to be carrying only a bag of Skittles and an iced tea). See Barry, Kovaleski, Robertson, & Alvarez, 2012.

[11]   Rich, 1999.

[12]   Details of the case are from reports in *Time* (September 2000) and Dan Stober and Ian Hoffman's book *A Convenient Spy* (2001).

[13]   Gilbert, 1991.

[14]   For this reason "innocent until proven guilty" is a principle that must be consciously implemented; it doesn't occur naturally.

[15]   Steele, 1997; Steele, 2010.

[16]   There are many potential reasons for gender parity at this time, including the loss of

jobs, starting with the 2008 recession, in the construction and manufacturing sectors that employ more men, but it does look as though gender parity in the workplace is here to stay; see Bureau of Labor Statistics reports at www.bls.gov/cps/wlf-intro-2009.htm and http://www.bls.gov/cps/wlf-databook-2006.pdf. It should also be noted that women are far more likely than men to be doing part-time work, do not draw the same benefits, and are compensated 80 percent of what men are compensated. See the gender wage gap report from the Institute for Women's Policy Research at www.iwpr.org.

[17]   The gender-career IAT is a measure of automatic stereotype, which is not the same thing as a gender preference (or attitude) test, which measures the association of *male* and *female* with *good* and *bad*. On the latter test, *female* is more associated with *good* than with *bad* (relative to *male*), especially by women.

[18]   Nosek, Banaji, & Greenwald, 2002a.

[19]   Some IATs, such as the gender-career test, in showing that younger people are less biased than older people signal a shift in cultural stereotypes that is encouraging, if one is of the opinion that equality in mental association is a step toward equality in action. The lack of an equivalent age effect on the Race IAT, though, is surprising, given that younger people do express less biased views about race and parents often tell us that they view their children to be more race-neutral than they themselves are. So why do older and younger Americans look identical in their race preferences? Why is there no greater neutrality of attitude among the young? One possible answer is that women have entered the workforce in sufficiently large numbers that daily experience has translated into lowering automatic gender stereotypes in younger minds. By contrast, racial groups in the United States are still substantively segregated in housing, in professions, and in friendship patterns. That being the case, even young Americans have not had the experiences that are needed to achieve parity in racial preferences, at least implicit preferences.

[20]   Rudman & Heppen, 2003.

[21]   Rudman is careful to note that, this being a correlation, the opposite possibility remains open: that women less inclined to want personal power and professional satisfaction may be more likely to develop this fantasy view of their partner.

[22]   Caruso, Rahnev, & Banaji, 2009.

[23]   Dolly Chugh coined the term *stereotype tax* to capture the penalty that is levied upon oneself for holding the stereotype (Chugh, 2004).

[24]   Jost & Banaji, 1994. Also see Jost, Banaji, & Nosek, 2004.

[25]   Nosek, Banaji, & Greenwald, 2002b.

[26]   Smyth, Greenwald, & Nosek, 2009.

[27]   Kay, Gaucher, Peach, Zanna, & Spencer, 2008.

[28]   In Kanner's 1943 study of a small group of children with autistic syndrome, there were four times as many boys as girls. In their much larger study of Asperger syndrome in mainstream schools in Sweden in 1993, Ehlers and Gillberg found the same male-to-female ratio of 4:1.

[29]   Goldstein & Stocking, 1994.

[30]   Spelke, 2005. See also Ceci & Williams, 2007.

[31]   Nosek et al., 2009.

7 Us and Them

[1] See Bowles and Gintus, 2011. Also, Steven Pinker offers evidence for the idea of decreasing violence in the world, but he doesn't say that the levels today are tolerable. In fact, reading his book only reminded us further of our gruesome past, the continued dissatisfaction with our state today, and the struggle toward civility (Pinker, 2011).

[2] Hoffman, 1996.

[3] Grier, Counter, & Shearer, 1967.

[4] Breger, 1974.

[5] A good review of the work on face processing in infants can be found in Pascalis & Kelly, 2009.

[6] Quinn, Yahr, Kuhn, Slater, & Pascalis, 2002; Banaji & Heiphetz, 2010.

[7] Park & Rothbart, 1982.

[8] Sangrigoli & de Schonen, 2004.

[9] Looking time is a standard measure in research with infants, developed by Fantz (1964) and used extensively since (Spelke, 1985), in spite of some criticisms.

[10] Kinzler, Dupoux, & Spelke, 2007.

[11] Devine, 1995.

[12] Baron, Dunham, Banaji, & Carey, 2009.

[13] Thomson, 1975.

[14] Olsson, Ebert, Banaji, & Phelps, 2005.

[15] Öhman, 2005.

[16] Tajfel, 1970.

[17] Tajfel, Billig, Bundy, & Flament, 1971; but see Gaertner & Insko, 2001.

[18] Since the original minimal group experiment, hundreds of other studies have been conducted that verify the fact of minimal group discrimination. Telling people they are Kandinsky lovers while others are Klee lovers is sufficient to make one group discriminate against the other. Teachers can routinely create it in their classrooms by simply making the left side and right side of the class see themselves as two groups.

[19] Abrams, Frings, & de Moura, 2005.

[20] Mitchell, Macrae, & Banaji, 2006.

[21] Kelley, Macrae, Wyland, Caglar, Inati, & Heatherton, 2002.

8 Outsmarting the Machine

[1] Thanks to William Kaplan for the insight that became this chapter's title.

[2] A Dutch website, www.muzieklijstjes.nl/100players.htm, presents a listing of the one hundred greatest instrumental virtuosos. All of the top ten are men—the names given in the text. Of the top twenty-five, twenty-three are men. Of the top fifty, forty-four are men. Nine of the fifteen women in the top hundred were in the last thirty places.

³ This symphony orchestra example also appears in Malcolm Gladwell's (2005) tribute to automatic mental processes, *Blink*. The screen was adopted by the Boston Symphony Orchestra in 1952, well before other orchestras. Both historical and statistical analyses of time trends in hiring of women by orchestras were documented in an article by Goldin and Rouse (2000). Goldin and Rouse also pointed out that the proportion of women graduating from music conservatories increased along with the increase in hiring, but the rate of increase in graduations was much too small to explain women's increased success after blind auditions were adopted.

⁴ The research using exposure to admirable Black Americans and admirable elders was reported by Dasgupta and Greenwald (2001). Because of the way the IAT is designed, the finding described as weakened *White = good* associations could equally have been described as strengthened *Black = good* associations, strengthened *White = bad* associations, and/or weakened *Black = bad* associations. As we explained in Chapter 3, this is because the IAT assesses the relative strengths of these associations rather than the absolute strengths of each.

⁵ Irene Blair's research was reported in Blair, Ma, and Lenton (2001). Blair also provided a useful review of others' research that had demonstrated similar brief interventions that effectively modified implicit attitudes and stereotypes in laboratory studies (Blair, 2002).

⁶ The spider phobia study was by Teachman and Woody (2003).

⁷ The studies showing that women's *female = leader* and *self = leader* associations could be strengthened by exposure to women role models on a college campus were by Dasgupta and Asgari (2004) and by Asgari, Dasgupta, and Cote (2010). Studies showing that women's *female = math* and *self = math* associations could be strengthened by sustained exposure to women mathematicians and engineers were reported by Stout, Dasgupta, Hunsinger, and McManus (in press). Phelan (2010) recently completed a similar study involving *female = science* and *self = science* associations in which the subjects were high school girls. The Wisconsin study involving the Race IAT is by Devine, Forscher, Austin, and Cox (2011).

⁸ "Pit bull" encompasses multiple breeds and may also be applied to various mixtures. This flexibility of the pit bull label can itself influence the publicity received by pit bulls. Consider a dog bred as a 50:50 mixture of American pit bull terrier and Labrador retriever. If this mixed-breed dog protects a child by aggressively driving off a threatening person, its pit bull parentage may be left unmentioned in the local news report. But if it should bite a child, the odds are that it will be reported as a pit bull, with no mention of the other 50 percent of its parentage.

Confident estimates of the number of pit bulls in the United States and of the proportion of dog bites attributable to pit bulls are difficult to come by. The information about pit bulls in Seattle was gleaned from hwwright.pbworks.com/f/1.6.08PitBullPopulationgraph.doc and www.kirotv.com/news/14354189/detail.html.

⁹ Some recent attention to testing of pit bulls for aggressiveness was generated in the wake of the highly publicized arrest and prosecution, in 2007, of professional football quarterback Michael Vick for operating an illegal dog fighting operation. Vick's case focused on forty-nine pit bulls who were discovered at the time of his arrest. Under supervision of a federal court and the American Society for the Prevention of Cruelty to Animals (ASPCA), all of these dogs were tested for aggressiveness. Only one of the forty-nine

was deemed a candidate for euthanasia because of aggressiveness. The other forty-eight qualified for rescue and rehabilitation. About half of these pit bulls were eventually judged fit for adoption, and most of those were subsequently placed with families in which they became most welcome as pets. The remaining ones were judged to have suffered sufficient mistreatment while in Vick's possession to raise questions about the likelihood of their successful adoption as pets—those others have remained in shelters. More detail on the evaluation and relocation of these pit bulls can be found at www. badrap.org/vick-dogs.

[10] Several other competitive sports have taken steps in recent years to minimize subjectivity in their more challenging refereeing decisions. In tennis, ice hockey, gridiron football, and basketball, video replay analysis has come very close to eliminating subjectivity from difficult judgments. Further detail on the skating scandal can be found at en.wikipedia.org/wiki/2002_Olympic_Winter_Games_figure_skating_scandal.

[11] Gaertner and Dovidio's concept of aversive racism and its relation to in-group favoritism can be found in Gaertner et al. (1977). Brewer (1999) has similarly identified an important role for in-group favoritism in discrimination. The Matthew effect was described by Merton (1968). The biblical reference is to a passage in Matthew (25:29). "Unto every one that hath shall be given, and he shall have abundance: but from him that hath not shall be taken away even that which he hath." Actions that selectively help those with whom one has an in-group connection were treated as a major class of ethical problems in a *Harvard Business Review* article by Banaji, Bazerman, and Chugh (2003).

[12] See the research by Levy (2009) on health in the elderly and the research (mentioned in Chapter 5) by Steele, Spencer, and Aronson (2002) on stereotype threat affecting African Americans.

[13] Cheryan, Plaut, Davies, and Steele, 2009.

Appendix 1 Are Americans Racist?

[1] "1959 Tuskegee Institute Lynch Report," *Montgomery Advertiser,* April 26, 1959, reprinted in *100 Years of Lynching* by Ralph Ginzburg (1962, 1988).

[2] The original sources of these procedures to measure race bias are Bogardus (1925, 1928), Thurstone (1928), and Hinckley (1932).

[3] Surveys of race attitudes have been done regularly by the National Opinion Research Center, the Gallup Poll, and the Institute for Survey Research. The time trends in responses can be found in the book by Schuman, Steeh, Bobo, and Krysan (1997). Over the last half of the twentieth century, declining race bias like that shown in regard to segregation in housing and education (Figure 5) has been observed also in responses to questions about segregation in public places and in commercial establishments, as well as in responses to questions about the acceptability of a Black presidential candidate, approval of racial intermarriage, and support for equal opportunity in employment. The flat pattern of steady opposition to government intervention to benefit minorities (Figure 6) appears additionally in affirmative action questionnaires toward Blacks in college admissions and in job hiring. For the two questions in Figure 6, survey respondents had a noncommittal option. Half of the noncommittal responses were included in the rejection percentages shown in the figure.

[4] In Appendix 2 we consider large bodies of evidence showing that America's playing

fields are considerably less than level in employment, education, medicine, and law enforcement.

5   The survey experiment described in the text was reported by Reyna et al. (2005). The principled conservative view of opposition to government intervention on behalf of minorities was advanced by Sniderman and Tetlock (1986). Variations of the covert bias view have been developed under the labels of symbolic racism (Sears, 1988), modern racism (McConahay, Hardee, & Batts, 1981), aversive racism (Gaertner & Dovidio, 1977; Dovidio, 2001), and subtle prejudice (Pettigrew & Meertens, 1995).

6   The 1930s experiments were by LaPiere (1934; with Chinese tourists) and by Clark and Clark (1947; with Black and White dolls). The 1954 Supreme Court decision that cited the doll studies was written by Chief Justice Earl Warren (*Brown v. Board of Education*, 347 U.S. 483).

7   The telephone wrong-number experiment that revealed race bias was reported by Gaertner and Bickman (1971). Interestingly, in that experiment Black recipients also completed more calls for White callers (67 percent) than for Black callers (60 percent).

    The lost-letter experiment was by Benson, Karabenick, and Lerner (1976). The review of these and other studies was by Crosby, Bromley, and Saxe (1980). In a recent unobtrusive-measure study, Kunstman and Plant (2008) found greater help for a White person than a Black person who appeared to have suffered an accidental injury.

8   The preelection and exit poll data were obtained from Pew Research Center and cnn .com, respectively. Further evidence that racial attitudes played significant roles in the 2008 presidential vote has appeared in published research (e.g., Greenwald, Smith, Sriram, Bar-Anan, & Nosek, 2009).

Appendix 2 Race, Disadvantage, and Discrimination

1   Few scholars are willing to publicly espouse the theory that genes predispose to violence. However, a search on the Internet for "Black genetic predisposition to violence" (or some similar query) will produce numerous nonscholarly sites that proclaim the validity of this group-responsible theory.

2   The ultimately decisive state of Florida in the 2000 U.S. presidential election provided multiple examples of institutional race discrimination in vote counting. A July 2001 report by the U.S. Commission on Civil Rights, titled *Voting Irregularities in Florida During the 2000 Presidential Election,* reported: "Poorer counties, particularly those with large minority populations, were more likely to use voting systems with higher spoilage [i.e., vote discard] rates than more affluent counties with significant White populations. For example, in Gadsden County, the only county in the state with an African American majority, approximately one in eight voters was disenfranchised. In Leon County, on the other hand, which is home to the prosperous state capital and two state universities, fewer than two votes in 1,000 were not counted. In Florida, of the 100 precincts with the highest numbers of disqualified ballots, 83 of them are majority-Black precincts." (retrieved from www.usccr.gov/pubs/pubsndx.htm).

3   From the start, audit studies aimed to rule out factors other than race as possible explanations for observed disadvantages to Black or Hispanic testers. Some of the other factors that might affect a person's qualification for housing include income, assets, debt levels, family circumstances, current and past employment, education and school rec-

ord, housing preference, employment history, credit record, and neatness of appearance. These were all allowed to vary among applicants, but in ways that created no systematic differences that should have made one of the two testers in each matched pair appear more qualified.

When experimental control is imposed, as in well-done audit studies, there remain only two possible causes of race differences in outcomes to Black and White paired testers. The more plausible explanation is race discrimination. The less plausible explanation is statistical fluke—that the result is an extremely rare occurrence such as repeatedly tossing a coin and getting heads to come up ten times in a row, something expected to occur only once in 1,024 attempts. Even though statistical fluke can never be ruled out entirely, the combination of proper experimental control and a large number of observations leaves the possibility of statistical fluke extremely low. The possibility of statistical fluke becomes much lower still when, as is true in the history of audit studies, numerous studies report similar findings.

[4]   The history of housing audits, starting in the 1950s, is described in a report by Yinger (1998). That report includes documentation of redlining, including a racially reversed form—Whites encountering difficulty in obtaining insurance for homes when they were interested in buying in a non-White residential area. The quote from the 2000 Housing Discrimination Study was taken from its report (Turner, Ross, Galster, & Yinger, 2002, p. i). The figures that we described as "net estimates" of discrimination are the "hierarchical" estimates in Exhibits 3-5 and 3-16 of that report. The corresponding estimates for discrimination against Hispanic apartment and home seekers were 15 percent and 5 percent.

[5]   The studies on employment discrimination summarized in the text are by Bendick (2004), Bertrand and Mullainathan (2004), and Pager (2003).

[6]   The IOM's conclusion about implicit bias as a possible cause of health care disparities appears on p. 178 of their report (Institute of Medicine, 2002).

[7]   Green et al., 2007; Penner et al., 2010; Cooper et al., 2012.

[8]   Statistics on prison populations by race are from James (2006). The Department of Justice study of traffic stops (Smith & Durose, 2006) was based on the "2002 Police-Public Contact Survey." Its report states that this survey was "administered to 76,910 individuals throughout the United States, and it questioned respondents about face-to-face encounters with police, including, but not limited to, personal experiences with traffic stops."

After Lamberth's (1994) study of state police actions on the New Jersey Turnpike, a subsequent study by the New Jersey attorney general's office found that "while the New Jersey State Police has never issued an official policy to engage in racial profiling or any other discriminatory enforcement practices, minority motorists have been treated differently than non-minority motorists at various stages of motor vehicle stops" (Verniero & Zoubek, 1999, p. 112).

Among numerous other available reports, we mention just two more: A report on arrests by New York City police who were conducting "stop and frisk" operations revealed that Blacks were arrested in proportions greater than their apparent proportion of criminal activity in the observed jurisdictions (Office of the Attorney General, 1999). And a recent report on activities of police units throughout Illinois described harsher enforcement against minority drivers, especially African Americans and Hispanics (Weiss & Rosenbaum, 2009).

[9]   The taxicab tipping study was reported by Ayres, Vars, and Zakariya (2005). The restaurant tipping study was by Lynn, Sturman, Ganley, Adams, Douglas, and McNeal (2006). The study of proffered selling prices for automobiles was described in Ayres and Siegelman (1995).

[10]   Group-responsible explanations are at a decided disadvantage when it comes to establishing convincing research evidence for them. The only available strategy is to show that all conceivable others-responsible interpretations can be ruled out, and this is a nearly impossible task.

[11]   The attention given by social scientists to cumulative impact of small acts of discrimination is indicated by the coining of three terms to label it. Mary Rowe, then ombudsperson at the Massachusetts Institute of Technology, first used *microinequities* in 1973. Barbara Reskin (2002), at the University of Washington, introduced the concept of *micro acts of discrimination*. The concept of *microaggressions* was developed by Derald Wing Sue et al. (2007). Virginia Valian (1998) developed the idea that minor acts of discrimination can accumulate to have a major impact on women's professional careers. Sociologist Robert K. Merton (1968) described the Matthew effect, as a "cumulative advantage" that "operates in many systems of social stratification to produce the same result: the rich get richer at a rate that makes the poor become relatively poorer."

[12]   The formula for computing survival percentage is p^k, where p is the probability of survival at each evaluation and k is the number of times that probability is applied. In the example, with $p = .995$ and $k = 72$, the result is .697 (70 percent). When $p = .985$ and $k = 72$, the result is .337 (34 percent).

[13]   The figures on high school graduation rates were obtained from Mishel and Roy (2006). The population statistics are from the 2012 Statistical Abstract of the United States Census Bureau, which can be found at www.census.gov/compendia/statab/cats /population/estimates_and_projections_by_age_sex_raceethnicity.html. We computed the impact by taking 1 percent (the hypothetical discrimination figure) of 71.5 percent (the proportion of Black Americans past high school age) of 39.64 million (the number of Black Americans as of July 2009). The result (.01 x .715 x 39,641,000) is 283,433.

[14]   The estimate that 10–15 percent of Americans express overt prejudice against Blacks is based on the proportions found to endorse views such as that White-Black intermarriage should be illegal or that Blacks are deficient in inborn ability (Schuman, Steeh, Bobo, & Krysan, 1997). See also Krysan's (2008) update of Schuman et al.'s book.

REFERENCES

1 Mindbugs

Adelson, E. (n.d.). *Checkershadow illusion.* Retrieved July 10, 2010, from web.mit.edu/persci/people/adelson.

Ariely, D. (2009). *Predictably irrational: The hidden forces that shape our decisions.* New York: HarperCollins.

Correll, J., Park, B., Judd, C. M., & Wittenbrink, B. (2002). The police officer's dilemma: Using ethnicity to disambiguate potentially threatening individuals. *Journal of Personality and Social Psychology, 83,* 1314–1329.

Creswell, J., & Thomas, L., Jr. (2009, January 24). The talented Mr. Madoff. *New York Times.*

Fiske, S. T., Cuddy, A. J., & Glick, P. (2007). Universal dimensions of social perception: Warmth and competence. *Trends in Cognitive Science, 11,* 77–83.

Frith, C. D. (2007). The social brain? *Philosophical Transactions of the Royal Society B 362,* 671–678.

Gallo, D. A., Roediger, H. L., III, & McDermott, K. B. (2001). Associative false recognition occurs without liberal criterion shifts. *Psychonomic Bulletin & Review, 8,* 579–586.

Garrett, B. L. (2011). *Convicting the innocent: Where criminal prosecutions go wrong.* Cambridge, MA: Harvard University Press.

Gilovich, T., Griffin, D., & Kahneman, D. (2002). *Heuristics and biases: The psychology of intuitive judgment.* New York: Cambridge University Press.

Helmholtz, H. V. (1924). *Helmholtz's treatise on physiological optics,* vol. 1. New York: Optical Society of America.

Janis, I. L. (1972). *Victims of groupthink.* New York: Houghton Mifflin.

Kahneman, D. (2011). *Thinking fast and slow.* New York: Farrar, Straus & Giroux.

Lamb, T. D. (2007). Evolution of the vertebrate eye: Opsins, photoreceptors, retina and eye cup. *Nature Reviews Neuroscience, 8,* 960–975.

Levy, B. R., Zonderman, A. B., Slade, M. D., & Ferrucci, L. (2009). Age stereotypes held earlier in life predict cardiovascular events in later life. *Psychological Science, 20,* 296–298.

Loftus, E. F., & Palmer, J. C. (1974). Reconstruction of automobile destruction: An example of the interaction between language and memory. *Journal of Verbal Learning and Verbal Behavior, 13,* 585–589.

Malpass, R. S., & Devine, P. G. (1980). Realism and eyewitness identification research. *Law and Human Behavior, 4,* 347–358.

Malpass, R. S., & Devine, P. G. (1981). Guided memory in eyewitness identification. *Journal of Applied Psychology, 66,* 343–350.

Marsat, S., & Williams, B. (2009). *Does the price influence the assessment of fundamental value? Experimental evidence.* Paper presented at the European Financial Management Association annual meeting, Milan, Italy.

Mitchell, J. P., Banaji, M. R., & Macrae, C. N. (2005). The link between social cognition and self-referential thought in the medial prefrontal cortex. *Journal of Cognitive Neuroscience, 17,* 1306–1315.

Mitchell, J. P., Macrae, C. N., & Banaji, M. R. (2004). Encoding-specific effects of social cognition on the neural correlates of subsequent memory. *Journal of Neuroscience, 24,* 4912–4917.

Mitchell, J. P., Macrae, C. N., & Banaji, M. R. (2005). Forming impressions of people versus inanimate objects: Social-cognitive processing in the medial prefrontal cortex. *NeuroImage, 26,* 251–257.

Mussweiler, T., & Englich, B. (2003). Adapting to the euro: Evidence from bias reduction. *Journal of Economic Psychology, 24,* 285–292.

Northcraft, G., & Neale, M. (1987). Experts, amateurs, and real estate: An anchoring and adjustment perspective on property pricing decisions. *Organizational Behavior and Human Decision Processes, 39,* 84–97.

Powell, M. (2009, May 31). On diverse force, blacks still face special peril. *New York Times.*

Reyes, R. M., Thompson, W. C., & Bower, G. H. (1980). Judgmental biases resulting from differing availabilities of arguments. *Journal of Personality and Social Psychology, 39,* 2–12.

Roediger, H. L., III, & Gallo, D. A. (2002). Processes affecting accuracy and distortion in memory: An overview. In M. L. Eisen, J. A. Quas, & G. S. Goodman (eds.), *Memory and suggestibility in the forensic interview* (pp. 3–28). London: Lawrence Erlbaum.

Schwartz, N. (2009, January 3). Personal communication.

Schwartz, N., Bless, H., Strack, F., Klumpp, G., Rittenauer-Schatka, H., & Simons, A. (1991). Ease of retrieval as information: Another look at the availability heuristic. *Journal of Personality and Social Psychology, 61,* 195–202.

Shores, M. (2010). *Informal networks and white collar crime: An extended analysis of the Madoff scandal.* Unpublished manuscript, Cornell University.

Simon, H. A. (1983). *Reason in human affairs.* Stanford, CA: Stanford University Press.

Sporer, S. L., Penrod, S., Read, D., & Cutler, B. (1995). Choosing, confidence, and accuracy: A meta-analysis of the confidence-accuracy relation in eyewitness identification studies. *Psychological Bulletin, 118,* 315–327.

Todorov, A., Mandisodza, A. N., Goren, A., & Hall, C. C. (2005). Inferences of competence from faces predict election outcomes. *Science, 308,* 1623–1626.

Tversky, A., & Kahneman, D. (1973). Availability: A heuristic for judging frequency and probability. *Cognitive Psychology, 5,* 207–232.

Tversky, A., & Kahneman, D. (1974). Judgment under uncertainty: Heuristics and biases. *Science, 185,* 1124–1130.

VanLehn, K. (1990). *Mindbugs: The origins of procedural misconceptions.* Cambridge, MA: MIT Press.

Wells, G. L., Olson, E. A., & Charman, S. D. (2002). The confidence of eyewitnesses in their identifications from lineups. *Current Directions in Psychological Science, 11*, 151–154.

2 Shades of Truth

Abelson, R. P., Loftus, E. F., & Greenwald, A. G. (1992). Attempts to improve the accuracy of self-reports of voting. In J. M. Tanur (ed.), *Questions about survey questions: Meaning, memory, expression, and social interactions in surveys* (pp. 138–153). New York: Russell Sage Foundation.

Allison, A. C. (1964). Polymorphism and natural selection in human populations. *Cold Spring Harbor Symposium in Quantitative Biology, 29*, 137–149.

Enattah, N. S., et al. (2008). Independent introduction of two lactase-persistence alleles into human populations reflects different history of adaptation to milk culture. *American Journal of Human Genetics, 82*, 57–72.

Jones, E. E., & Sigall, H. (1971). The bogus pipeline: A new paradigm for measuring affect and attitude. *Psychological Bulletin, 75*, 349–364.

McConahay, J. B., Hardee, B. B., & Batts, V. (1981). Has racism declined in America? It depends on who is asking and what is asked. *Journal of Conflict Resolution, 25*, 563–579.

Perry, G. H., et al. (2007). Diet and the evolution of human amylase gene copy number variation. *Nature Genetics, 39*, 1256–1260.

Rowland, M. L. (1990). Self-reported weight and height. *American Journal of Clinical Nutrition, 52*, 1125–1133.

Saxe, L., & Ben-Shakhar, G. (1999). Admissibility of polygraph tests: The application of scientific standards post-Daubert. *Psychology, Public Policy, and Law, 5*, 203–223.

Smith, D. L. (2004). *Why we lie.* New York: St. Martin's Press.

Spencer, E. A., Appleby, P. N., Davey, G. K., & Key, T. J. (2002). Validity of self-reported height and weight in 4808 EPIC-Oxford participants. *Public Health Nutrition, 5*, 561–565.

Tedeschi, J. T., Schlenker, B. R., & Bonoma, T. V. (1971). Cognitive dissonance: Private ratiocination or public spectacle? *American Psychologist, 26*, 685–695.

Trivers, R. (1985). *Social evolution.* Menlo Park, CA: Benjamin/Cummings.

Trivers, R. (2000). The elements of a scientific theory of self-deception. *Annals of the New York Academy of Sciences, 907*, 114–131.

3 Into the Blindspot

Green, A. R., Carney, D. R., Pallin, D. J., Ngo, L. H., Raymond, K. L., Iezzoni, L. I., & Banaji, M. R. (2007). The presence of implicit bias in physicians and its prediction of thrombolysis decisions for black and white patients. *Journal of General Internal Medicine, 22*, 1231–1238.

Greenwald, A. G., McGhee, D. E., & Schwartz, J. L. K. (1998). Measuring individual differences in implicit cognition: The Implicit Association Test. *Journal of Personality and Social Psychology, 74*, 1464–1480.

Greenwald, A. G., Poehlman, T. A., Uhlmann, E., & Banaji, M. R. (2009). Understanding and using the Implicit Association Test: III. Meta-analysis of predictive validity. *Journal of Personality and Social Psychology, 97*, 17–41.

Greenwald, A. G., Smith, C. T., Sriram, N., Bar-Anan, Y., & Nosek, B. A. (2009). Race attitude measures predicted vote in the 2008 U.S. presidential election. *Analyses of Social Issues and Public Policy, 9,* 241–253.

Hugenberg, K., & Bodenhausen, G. V. (2003). Facing prejudice: Implicit prejudice and the perception of facial threat. *Psychological Science, 14,* 640–643.

Lynch, R. (2010). It's funny because we think it's true: Laughter is augmented by implicit preferences. *Evolution and Human Behavior, 31,* 141–148.

McConnell, A. R., & Leibold, J. M. (2001). Relations among the Implicit Association Test, discriminatory behavior, and explicit measures of racial attitudes. *Journal of Experimental Social Psychology, 37,* 435–442.

Penner, L. A., Dovidio, J. F., West, T. V., Gaertner, S. L., Albrecht, T. L., Dailey, R. K., & Markova, T. (2010). Aversive racism and medical interactions with black patients: A field study. *Journal of Experimental Social Psychology, 46,* 436–440.

Rosenthal, R., & Rubin, D. B. (1982). A simple general purpose display of magnitude of experimental effect. *Journal of Educational Psychology, 74,* 166–169.

Ziegert, J. C., & Hanges, P. J. (2005). Employment discrimination: The role of implicit attitudes, motivation, and a climate for racial bias. *Journal of Applied Psychology, 90,* 554–562.

4 "Not That There's Anything Wrong with That!"

Ayan, S. (2008, October). Speaking of memory: Q&A with neuroscientist Eric Kandel. *Scientific American Mind.*

Bargh, J. (1997). Reply to the commentaries. In R. J. Wyer (ed.), *The automaticity of everyday life: Advances in social cognition,* vol. 10 (pp. 231–246). Mahwah, NJ: Erlbaum.

Begnaud, D. (2010, March 8). Senator Roy Ashburn says "I am gay." Retrieved September 5, 2010, from bs13.com/local/ashburn.admits.gay.2.1545432.html.

Chesterton, G. K. (1908) *Orthodoxy.* archive.org/stream/orthodoxy16769gut/16769.txt.

DiMartino, M. D. (director). (2003). *King of the Hill, 7, 20:* "Racist Dawg" [motion picture].

Festinger, L. (1957). *A theory of cognitive dissonance.* Evanston, IL: Row, Peterson.

Gladwell, M. (2007, June 6). [Interview, O. Winfrey, interviewer].

Harvey, E. (2010, May 20). Labor MP David Campbell resigns for "personal reasons." Retrieved September 5, 2010, from www.smh.com.au/nsw/labor-mp-david-campbell-resigns-for-personal-reasons-20100520-vm58.html.

Hummert, M. L., Garstka, T. A., O'Brien, L. T., Greenwald, A. G., & Mellott, D. S. (2002). Using the implicit association test to measure age differences in implicit social cognitions. *Psychology and Aging, 17,* 482–495.

Hungary's far right makes strong gains in parliamentary elections. (2010, April 12). Retrieved September 5, 2010, from www.inthenews.co.uk/news/world/europe/hungary-s-far-right-makes-strong-gains-in-parliamentary-elections-$1370724.htm.

Johnson, M., Kim, J., & Risse, G. (1985). Do alcoholic Korsakoff's syndrome patients acquire affective reactions? *Journal of Experimental Psychology: Learning, Memory, and Cognition, 11,* 22–36.

Lynch, R. (2010). It's funny because we think it's true: Laughter is augmented by implicit preferences. *Evolution and Human Behavior, 31,* 141–148.

Lynch, R. (2010). Videos for "It's funny because we think it's true: Laughter is augmented by implicit preferences." Retrieved September 5, 2010, from www.ehbonline.org/article/PIIS1090513809000683/addOns.

Nelson, T. D. (2002). *Ageism: Stereotypes and prejudice against older persons.* Cambridge, MA: MIT Press.

Nisbett, R., & Wilson, T. (1977). Telling more than we can know: Verbal reports on mental processes. *Psychological Review, 84,* 231–259.

Nosek, B. A., Smyth, F. L., Hansen, J. J., Devos, T., Lindner, N. M., Ranganath, K. A., et al. (2007). Pervasiveness and correlates of implicit attitudes and stereotypes. *European Review of Social Psychology, 18,* 36–88.

Trivers, R. (2000). The elements of a scientific theory of self-deception. *Annals of the New York Academy of Sciences, 907,* 114–131.

van Veen, V., Krug, M. K., Schooler, J. W., & Carter, C. S. (2009). Neural activity predicts attitude change in cognitive dissonance. *Nature Neuroscience, 12, 11,* 1469–1475.

Vargas, J. A. (2007, September 4). The most feared man on the hill? *Washington Post.* Retrieved September 5, 2010, from www.washingtonpost.com/wp-dyn/content/article/2007/09/03/AR2007090301396.html.

Vedantam, S. (2005, January 23). See no bias. *Washington Post.*

Zajonc, R. (1980). Feeling and thinking: Preferences need no inferences. *American Psychologist, 35,* 151–175.

5 Homo Categoricus

Allport. G. W. (1954). *The nature of prejudice.* Cambridge, MA: Perseus.

Brown, D. E. (1982). Sex ratios, sexual selection and sexual dimorphism in waterfowl. *American Birds, 36,* 259–260.

Bruner, J. S. (1957). Going beyond the information given. In H. Gruber et al. (eds.), *Contemporary approaches to cognition* (pp. 41–69). Cambridge, MA: Harvard University Press.

Dovidio, J. F., Glick, P., & Rudman, L. A. (eds.) (2005). *On the nature of prejudice: Fifty years after Allport.* Malden, MA: Blackwell.

Eagly, A. H., & Kite, M. E. (1987). Are stereotypes of nationalities applied to both women and men? *Journal of Personality and Social Psychology, 53,* 451–462.

Katz, D., & Braly, K. (1933). Racial stereotypes of one hundred college students. *Journal of Abnormal and Social Psychology, 28,* 280–290.

Khemlani, S., Glucksberg, S., & Rubio Fernandez, P. (2007). Do ducks lay eggs? How people interpret generic assertions. In D. S. McNamara & J. G. Trafton (eds.), *Proceedings of the 29th Annual Cognitive Science Society,* 64–70. Austin, TX: Cognitive Science Society.

Levy, B. (2009). Stereotype embodiment: A psycho-social approach to aging. *Current Directions in Psychological Science, 18,* 332–336.

Lippmann, W. (1922). *Public opinion.* New York: Harcourt, Brace.

Madon, S., et al. (2001). Ethnic and national stereotypes: The Princeton trilogy revisited and revised. *Personality and Social Psychology Bulletin, 27,* 996–1010.

Rice, S. A. (1926). "Stereotypes": A source of error in judging human character. *Journal of Personnel Research, 5,* 267–276.

Schneider, D. J. (2004). *The psychology of stereotypes.* New York: Guilford.

Steele, C. M., Spencer, S. J., & Aronson, J. (2002). Contending with group image: The psychology of stereotype and social identity threat. In M. P. Zanna (ed.), *Advances in experimental social psychology,* vol. 34 (pp. 379–440). San Diego, CA: Academic Press.

6 The Hidden Costs of Stereotypes

Allport, G., & Postman, J. (1947). *The psychology of rumor*. New York: Rinehart & Wilson.

Aronson, E. (1968). Dissonance theory: Progress and problems. In R. Abelson, E. Aronson, W. McGuire, & T. Newcomb, *Theories of cognitive consistency: A sourcebook*. Chicago: Rand McNally.

Barry, D., Kovaleski, S. F., Robertson, C., & Alvarez, L. (2012, April 2). Race, tragedy and outrage collide after a shot in Florida. *New York Times*.

Caruso, E., Rahnev, D., & Banaji, M. (2009). Using conjoint analysis to detect discrimination: Revealing covert preferences from overt choices. *Social Cognition, 27*, 128–137.

Ceci, S., & Williams, W. (2007). *Why aren't more women in science: Top researchers debate the evidence*. Washington, DC: American Psychological Association.

Chugh, D. (2004). Societal and managerial implications of implicit social cognition: Why milliseconds matter. *Social Justice Research, 17, 2*, 203–222.

Correll, J., Park, B., Judd, C., & Wittenbrink, B. (2002). The police officer's dilemma: Using ethnicity to disambiguate potentially threatening individuals. *Journal of Personality and Social Psychology, 83, 6*, 1314–1329.

Ehlers, S., & Gillberg, C. (1993). The epidemiology of Asperger syndrome. *Journal of Child Psychology and Psychiatry, 34, 8*, 1327–1350.

Gilbert, D. (1991). How mental systems believe. *American Psychologist, 46, 2*, 107–119.

Goldstein, D., & Stocking, V. (1994). TIP studies of gender differences in talented adolescents. In K. Heller & E. Hany (eds.), *Competence and responsibility*, vol. 2 (pp. 190–203). Ashland, OH: Hofgreve.

Greenwald, A., Oakes, M., & Hoffman, H. (2003). Targets of discrimination: Effects of race on responses to weapons holders. *Journal of Experimental Social Psychology, 39, 4*, 399–405.

Hartmann, H., Hegewisch, A., Liepmann, H., & Williams, C. (2010, March). *The gender wage gap: 2009*. Retrieved September 7, 2010, from www.iwpr.org/pdf/C350.pdf.

Hugenberg, K., & Bodenhausen, G. (2003). Facing prejudice: Implicit prejudice and the perception of facial threat. *Psychological Science, 14, 6*, 640–643.

Hugenberg, K., & Bodenhausen, G. (2004). Ambiguity in social categorization: The role of prejudice and facial affect in race categorization. *Psychological Science, 15, 5*, 342–345.

Jacoby, L., Kelley, C., Brown, J., & Jasechko, J. (1989). Becoming famous overnight: Limits on the ability to avoid unconscious influences of the past. *Journal of Personality and Social Psychology, 56*, 326–338.

Jost, J., & Banaji, M. (1994). The role of stereotyping in system-justification and the production of false consciousness. *British Journal of Social Psychology, 33*, 1–27.

Jost, J., Banaji, M., & Nosek, B. (2004). A decade of system justification theory: Accumulated evidence of conscious and unconscious bolstering of the status quo. *Political Psychology, 25*, 881–919.

Kanner, L. (1943). Autistic disturbances of affective contact. *Nervous Child, 2*, 217–250.

Katz, D., & Braly, K. (1933). Racial stereotypes of one hundred college students. *The Journal of Abnormal and Social Psychology, 28*, 280–290.

Kay, A., Gaucher, D., Peach, J., Zanna, M., & Spencer, S. (2008). Towards an understanding of the naturalistic fallacy: System justification and the shift from is to ought. *Under review*.

Madon, S., Guyll, M., Aboufadel, K., Montiel, E., Smith, A., Palumbo, P., et al. (2001). Ethnic and national stereotypes: The Princeton trilogy revisited and revised. *Personality and Social Psychology Bulletin, 27*, 996–1010.

Meissner, C., & Brigham, J. (2001). Thirty years of investigating the own-race bias in memory for faces: A meta-analytic review. *Psychology, Public Policy, and Law, 7,* 3–35.

Nosek, B., Banaji, M., & Greenwald, A. (2002a). Harvesting intergroup attitudes and stereotypes from a demonstration website. *Group Dynamics, 6,* 101–115.

Nosek, B., Banaji, M., & Greenwald, A. (2002b). Math = male, me = female, therefore math ≠ me. *Journal of Personality and Social Psychology, 83,* 44–59.

Nosek, B., Smyth, F., Sriram, N., Lindner, N., Devos, T., Ayala, A., et al. (2009). National differences in gender-science stereotypes predict national sex differences in science and math achievement. *Proceedings of the National Academy of Sciences of the United States of America, 106, 26,* 10593–10597.

Payne, B. (2006). Weapon bias: Split-second decisions and unintended stereotyping. *Current Directions in Psychological Science, 15, 6,* 287–291.

Rahnev, D. (2007). *Conjoint analysis: A new method of investigating stereotypes.* Unpublished undergraduate thesis. Cambridge, MA: Harvard University.

Rich, A. (1999). *Midnight salvage, poems 1995–1998.* New York: W. W. Norton.

Rudman, L., & Heppen, J. (2003). Implicit romantic fantasies and women's interest in personal power: A glass slipper effect? *Personality and Social Psychology Bulletin, 29, 11,* 1357–1370.

Smyth, F., Greenwald, A. G., & Nosek, B. (2009). *Implicit gender-science stereotype outperforms math scholastic aptitude in identifying science majors.* Unpublished manuscript. University of Virginia.

Spelke, E. (2005). Sex differences in intrinsic aptitude for mathematics and science?: A critical review. *American Psychologist, 60, 9,* 950–958.

Staples, B. (1986, December). Black men and public space. *Harper's.*

Steele, C. M. (1997). A threat in the air: How stereotypes shape intellectual identity and performance. *American Psychologist, 52,* 613–629.

Steele, C. (2010). *Whistling Vivaldi: And other clues to how stereotypes affect us.* New York: W. W. Norton.

Stober, D., & Hoffman, I. (2001). *A convenient spy: Wen Ho Lee and the politics of nuclear espionage.* New York: Simon & Schuster.

Women in the labor force: A databook. (2006). Retrieved September 7, 2010, from www.bls.gov/cps/wlf-databook-2006.pdf.

Women in the labor force: A databook (2009 edition). (2009). Retrieved September 7, 2010, from www.bls.gov/cps/wlf-intro-2009.htm.

Zawitz, M., & Strom, K. (2000, October). *Firearm injury and death from crime (1993–1997).* Retrieved September 7, 2010, from U.S. Department of Justice: bjs.ojp.usdoj.gov/content/pub/pdf/fidc9397.pdf.

7 Us and Them

Abrams, D., Frings, D., & Moura, G. R. (2005). Group identity and self definition. In S. Wheelen, *Handbook of Group Research and Practice.* Thousand Oaks, CA: Sage.

Banaji, M. R., & Heiphetz, L. (2010). Attitudes. In S. T. Fiske, D. T. Gilbert, & G. Lindzey G. (eds.) *Handbook of Social Psychology,* (pp. 348–388). New York: John Wiley & Sons.

Baron, A., Dunham, Y., Banaji, M. R., & Carey, S. (2009). Examining the effect of labels and visual cues on social categorization. Unpublished manuscript, Harvard University.

Bowles, S., & Gintus, H. (2011). *A cooperative species: human reciprocity and its evolution.* Princeton, NJ: Princeton University Press.

Breger, L. (1974). *From instinct to identity: The development of personality.* Prentice Hall.

Devine, P. G. (1995). Distinguished scientific award for an early career contribution to psychology. *American Psychologist, 50, 4,* 227–229.

Fantz, R. L. (1964). Visual experience in infants: Decreased attention to familiar patterns relative to novel ones. *Science, 146,* 668–670.

Gaertner, L., & Insko, C. A. (2001). On the measurement of social orientations in the minimal group paradigm: norms as moderators of the expression of intergroup bias. *European Journal of Social Psychology, 31,* 143–154.

Grier, J. B., Counter, S. A., & Shearer, W. M. (1967). Prenatal auditory imprinting in chickens. *Science, 155,* 1692–1693.

Hoffman, H. (1996). *Amorous turkey and addicted ducklings: A search for the causes of social attachment.* Authors Cooperative.

Kelley, W. M., Macrae, C. N., Wyland, C. L., Caglar, S., Inati, S., & Heatherton, T. F. (2002). Finding the self? An event related fMRI study. *Journal of Cognitive Neuroscience, 14,* 785–794.

Kinzler, K. D., Dupoux, E., & Spelke, E. S. (2007). The native language of social cognition. *Proceedings of the National Academy of Sciences of the United States of America, 104,* 12577–12580.

Mitchell, J. P., Macrae, C. N., & Banaji, M. R. (2006). Dissociable medial prefrontal contributions to judgments of similar and dissimilar others. *Neuron, 50,* 655–663.

Öhman, A. (2005). Conditioned fear of a face: A prelude to ethnic enmity? *Science, 309,* 711–713.

Olsson, A., Ebert, J. P., Banaji, M. R., & Phelps, E. A. (2005). The role of social groups in the persistence of learned fear. *Science, 309,* 785–787.

Park, B., & Rothbart, M. (1982). Perception of out-group homogeneity and levels of social categorization: Memory for the subordinate attributes of in-group and out-group members. *Journal of Personality and Social Psychology, 42,* 1051–1068.

Pascalis, O., & Kelly, D. (2009). Origins of face processing in humans: Phylogeny and ontogeny. *Perspectives on Psychological Science, 4,* 200–209.

Pinker, S. (2011). *The better angels of our nature: Why violence has declined.* New York: Viking.

Quinn, P. C., Yahr, J., Kuhn, A., Slater, A. M., & Pascalis, O. (2002). Representations of the gender of human faces by infants: A preference for female. *Perception, 31,* 1109–1121.

Sangrigoli, S., & de Schonen, S. (2004). Recognition of own-race and other-race faces by three-month-old infants. *Journal of Child Psychology and Psychiatry, 45, 7,* 1219–1227.

Smyth, F. L., Greenwald, A. G., & Nosek, B. A. (2009). *Implicit gender–science stereotype outperforms math scholastic aptitude in identifying science majors.* Unpublished manuscript, University of Virginia.

Spelke, E. S. (1985). Preferential-looking methods as tools for the study of cognition in infancy. In G. Gottlieb & N. Krasnegor (eds.), *Measurement of audition and vision in the first year of postnatal life* (pp. 323-363). Norwood, NJ: Ablex.

Tajfel, H. (1970). Experiments in intergroup discrimination. *Scientific American, 223,* 96–102.

Tajfel, H., Billig, M. G., Bundy, R. P., & Flament, C. (1971). Social categorization and intergroup behaviour. *European Journal of Social Psychology, 1, 2,* 149–178.

Thomson, S. K. (1975). Gender labels and early sex role development. *Child Development, 46,* 339–347.

8 Outsmarting the Machine

Asgari, S., Dasgupta, N., & Cote, N. G. (2010). When does contact with successful ingroup members change self-stereotypes? A longitudinal study comparing the effect of quantity vs. quality of contact with successful individuals. *Social Psychology, 41,* 203–211.

Banaji, M. R., Bazerman, M., & Chugh, D. (2003). How (un)ethical are you? *Harvard Business Review, 81,* 56–64.

Blair, I. V. (2002). The malleability of automatic stereotypes and prejudice. *Personality and Social Psychology Review, 6,* 242–261.

Blair, I. V., Ma, J. E., & Lenton, A. P. (2001). Imagining stereotypes away: The moderation of implicit stereotypes through mental imagery. *Journal of Personality and Social Psychology, 81,* 828–841.

Brewer, M. B. (1999). The psychology of prejudice: Ingroup love or outgroup hate? *Journal of Social Issues, 55,* 429–444.

Cheryan, S., Plaut, V. C., Davies, P. G., & Steele, C. M. (2009). Ambient belonging: How stereotypical cues impact gender participation in computer science. *Journal of Personality and Social Psychology, 97, 6,* 1045–1060.

Dasgupta, N., & Asgari, S. (2004). Seeing is believing: Exposure to counterstereotypic women leaders and its effect on the malleability of automatic gender stereotyping. *Journal of Experimental Social Psychology, 40,* 642–658.

Dasgupta, N., & Greenwald, A. G. (2001). Exposure to admired group members reduces automatic intergroup bias. *Journal of Personality and Social Psychology, 81,* 800–814.

Devine, P. G., Forscher, P. S., Austin, A. J., & Cox, W. T. L. (2011). Long-term reduction in implicit racial prejudice: A prejudice habit-breaking intervention. Unpublished manuscript, University of Wisconsin, Madison.

Gaertner, S. L., Dovidio, J. F., Banker, B., Rust, M., Nier, J., Mottola, G., & Ward, C. M. (1997). Does racism necessarily mean anti-blackness? Aversive racism and pro-whiteness. In M. Fine, L. Powell, L. Weis, & M. Wong (eds.), *Off white* (pp. 167–178). London: Routledge.

Gladwell, M. (2005). *Blink: The power of thinking without thinking.* New York: Little Brown.

Goldin, C., & Rouse, C. (2000). Orchestrating impartiality: The impact of "blind" auditions on female musicians. *American Economic Review, 90,* 715–741.

Levy, B. (2009). Stereotype embodiment: A psycho-social approach to aging. *Current Directions in Psychological Science, 18,* 332–336.

Merton, R. K. (1968). The Matthew effect in science. *Science, 159,* 56–63.

Phelan, J. E. (2010). The effect of role models on implicit cognitions. Doctoral dissertation, Rutgers University.

Steele, C. M., Spencer, S. J., & Aronson, J. (2002). Contending with group image: The psychology of stereotype and social identity threat. In M. P. Zanna (ed.), *Advances in experimental social psychology,* vol. 34 (pp. 379–440). San Diego, CA: Academic Press.

Stout, J. G., Dasgupta, N., Hunsinger, M., & McManus, M. (in press). STEMing the tide: Using ingroup experts to inoculate women's self-concept and professional goals in science, technology, engineering, and mathematics (STEM). *Journal of Personality and Social Psychology.*

Teachman, B., & Woody, S. (2003). Automatic processing in spider phobia: Implicit fear associations over the course of treatment. *Journal of Abnormal Psychology, 112,* 100–109.

Appendix 1 Are Americans Racist?

Benson, P. L., Karabenick, S. A., & Lerner, R. M. (1976). Pretty pleases: The effects of physical attractiveness, race, and sex on receiving help. *Journal of Experimental Social Psychology, 12,* 409–415.

Bogardus, E. S. (1925). Measuring social distance. *Journal of Applied Sociology, 9,* 299–308.

Bogardus, E. S. (1928). *Immigration and race attitudes.* Boston: D. C. Heath.

Clark, K. B., & Clark, M. P. (1947). Racial identification and preference in Negro children. In T. N. Newcomb et al. (eds.), *Readings in Social Psychology* (pp. 169–178). New York: Henry Holt.

Crosby, F., Bromley, S., & Saxe, L. (1980). Recent unobtrusive studies of black and white discrimination and prejudice: A literature review. *Psychological Bulletin, 87,* 546–563.

D'Souza, D. (2002). *What's so great about America?* New York: Penguin Books.

Gaertner, S., & Bickman, L. (1971). Effects of race on the elicitation of helping behavior: The wrong number technique. *Journal of Personality and Social Psychology, 20,* 218–222.

Gaertner, S. L., & Dovidio, J. F. (1977). The subtlety of white racism, arousal, and helping behavior. *Journal of Personality and Social Psychology, 35, 10,* 691–707.

GAO (1993). *Homosexuals in the military: Policies and practices of foreign countries.* Washington, DC: GAO, NSIAD-93-215.

Greenwald, A. G., Smith, C. T., Sriram, N., Bar-Anan, Y., & Nosek, B. A. (2009). Race attitude measures predicted vote in the 2008 U.S. presidential election. *Analyses of Social Issues and Public Policy, 9,* 241–253.

Hinckley, E. D. (1932). The influence of individual opinion on construction of an attitude scale. *Journal of Social Psychology, 3,* 283–296.

Kier, E. (1998). Homosexuals in the military: Open integration and combat. *International Security, 23,* 5–39.

Kier, E. (2006). Declaration of Professor Elizabeth Kier in Case C06-cv-05195-RBL. United States District Court, Western District of Washington.

Kunstman, J. W., & Plant, E. A. (2008). Racing to help: Racial bias in high emergency helping situations. *Journal of Personality and Social Psychology, 95,* 1499–1510.

LaPiere, R. T. (1934). Attitudes versus actions. *Social Forces, 13,* 230–237.

McConahay, J. B., Hardee, B. B., & Batts, V. (1981). Has racism declined in America? It depends upon who is asking and what is asked. *Journal of Conflict Resolution, 25,* 563–579.

McMichael, W. R., & McGarry, B. (2010, February 15). "Exclusive militarywide survey: How troops really feel about gays serving openly." *Military Times.*

Moradi, B., & Miller, L. (2010). Attitudes of Iraq and Afghanistan war veterans toward gay and lesbian service members. *Armed Forces & Society, 36,* 397–419.

Pettigrew, T. F., & Meertens, R. W. (1995). Subtle and blatant prejudice in Western Europe. *European Journal of Social Psychology, 25,* 57–75.

Reyna, C., Henry, P. J., Korfmacher, W., & Tucker, A. (2005). Examining the principles in principled conservatism: The role of responsibility stereotypes as cues for deservingness in racial policy decisions. *Journal of Personality and Social Psychology, 90,* 109–128.

Rule, N. O., Macrae, C. N., & Ambady, N. (2009). Ambiguous group membership is extracted automatically from faces. *Psychological Science, 20,* 441–443.

Schuman, H., Steeh, C., Bobo, L., & Krysan, M. (1997). *Racial attitudes in America.* Cambridge, MA: Harvard University.

Sears, D. O. (1988). Symbolic racism. In P. Katz & D. Taylor (eds.), *Eliminating racism: Profiles in controversy* (pp. 53–84). New York: Plenum Press.

Sidanius, J., & Pratto, F. (1999). *Social dominance*. Cambridge: Cambridge University Press.

Sniderman, P. M., & Tetlock, P. E. (1986). Symbolic racism: Problems of motive attribution in political analysis. *Journal of Social Issues, 42,* 129–150.

Thurstone, L. L. (1928). An experimental study of nationality preferences. *Journal of General Psychology, 1,* 405–425.

Appendix 2 Race, Disadvantage, and Discrimination

Ayres, I., & Siegelman, P. (1995). Race and gender discrimination in bargaining for a new car. *American Economic Review, 85,* 304–321.

Ayres, I., Vars, F. E., & Zakariya, N. (2005). To insure prejudice: Racial disparities in taxicab tipping. *Yale Law Journal, 114,* 7.

Bendick, M. (2004, June). Using paired-comparison testing to develop a social psychology of civil rights. Paper presented at the biennial conference of the Society for the Psychological Study of Social Issues.

Bertrand, M., & Mullainathan, S. (2004). Are Emily and Greg more employable than Lakisha and Jamal? A field experiment on labor market discrimination. Chicago: University of Chicago Business School.

Cooper, L. A., Roter, D. L., Beach, M. C., Sabin, J. A., Carson, K. A., Greenwald, A. G., & Inui, T. S. (2012). Implicit racial bias among clinicians, communication behaviors, and clinician and patient ratings of interpersonal care. *American Journal of Public Health, 102,* 979–987.

Green, A. R., Carney, D. R., Pallin, D. J., Ngo, L. H., Raymond, K. L., Iezzoni, L. I., & Banaji, M. R. (2007). The presence of implicit bias in physicians and its prediction of thrombolysis decisions for black and white patients. *Journal of General Internal Medicine, 22,* 1231–1238.

Institute of Medicine (2002). *Unequal treatment: Confronting racial and ethnic disparities in health care.* Washington, DC: National Academy of Sciences.

James, D. J. (2006). Profile of jail inmates, 2002. Washington, DC: U.S. Department of Justice, Bureau of Justice Statistics.

Krysan, M. (2008). Racial attitudes in America: A brief summary of the updated data. Institute of Government and Public Affairs, University of Illinois. Retrieved from www.igpa.uillinois.edu/programs/racial-attitudes/brief.

Lamberth, J. (1994). Revised statistical analysis of the incidence of police stops and arrests of black drivers/travelers on the New Jersey Turnpike between Exits or Interchanges 1 and 3 from the years 1988 through 1991. Unpublished report, Temple University.

Lynn, M., Sturman, M., Ganley, C., Adams, E., Douglas, M., & McNeal, J. (2006). Consumer racial discrimination in tipping: A replication and extension. Unpublished manuscript, Cornell University.

Merton, R. K. (1968). The Matthew effect in science. *Science, 159,* 56–63.

Mishel, L., & Roy, J. (2006). *Rethinking high school graduation rates and trends.* Washington, DC: Economic Policy Institute.

Office of the Attorney General (1999). The New York City Police Department's "stop & frisk" practices: A report to the people of the State of New York. Retrieved from www.oag.state.ny.us/bureaus/civil_rights/pdfs/stp_frsk.pdf.

Pager, D. (2003). The mark of a criminal record. *American Journal of Sociology, 108,* 937–935.

Penner, L. A., Dovidio, J. F., West, T. V., Gaertner, S. L., Albrecht, T. L., Dailey, R. K., & Markova, T. (2010). Aversive racism and medical interactions with black patients: A field study. *Journal of Experimental Social Psychology, 46,* 436–440.

Reskin, B. F. (2002). Rethinking employment discrimination and its remedies. In M. Guillen, R. Collins, P. England, & M. Meyer (eds.), *The new economic sociology: Developments in an emerging field* (pp. 218–244). New York: Russell Sage Foundation.

Schuman, H., Steeh, C., Bobo, L., & Krysan, M. (1997). *Racial attitudes in America,* rev. ed. Cambridge, MA: Harvard University.

Smith, E. L., & Durose, M. R. (2006). Characteristics of drivers stopped by police, 2002. Washington, DC: U.S. Department of Justice, Bureau of Justice Statistics.

Sue, D. W., Capodilupo, C. M., Torino, G. C., Bucceri, J. M., Holder, A. M. B., Nadal, K. L., & Esquilin, M. (2007). Racial microaggressions in everyday life: Implications for clinical practice. *American Psychologist, 62,* 271–286.

Turner, M. A., Ross, S. L., Galster, G. C., & Yinger, J. (2002). *Discrimination in metropolitan housing markets: National results from Phase I HDS 2000.* Washington, DC: Urban Institute.

Valian, V. (1998). *Why so slow? The advancement of women.* Cambridge, MA: MIT Press.

Verniero, P., & Zoubek, P. H. (1999). Interim report of the state police review team regarding allegations of racial profiling. Paper presented at the Race, Police and the Community Conference sponsored by the Criminal Justice Institute of Harvard Law School, December 7–9, 2000, Cambridge, MA.

Weiss, A., & Rosenbaum, D. P. (2009). *Illinois traffic stops statistics study: 2008 annual report.* Center for Research in Law and Justice, University of Illinois at Chicago. Downloaded from www.dot.state.il.us/travelstats/ITSS 2008 Annual Report.pdf.

Yinger, J. (1998). Testing for discrimination in housing and related markets. In M. Fix & M. A. Turner (eds.), *A national report card on discrimination in America: The role of testing* (pp. 27–68). Washington, DC: Urban Institute.

INDEX

MAHZARIN R. BANAJI received her PhD from Ohio State University and was a postdoctoral fellow at University of Washington. She taught at Yale University for fifteen years, receiving the Lex Hixon Prize for Teaching Excellence. She is currently Richard Clarke Cabot Professor of Social Ethics in the department of psychology at Harvard, and served as the first Carol K. Pforzheimer Professor at the Radcliffe Institute for Advanced Study. At present, she also serves as Cowan Chair in Human Social Dynamics at the Santa Fe Institute. She is the recipient of a Guggenheim Fellowship and the Diener Award for Outstanding Contributions to Social Psychology, and is Herbert Simon Fellow of the Association for Social and Political Psychology.

ANTHONY G. GREENWALD received his bachelor's degree from Yale University and his PhD from Harvard University. He was a postdoctoral fellow at Educational Testing Service. For twenty years he taught at Ohio State University (where Mahzarin was his student) and is currently professor of psychology at University of Washington, as well as adjunct professor of marketing and international business. Greenwald has received the Thomas M. Ostrom Award from the Person Memory Group, the Donald T. Campbell Award from the Society for Personality and Social Psychology, and the Distinguished Scientific Contribution Award from the Society for Experimental Social Psychology.

Both authors were elected fellows of the American Association for the Advancement of Science, the Society of Experimental Psychologists, and the American Academy for Arts and Science. Both were recognized with a Presidential Citation from the American Psychological Association.

people.fas.harvard.edu/~banaji
faculty.washington.edu/agg
blindspotthebook.com